No. 1906
$18.95

MICRO MANSION
USING YOUR COMPUTER TO HAVE A SAFER MORE CONVENIENT HOME

DAVID B. BONYNGE

TAB BOOKS Inc.
Blue Ridge Summit, PA 17214

Apple is a registered trademark of Apple Computer, Inc.
IBM is a registered trademark of International Business Machines Corp.
Commodore is a registered trademark of Commodore Business Systems, Inc.
HomeBrain is a trademark of HyperTek, Inc.
HomeMinder is a trademark of General Electric.

FIRST EDITION

FIRST PRINTING

Copyright © 1984 by David B. Bonynge

Printed in the United States of America

Library of Congress Cataloging in Publication Data

Bonynge, David B.
Micro mansion

Includes index.
1. Dwellngs—Automation—Data processing.
2. Microcomputers—Programming.   I. Title.
TH4812.B664   1985   643′.028′54   84-26759
ISBN 0-8306-0906-7

Cover illustration by Al Cozzi

Contents

Acknowledgments

I wish to express my thanks to Hannah Blank for encouraging the creation of this book; my sister, Cheryl Clark, for her artwork; and most of all, my wife, Kathleen, for her support and editorial efforts.

Introduction

Would you like a powerful yet easy way to reduce your heating and cooling costs, an inexpensive method to make your home safer, and a way to give yourself and your family greater convenience, comfort and enjoyment? The guide to help you do so is in your hands! It will explain how you can raise your home's IQ and make it come alive to work for you. Even if you've never changed a fuse or touched a computer before, the step-by-step instructions in this book will enable you to set up a highly sophisticated control system for your home. This book will show you how to transform a home computer and a few inexpensive gadgets into a Computer Home Control (CHC) system that will provide cost-savings, convenience, comfort, and enhanced safety for you and your family. Yet it will be easy for you to install and operate and reasonably inexpensive to acquire.

For those of you unfamiliar with personal computers, controlling your home by computer may sound far-out, complicated, and expensive. It can be, but with this book it need not be. Without this book, you might need to be an electronics wizard and computer hobbyist to gain computer control over your home's operations. With it, however, you need know little more than how to read and follow this step-by-step guide!

Controlling the operations of a home by computer for economy and efficiency is not new, but what is new—using this book—is the ease with which you can take advantage of this technology. There are a number of books available for the technical-minded (and you'll find mention of some of them in the Optional Reading Appendix), but you need not concern yourself with theory and detail in order to enjoy the benefits of Computer Home Control. The "techy" talk has been translated into plain English, the steps that need to be taken have been streamlined, and they are described simply and completely. Now regardless of your level of knowledge and experience with computers, you can install useful, cost-saving Computer Home Controls. And they can be fun, too!

Some of the controls described are as easy to

install as plugging a lamp into a socket and switching it on. Some do require simple skills and you'll be guided in performing these, so don't be concerned if you've never done them before. If you like to tinker and already have some experience with computers, there are still complicated challenging projects to do, and a few are provided. But it's not necessary to get involved with these unless you want to.

Besides the enjoyment you and your family will get from Computer Home Control, the savings you will obtain may be many times the size of your investment. This book tells everything you need to know to get the benefits of Computer Home Control in the most economical, trouble-free way. The general ideas of Computer Home Control are described in simple language.

☐ How and why it works, and what you need to know and do to get started.

☐ How to estimate your potential savings.

☐ How to decide what you need and how to select the best products to meet your needs.

☐ How to install the necessary gadgets in your home.

☐ What safety precautions you should take.

☐ How to manage and operate your system once it is installed.

The aim of this book is to reach as many people as possible with the benefits of CHC, and not let lack of experience with wiring or computers or both be a roadblock to installing or using these powerful systems. Therefore, each step is explained as if you had never done it before.

The few tools you will need for installing the controls that are described are probably in your home already: screwdriver, hammer, pliers, and wire-strippers. A drill, while not essential, is handy for starting screw-holes. Supplies and parts needed for a particular project are identified in the chapter describing the particular installation.

Before you turn to the pages describing the controls that particularly interest you, take a moment with the following overview of the contents of this book so that you can make the most of it. Some of you will be most interested in the extensive cost-savings that are possible with CHC, while others are most concerned about home security and safety. Still others just want to get going with a few fun projects to entertain friends and family and provide some luxurious conveniences—and perhaps find an excuse for buying a home computer! A few of you will want a complete CHC system that has it all: control of heating and cooling for cost-savings; improved security with burglar alarms, basement flood sensing, and smoke and heat detection; convenience with control of lights and appliances; the luxury of letting your computer decide when and how much to water your lawn, and more. So the book is organized according to these interests.

Chapter 1 gives you a bird's-eye view of Computer Home Control: how you can save money; how you can improve home safety, security, convenience, etc.; what you need to know and do to select and install CHC; concerns you may have.

Chapter 2 is a simple nontechnical overview of how Computer Home Control works. It explains the basic concepts that will help you understand whichever of the specific controls you decide to install in your home. It describes how the computer finds out what's going on around your house, how you can order it to perform various control operations, how the computer affects what's happening based on your orders, and how you orchestrate all the pieces which must work together.

Chapter 3 surveys those controls that help you save money—controls for home heating and cooling and electric hot water heating. By following the methods presented in this chapter you can discover whether Home Control is worthwhile financially in your particular situation.

By the time you reach Chapter 4, you will have quite a good idea of the kind of controls that are possible and that make the most sense for you and your family. You will be ready for the tour of your home on which Chapter 4 takes you. As a result of this tour, you will have identified the types and locations of controls appropriate for your particular home. This chapter also begins to provide you with an overview of the Home Control products available commercially for your use.

You are almost ready to seize control of your house! Chapter 5 gives you the basics you need in order to hook up a Home Control system to a personal computer. This is done by actually looking at how a few representative products work, and noting the differences between these products and others that are currently available.

Now you're ready to begin installation. For those of you with no prior computer experience, or experience with home electrical wiring, Chapter 6 starts off with the easiest controls to install. Even if these are not your main interest, you may want to install one or two light or appliance controls just for some simple experience with CHC.

If cost-savings are your primary interest, then follow the step-by-step instructions in Chapter 7 to control your home heating and cooling, and in Chapter 8, if you have an electric hot water heater, to control another big energy-guzzler.

Safety of your family, yourself and your valuables is another important area where CHC can, at low cost, provide valuable service. Although surveys have shown that homeowners are most likely to install safety systems in their homes only after misfortune has struck, hopefully the ease and low cost of CHC will encourage you to install these measures before anything happens. Each of the important types of safety systems is explained step-by-step in its own chapter. Basement flood detection is explained in Chapter 9, burglar alarm systems in Chapter 10, and smoke and heat detection in Chapter 11. Chapter 12 explains how you can connect any of your CHC safety systems to contact the outside world: yourself at work, a neighbor, the police or fire department.

And for comfort and convenience, Chapters 13, 14, 15, and 16 take you through the steps to install the necessary equipment for sensing light and temperature, watering your lawn, controlling your swimming pool, and controlling your audio/video system.

Finally, when it's time to fully integrate all the features of your system, Chapter 17 discusses getting it all together. Chapter 18 then explores a complete Home Control case study—the Preston home. The last Chapter, 19, looks to the future of Computer Home Control including some examples of experimental futuristic houses.

An extensive product directory, with names and addresses of manufacturers and distributors for each of the types of controls discussed in this book, can be found in Appendix A. Alternative methods for controlling home heating and cooling, more complex than those which are described in Chapter 7, are found in Appendix B. A simple BASIC program you can enter into your own computer is listed in Appendix C. It will help you monitor your home's energy consumption. Books and articles on related subjects you might find helpful are listed in Appendix D.

1. Controlling Your Home with a Computer

LONG BEFORE THE COMPUTER AGE, PEOPLE fantasized about sophisticated control devices which could provide them with greater power over their environment. Science fiction books, movies, and television programs abound with examples where either magic or some future era's science has given man a god-like power to simplify, entertain, protect, or in some way improve the control over life. But while the level of interest in such devices and capabilities is clear from the sheer volume of the fantasy projections of the future, their practicality has seemed remote. Today, except to a few "techy" hobbyists, and a handful of tiny, unheard of product manufacturers, actually having such controls still appears unrealistic.

The problem, however, is not technology. The problem is that the average consumer is not aware of the availability of these products, their compatibility with a home computer, or the ease with which they may be installed.

Up until now, the home computer has been used for basically three things—entertainment, education, and business applications (word process-ing, spreadsheets, etc.). But the computer can be integrated into the basic functions of the home. A new technology is unfolding today which makes three important things possible.

☐ Cost savings.
☐ Increased safety and security.
☐ Increased convenience and free time (and some fun, too!).

Before going any further, however, let's discuss a bit about how complex this book is going to be.

IS IT DIFFICULT?

Many of you who have read this far may be getting anxious that this book is going to become very technical in just a few short chapters. Well, relax. It isn't. This book has been carefully structured with ideas and products so even the beginner can use it.

You may be thinking that since you don't have the time to become an electrical engineer and a computer programmer, Computer Home Control is not for you. Perhaps if you've already started using a personal computer, you may have had some disappointing experiences. And no doubt you've been told by someone that something was really simple, when it wasn't at all. And now this book comes along and tells you how easy this is to do. But Computer Home Control sounds more complex than most things. So which is right?

Both are correct! Overall, Computer Home Control (CHC) is a complex use of the computer. However, to draw an analogy, this book won't be describing how to do something like build a component stereo system from transistors and circuit boards. Instead, it will tell you how to plug the components together and then how to operate it. Everything in this book will be explained using simple, step by step guidelines and can be easily installed with just a few common household tools.

Enough said about ease. What about the benefits?

CAN I SAVE MONEY?

CHC saves you money by turning your energy-consuming equipment off when it is not really needed and on only when it is needed. But, you ask, who needs a computer to do that? I can do it myself. And besides, my thermostat does it for me.

That is certainly true as far as it goes. You could turn your heating system off or down as you wished, and you do control the level of heat in your home by setting the thermostat at a selected temperature. But in your daily life, there are doubtless times when the level of heat required is lower than the thermostat is actually set for, because no one was around to turn it down.

Proponents of Home Control claim that their system can make sound financial sense. Some users of CHC claim up to a 35 percent reduction in their heating fuel usage. In areas with high heating costs, it is estimated that CHC can pay for itself well within a year's time.

You may already obtain some savings by turning down the thermostat at night when all are asleep. This alone can have a significant effect on fuel savings. CHC works much the same way,

though much more efficiently, and conveniently. CHC turns a "dumb" heating system into a "smart" one, while maintaining comfort levels similar to or better than you now have. CHC senses the heat necessary, and only when necessary, and provides no more. Although Chapter 7 describes more thoroughly how the computer does this, the following is a preview explanation:

Your thermostat controls the operation of your heating system and maintains the desired temperature by opening or temporarily disconnecting the circuit when the desired temperature and the actual temperature of your house match. CHC uses the same principle, but works with the thermostat to tell such things as the time of day, the day of the week, whether someone is at home, what time someone is expected home, and even what part of the house is occupied. Your computer, in effect, is able to interpret many pieces of information, and automatically adjust the thermostat accordingly. It can control execution of your orders whether you are at home or away from home. This, of course, is an oversimplification, but nonetheless should help you understand just how useful your CHC system can be.

Computer control of home cooling, if you have either central air or separate window units, can affect other significant savings and operates similarly to the heating scenario described above. The computer can control the amount of cooling provided for different periods of the week or day. And you can change your orders whenever you wish, as well as giving the computer different orders to follow on weekends from those followed on weekdays. Once you tell it what to do, it will automatically follow those orders until they are changed. You can even make different schedules for different times of the year, or for extended times when no one will be occupying the house—such as vacations.

The next biggest energy-guzzler in the home is the hot water heater. (This book describes how to control an electric hot water heater only.) If you have an electric hot water heater, with CHC you can reduce its drain on your wallet, yet provide your family with all the hot water it needs, when it is needed. As with the other energy-saving (cost-reducing) areas, the basic principle is to turn it on when needed and off when not needed, and to do so automatically. Obviously, you don't need hot water when no one is at home, and you probably don't need it when you're asleep. You could have your heater started by the computer in time to have adequate hot water for the day's routine, such as showers in the morning, dishwashing and baths in the evening, and hot water for the laundry on the particular day(s) that it's done. The rest of the time the heater could be turned off by the computer, ticking off savings for you with every moment not in use.

Heating, cooling, and hot water are the biggest energy consumers in most private homes. By controlling these with your computer, you can save substantially on energy costs. Chapter 3 will delve into greater specifics in this area. You'll even be able to estimate your savings with the cost involved in setting up your CHC system, and you may be pleasantly surprised at how quickly your new equipment will pay for itself.

Also, having a CHC system can produce cost savings in a number of other areas. These include turning off your lights and appliances when not needed, protecting you from flood damage, discouraging a burglar, or preventing a fire in your home from going beyond control. CHC can provide the potential for savings (or loss reduction) in all these areas.

CAN I IMPROVE SAFETY AND SECURITY?

Safety and security controls are an extremely important use of CHC. You can set up a single kind of protection for your home, or a combination of security systems, and the total cost may be considerably less than a single purpose (noncomputerized) system. Also, your CHC system will likely be much more flexible.

Three basic types of security systems will be covered: basement flood, burglar, and fire protection systems.

Basement Flood Protection. If your home basement has ever flooded, you know what damage water can do. Not only is it a huge mess to clean out, but water can be very destructive and damage your furnishings, possessions, and even the structure of your home itself. The pain and cost can be enormous. While CHC may not be able to pump out your basement, it can be used to make you aware of the situation before it gets out of hand.

Burglar Protection. If your home is in an area where other homes have been broken into, you may be concerned that it could happen to you. Many previously safe neighborhoods are becoming more vulnerable to crime each year. Most people, of course, don't become interested in buying a burglar system until they, a relative, or a neighbor have been victimized. But doesn't it make sense to act with reasonable precautions before something happens rather than wishing you had in the aftermath? You may have even priced home burglar systems and, because of the high cost, deferred a decision to have one installed. Well, CHC has some good news! A burglar alarm capability connected to your Home Control system will be much less expensive than a stand-alone system, and again probably much more flexible.

Actually, this can be as simple or sophisticated as you would like. A classic method to discourage burglars is to give your home the appearance that it is occupied when no one is actually there. The computer can be used to randomly turn on lights (both indoors and outdoors) and a radio or television and thereby provide a "lived in" look. This is particularly useful if no one is home during the weekdays, or when you're on vacation.

A second type of burglar prevention system is to have your CHC system actually able to sense a variety of disturbances. This can range from sensors to detect if a door or window is being tampered with, to more sophisticated devices that can sense motion or sound. The computer can interpret these disturbances, and take action as necessary. The action could include sounding an alarm, flashing lights, broadcasting a recorded (or computer synthesized) message, or even alerting the police. One action or many can be handled by your Home Control system, and all can be made to happen in the appropriate order, or even simultaneously.

Fire Protection. Certainly everyone is aware of the advantages of smoke detectors in the house. CHC uses heat and/or smoke detectors similar to those that you may already own. But CHC is more efficient for two reasons. First, it can warn the entire house that the hazard is present. This can be especially important if your basement detector senses a fire while you're sleeping on the second floor. Just maybe you'll hear an ordinary smoke detector before any real damage is done! And second, suppose you have a fire and no one is home. With CHC you can have outdoor sirens attract attention, or even notify the fire department via your computer and the phone lines.

These three areas of safety and security (basement flood, burglar, and fire protection) can all be controlled with ease by your Computer Home Control system, and they can be yours with a modest amount of time, money and attention.

CAN I INCREASE CONVENIENCE AND COMFORT?

With some Home Control systems, you can actually have a conversation with your house! Home Control can include the capability for your computer to understand your voice, and by using your voice command the computer can react accordingly (turn on a light, or whatever). It can even reply that your wish has been carried out! At the current level of technology and cost, these conversations are certainly not intellectually stimulating, but they can be convenient and fun, and a godsend for the handicapped. If you choose, you can make such capabilities a requirement for your system. They are found, however, on only a few of the more sophisticated systems. Although most do not carry convenience to this degree, many practical applications (and some fun ideas) can be created with the more conventional Home Control systems as described in the following paragraphs:

Any light or appliance that plugs into an electrical outlet can be controlled by your computer. However, it is recommended that a little common sense be exercised in selecting the devices to be controlled, and in how they are controlled. For safe-

ty reasons, you may not wish to have your computer turn on items that heat up without making sure that the computer will also turn them off at the appropriate time. As an example, you may want to manually turn on your toaster oven for your morning Danish. If you are like me (at times a little forgetful!), you may wish your computer to check and, if necessary, turn the toaster oven off.

Bearing in mind such common sense safety precautions (and you'll be reminded more than once), you can have your computer start and stop any number of devices around your home to provide a more pleasurable environment. These might include:

☐ Turning on the front door light prior to your arriving home on a cold winter's night. And once you open your front door, a path of lights can automatically turn on your kitchen or den area. (Makes your computer seem kind of friendly doesn't it?)

☐ Watering your lawn after sensing the moisture content of the soil.

☐ Allowing you to turn your morning coffee on from your bedroom (so it's ready by the time you drag yourself to the kitchen), and checking later to make sure the coffeepot is off.

☐ During the summer, sensing that the outdoor air is cooler than the indoor air, and in turn, having the attic fan take advantage of the situation.

☐ Monitoring the water level in your swimming pool (if you have one), or having the pool filter turn on and off at the appropriate hours of the day.

☐ Shutting down your stereo or television after you have gone to bed and fallen asleep.

This list can go on and on. Only you can determine your specific needs and desires. Chapter 4 will help guide you in planning your overall CHC system. This list, however, should serve as a brief overview of the convenience and comfort items which can be handled automatically for you.

CONCERNS

Safety precautions have been hinted at more than once in just these few pages, and you may be concerned about something that requires so many safety reminders. Let's talk about that right now. Electricity is a potent force, and, if approached improperly, can cause disaster. However, we use electricity in every aspect of our lives, and as long as a few simple rules are followed, there will be no problems.

The first rule is to know your own limitations, and if you feel uncomfortable performing a given task, by all means, call in appropriate help (an electrician, etc.).

A second rule that should never be broken is: **always disconnect (shut off) the current before performing any electrical work**.

A third rule is: **always follow manufacturers' safety precautions and recommendations.** Be sure to follow details such as plugging grounded (three prong) plugs in appropriately and not going beyond recommended wattage or voltage levels (to be more fully explained later).

The fourth rule is: **make sure that electricity and water do not mix**. Always make certain that you only use electrical items that are specifically designed to be used around water when such work is being done.

Most of the electrical work to be done will be at 24 volts or less (normal house current is 120 volts), and this should minimize your fears. Where voltages are higher, it will be clear, and appropriate messages will be given.

You may be wondering how much wiring is necessary in order for your CHC system to work. Will your house become a mass of criss-crossing wires, and will this ruin its appearance? Well, it turns out that the majority of items controlled by (or linked to) the computer can be operated by sending signals over the wiring that is already in your home. Therefore, most things will need no wiring work at all. Other items connected to your computer will need some wiring, but this is generally at the low voltages noted above, and requires relatively thin wires that can easily be hidden from sight with very little effort. Actually, a very few wires can perform most of the tasks discussed in this book.

Does Home Control with a microcomputer mean that the computer is always going to be tied-up to the Home Control system, or can it be used for other things as well? This depends on your particular Home Control equipment. Most Home Control systems rely on the computer for the brain of the system, while others (those with their own microprocessors) only need to be programmed by the computer, and afterwards can run independently. This means your computer is free to do other tasks while your Home Control system is up and running. The other type of Home Control systems (those that need to be constantly tied to the computer) usually can only run other applications when not being used for Home Control.

And what about power failures? You may decide that you can handle the installation, but you're worried about relying on an electrical system that can fail at a critical time from a power outage. Be assured that this topic will be covered, and your system, if so desired, can provide for such contingencies.

Once set up, the operation of your CHC system can be simple too, and you'll be guided through this aspect. It will take very little time for you to give your computer its orders to control your house exactly as you desire; and, once you provide the orders, you need not touch it again, unless you want a change.

By following this step-by-step guide to Computer Home Control, you should soon be the proud owner of the smartest home on your block! Are you ready?

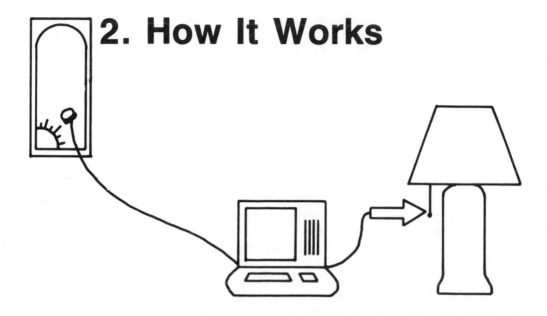

2. How It Works

YOU'RE CONVINCED! COMPUTER HOME CONtrol is useful. Now this chapter gives an overview of how it works. This is where you might expect to hear the nitty-gritty, the bits and bytes of machine language programming, the volts, ohms, and amps of electrical work, the redecoration of your home in sensors and wires. NOT TRUE! Take a deep breath and read on. You'll be pleasantly surprised.

This chapter assumes that you have little or no experience with computers. (For those of you who are experts in this area, please be patient with a few definitions and explanations.) Be assured that this will not make you into a technician. It will merely explain the concepts of Computer Home Control. The chapter is divided into two parts. The first section explains Computer Home Control "in theory" using an analogy to current Home Control—you! The second half of this chapter overviews the basic components and defines the terms that will be used throughout the rest of the book.

THE THEORY

Just in case you are worried that Computer Home Control means giving up the control of your house to your computer—reminiscent of the way HAL (the computer in the movie *2001*) took control over the spaceship—be assured this won't happen. It does mean, however, that you can delegate some of your responsibility for Home Control. In many ways, the computer can be a more efficient controller than we humans. Let's see why.

First of all, the computer doesn't need to sleep. This immediately makes it available to perform work while you cannot. The computer doesn't get tired or bored, it never needs a change of scenery or a coffeebreak. So a computer can keep on working—sensing and doing all its other chores as well—all day and all night, day in and day out, month after month, year after year.

Second, a computer can keep track of a lot of diverse activities at once. You or I might get confused if we tried to pay attention to seven things at once—someone talking, the temperature of another room, the degree of light outside, whether or not we turned off the coffeepot, all with one eye on the clock to see if it's time for our next chore, then checking the calendar to see if it's a workday or the weekend, and making sure no one is breaking in through any doors or windows. But a Computer Home Control system, if set up to do so, can do all these things at once, with the greatest of ease, and still have unused capabilities to do other things we might dream up for it later.

Third, a computer does not make mistakes. Period. With human nature what it is, we are all guilty occasionally of blaming someone or something else when we goof, and blaming the computer for mistakes is a favorite. It may appear that a computer made a mistake, but a computer mistake is always ultimately traceable to some human error.

How the Computer Senses

A computer controls the operations of your home much like you would do it yourself. Why do you turn on a light switch? Probably because it's too dark in a room, or in other words, your eyes could not sense enough light.

Just as a human control process begins with a perception, or a sensing of a particular condition, so does a Computer Home Control system. Your CHC system will use devices (sensors) which are designed to sense a particular condition. Each sensor is placed where it can perceive whatever you want it to sense. For instance, if you want your computer to know when it gets dark outside (so it can turn on a light), your sensor should be placed near a window. In this way, the computer will be able to see outside. Figure 2-1 illustrates this idea.

For many of the human senses there is a corresponding computer-controlled sensor.

Human Sense	Sensor
Seeing	Light sensor (senses degree of light and dark).
	Motion sensor (senses movement).
Hearing	Sound sensor (senses volume or pitch).
	Some can be sophisticated enough that when coupled with a computer they can understand spoken words.
Touch	Heat sensor (senses temperature).
	Moisture sensor (senses moisture or liquids).
Smell	Smoke sensor (smoke detector).

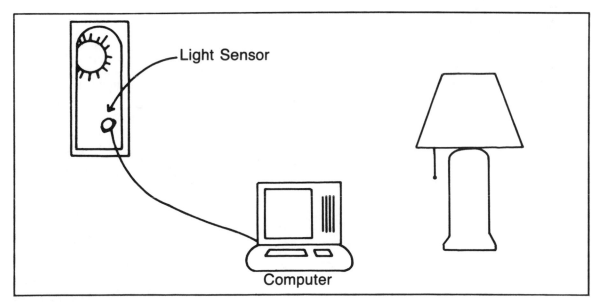

Fig. 2-1. Computer sensing light.

As you can see, while there is at least one (sometimes more than one) sensor for most human senses, the man-made version cannot do as much as the human sense can do (fortunately!). It can do enough, however, to be very useful in the home.

In computer terminology, the *sensor* is an input device to your computer, and the data which the sensor is gathering and sending is input just as surely as is the data you might key in at the keyboard or load from a tape cassette or from a diskette.

A special case of computer sensing is that of telling time. In CHC this is a very important function which your computer must be able to perform, since many control requirements are tied to a specific time of day, or day of the week, or both. There are two types of clocks to which your computer can refer. One is a *hardware* clock that is provided as part of the computer or as an add-on computer board. The other is a *software* clock—a program you can load into your computer which simulates the time keeping of a clock. For now all you need to know is that a computer, once given a hardware or software clock, will be able to execute your orders (by sensing time) at a given time of day, or (depending on sophistication) day of the week, etc.

The next step in the Home Control process is to get the needed information to the brain. When your eyes sensed the darkness, a message travelled from your eyes to your brain. When your brain received the message that it was too dark to see comfortably, it could begin to make the decision to switch on the light.

Having sensed something, a computer controlled sensor must be able to communicate its findings to the computer brain, or processor. Just as each of us has a network of nerves through which messages travel to our brain (not only from our eyes, but from our ears, fingertips, nose, and other sensing spots), computer sensors must have a network over which to send their messages to the computer. The network might be composed of visible wires, such as those you use to connect your table lamp to an electrical outlet (although usually a much smaller gauge of wire), or the network might be in-

visible, such as messages sent as radio frequencies.

How the Computer Thinks

You made the decision to turn on the light switch based on information beyond the fact that it was too dark—the information provided by your eyes. You already knew, for instance, that by flipping the light switch you could make the light go on. This information had to be learned. Another piece of information was the actual location of the light switch. In a dark, unfamiliar hotel room you may have difficulty locating the switch. In your house, it's usually second nature.

The computer processor also needs a certain amount of information in order to decide to take a specific action. Later, you'll learn what the computer needs to know, and how it can obtain (or at times, how you can provide) the necessary information. Just remember that part of the information the computer needs is what your wishes are. It doesn't decide things for itself!

How the Computer Takes Action

When your brain determined that it was too dark, it decided some sort of reaction was appropriate. In this case, the reaction was to move to the light switch, raise your hand, and manipulate your fingers in such a way that the switch was turned to the on position.

Similarly, a computer can be programmed to decide to take a particular action when and only when certain conditions are sensed. It can also be programmed to take into consideration many different conditions, and to have a plan of action for each. This is a rather abstract way of saying that you could control, for example, your lights, heating system, and burglar alarm, each with its own set of rules. Or you could have one dependent upon another. For instance, you might have your outside lights go on at sunset and go off at midnight—except when the burglar alarm system is triggered, where you may want all the lights in your house to go on at once.

The program can be as simple or as complex as you like. If you like to write programs, you can write your own. But you need not. Many of the products described in this book can be easily controlled with off-the-shelf programs that are often provided by the manufacturer of the control equipment.

Once the computer has decided that something should happen, based on your instructions and the conditions(s) it has sensed, it has to execute that action. It does so by transmitting the message (or output) to the device that will perform the action. In our light switch example, the computer must be able to signal (send a message) to a *control device* that can in effect operate the light switch, as illustrated in Fig. 2-2.

The computer can be made to signal a wide variety of actions by sending the appropriate messages to various types of control devices. These control devices can be simple to install and (as we will see) often require no additional wiring to run throughout the house.

THE BASICS

The basic components necessary for Computer Home Control are displayed in Fig. 2-3. The components shown in the figure are listed below in order of discussion:

1. The computer.
2. The sensors.
3. The sensor interface.
4. The software.
5. The control system.

For your reference a product directory is provided towards the end of this book (Appendix A) to help you match components to your particular situation.

The Computer

Almost any computer—including the IBM PC or PCjr.; and Apple *II+*, *IIe* or *IIc*; a Commodore 64 or VIC 20—can be used as part of your CHC system. All these brands can be linked with equipment described in this book and can control all of the functions described in Chapters 6 through 16. If you do not currently own a computer, you need not choose your computer solely on the basis of Home Control. Be sure to consider what other types

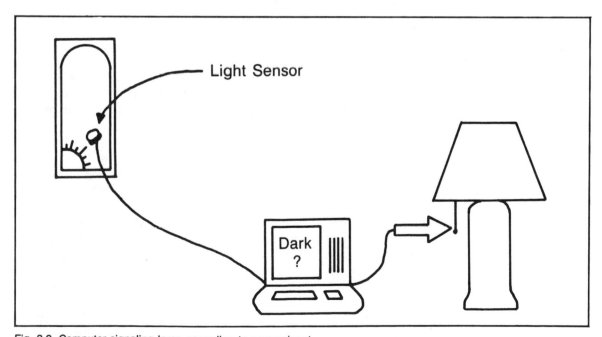

Fig. 2-2. Computer signaling lamp according to sensor input.

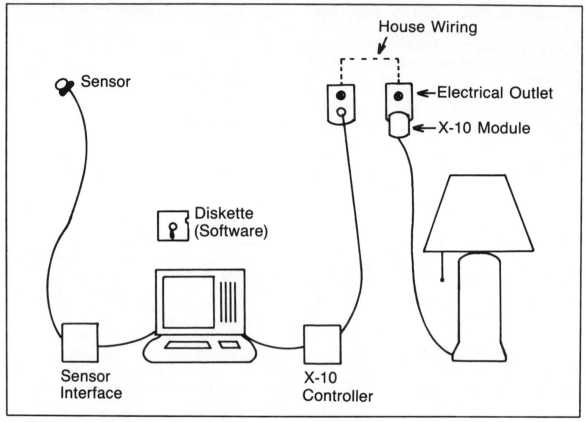

Fig. 2-3. The basic components of Home Control.

of computer applications you may wish to have available.

The basic rule of thumb is to first choose which applications you want to perform on your computer (such as Home Control, word processing, financial applications, games, child and adult education, etc.). Find out what software packages are available for these applications, which you prefer, and on which computers the packages will run (execute). Then choose the computer that fits all your needs the best. Remember: decide on software first, hardware second. You can find many good books and articles on choosing the best computer configuration for your personal needs.

The Sensors

Prior to discussing the sensors, a few notes on computer sensing in general are appropriate. Computer sensing can be of two basic kinds. The first kind is being able to sense whether something is on or off. The second is being able to tell "to what degree" something has happened. The on or off condition is the simplest and, as an example, is used for such a function as telling whether a door is opened or closed (for possible use in a burglar alarm system). This on or off sensing method is commonly referred to as a *digital* message to the computer.

The second kind of message tells the degree to which something is happening. It might be used for a temperature sensing purpose. The temperature should be measured not in terms of on or off, (hot or cold), but in terms of how hot or cold it is. A whole array of possibilities exist, and you may want to know any one of them. This type of sensing is commonly called an *analog* message.

As shown in Fig. 2-3, the equipment for sensing usually requires some wires to be run throughout the house. However, as you will see, this can be handled with reasonably few wires, and since all sensing described will be at low voltages, the types of wires used can be small and hardly noticeable.

The sensors themselves are usually quite small (some literally not much bigger than the head of a pin), and will be relatively unobtrusive when located around the house. As noted previously in this chapter, different sensors can be used to detect light, temperature, moisture or liquids, motion, sound, smoke, etc. Actually, there are many more sensors of various types than will be mentioned in this book. For the sake of brevity, only a selection of those that have been found useful in CHC will be described. You, of course, may wish to research a bit further and discover some sensors that are of particular interest for you.

The Sensor Interface

Unfortunately, sensors are not very good at communicating directly to a computer. Nor do most computers come with the capability to directly interpret sensors. Therefore, some sort of interface is necessary so that messages sent from the sensors can be interpreted into something the computer will understand. For this purpose, a *sensor interface* is needed. These devices are called by many different names, but usually they can be partially identified by the terms interface or digital interface or analog interface, etc. Some of the projects described in this book will use analog sensors, but most will use digital sensors. Since both are important depending on the particular project, it is recommended that your sensor interface have both capabilities and enough separate connection jacks (terminals) to interpret your various sensors. This may sound a bit confusing at present, but things will become clearer as we proceed.

The Software

The software (computer instructions) is necessary to tell your particular system what to do, how to do it, and when. Software makes your computer understand what it is sensing (whether it senses time, heat, light, etc.), and converts that information into the appropriate signal (turning on a light, signaling an alarm, etc.). Many of the sensor interfaces or control systems (sometimes sold together as one product) come with software, while a few come with only basic explanations and may require BASIC or machine language programming on your part.

In selecting your equipment, make sure you fully understand what type of programming may be required (none, BASIC, machine language, etc.). If you are not a programmer, buy equipment that includes fully documented and easy to run preprogrammed software. Packages that are simply hardware packages usually require a reasonable understanding of BASIC programming, and often at least a conceptual understanding of machine-language programming. Choose your equipment according to your programming capabilities and your interest in programming.

For those of you who are programmers, yet wish to purchase a package with complete software, most (if not all) of the packages which include software described in Appendix A also allow for self programming of software, if so desired.

Also, be sure that if you are buying equipment from different vendors, that the software provided can be used in conjunction with both the sensor interface and controller equipment purchased.

The Control System

There are a number of types of computer control (or signaling) methods available, some of which require wires to be running all over your house. This causes two problems: the added difficulty of wiring, and the poor aesthetics of a jumble of wires around the house. Therefore, it is highly recommended for any extensive control signaling system that you can use an *X-10 Control System*. Almost all of the control applications in this book are handled using this method, because it is the easiest and most flexible, and because it is reasonably cost effective.

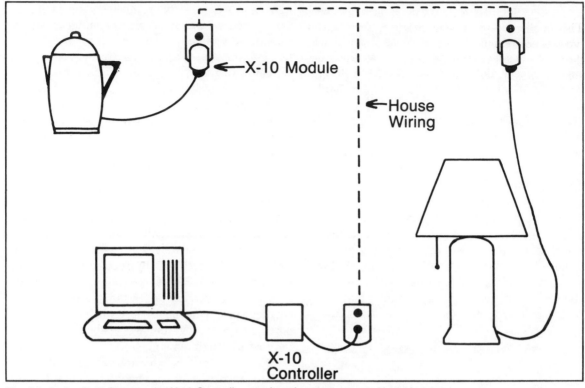

X-10 Module

←House Wiring

X-10 Controller

Fig. 2-4. In the X-10 System, the X-10 Controller sends pulse messages to X-10 Modules.

As noted in Fig. 2-4, X-10 Systems transmit signals from your computer and X-10 Controller via your existing house electrical system simply by connecting the X-10 Controller to your computer and plugging it into a wall outlet. That's all there is to it! The signals are sent as pulse messages through your house electrical system and are received by X-10 Modules. The modules, in their most basic form, are usually small boxes (roughly a cube measuring about 2 inches in each direction) that contain both a plug (to be inserted into a wall outlet) and a socket which can receive the plug from a lamp, a radio, etc. The best part about using the X-10 System is its great ability to control many, many household functions—up to 256 separately controlled items. Each module has 16 House Code settings from A-P, and 16 Unit Code settings from 1-16. The sixteen House Codes times the 16 Unit codes equals 256 separate messages that can be understood, and therefore, 256 items can be con-

trolled independently. That's a lot of control!

Another advantage of the X-10 System is that the modules are widely available from AT&T Phone Stores, Sears, and Radio Shack to name just a few outlets.

You may also want to consider equipment which includes *relays* as part of the Control System. Relays can be used where electrical items need to be switched on or off, similar to the X-10 System, except that hard-wiring is necessary. Mechanical relays work by turning on or off an electro-magnet. This magnet in turn is able to operate an electric switch that actually turns on or off the item (lamp, appliance, etc.) to which it is connected. A relay system can be particularly helpful for applications (such as a burglar alarm system) where a Home Control function is desired to operate during a power outage of normal house current. Unfortunately, the X-10 System will not work at such times.

AVAILABILITY

This book tries to present only readily available types of equipment and will suggest retailers where these items can be obtained. Also, some of the Sensor Interface and X-10 manufacturers and distributors are sources for peripheral devices, and they will sell those that are readily adaptable to their specific systems. Many devices are also available locally. Refer to the Product Directory in Appendix A.

3. You Can Save Money

A LITTLE OVER A DECADE AGO, BETWEEN 1973 and 1974, a barrel of oil rose from about $3.50 to over $11.00. And the nation's awareness of energy costs and consumption rose accordingly. Since then, many books have been written on how to handle energy costs more efficiently. Computer Home Control can be a significant step towards helping you better control these costs over time.

This chapter will show you just how CHC can assist as one of a number of potential steps to help you keep your energy costs down. Other valuable steps might include sealing and insulation, maintaining your furnace and water heater to work efficiently, and alternative energy sources such as solar, wind, and wood-burning stoves. Computer Home Control is one step, taken alone or with others, that offers better comfort, pays for itself and saves money for years to come. CHC saves money by using energy only when it is needed. At all other times, when energy is normally wasted, CHC shuts down or lowers energy consumption according to

your wishes—automatically.

Keep in mind that in this chapter only the money savings related to saving energy will be discussed. However, as was stated in Chapter 1, CHC can also be a money saver by helping to protect your home from the disaster of a fire, burglary, or flood. CHC also saves on the smaller energy users by turning off lights, TVs, radios, and other appliances when not needed.

TAX INCENTIVES

If your main interest in CHC is financial, here are the facts and figures needed to convince you. For many energy conservation projects for the home, federal and state governments offer tax incentives that may cut your costs significantly. Some utility companies offer loans at low rates for such projects, so you may wish to contact them, as well.

The laws which affect these tax incentives vary from state to state and tend to change at a fairly rapid pace. Therefore, it's recommended that you contact the appropriate agencies (see Fig. 3-1) to

Federal
National Solar Heating
  and Cooling Information
  Center:
800-523-2929

IRS Information
800-772-2345

Alabama
Development Office
Office of Governor
State Office Building
Montgomery, AL 36104
(205) 832-6960

Alaska
Division of Energy and Power
  Development
Department of Commerce
338 Denali Street
Anchorage, AK 99501
(907) 276-0508

Arizona
Energy Programs Office
Office of Economic Planning
  and Development
1700 W. Washington
Phoenix, AZ 85007
(602) 255-3303

Arkansas
Arkansas Energy Conservation
  and Policy Office
960 Plaza West Building
Lee & McKinley Streets
Little Rock, AR 72205
(501) 371-1379

California
Energy Resources
  Conservation and
  Development Commission
Resources Agency
704 11th & L Building
Sacramento, CA 95814
(916) 920-6811

Colorado
Office of Energy Conservation
1600 Downing
Denver, CO 80218
(303) 839-2507

Connecticut
Office of Planning and
  Management
Energy Division
20 Grand Street
Hartford, CT 06115
(203) 566-2800

Delaware
Delaware Energy Office
P.O. Box 1401
56 The Green
Dover, DE 19901
(302) 736-5647

Florida
State Energy Office of Florida
301 Bryant Building
Tallhassee, FL 32301
(904) 488-6764

Georgia
Office of Energy Resources
270 Washington Street, S.W.
Atlanta, GA 30334
(404) 656-5176

Hawaii
Energy Management and
  Conservation Office
Department of Planning and
  Economic Development
1164 Bishop Street, Suite 1515
Honolulu, HI 96813
(808) 548-4090

Idaho
Office of Energy
State House
Boise, ID 83720
(208) 334-3800

Illinois
Institute for Environmental
  Quality
222 South College
Springfield, IL 62706
(217) 785-2800

Indiana
Indiana Energy Office
Department of Commerce.
  Seventh Floor
Consolidated Building
Indianapolis, IN 46204
(317) 232-8940

Iowa
Iowa Energy Policy Council
215 East 7th Street
Des Moines, IA 50309
(515) 281-6679

Kansas
Kansas Energy Office
503 Kansas Avenue
Topeka, KS 66603
(913) 296-2910

Kentucky
Kentucky Department of
  Energy
P.O. Box 11888
Iron Works Pike
Lexington, KY 40578
(606) 252-5535
1-800-432-9014

Louisiana
Office of Conservation
Department of Natural
  Resources
P.O. Box 44275
Baton Rouge, LA 70804
(504) 342-5540

Maine
Office of Energy Resources
55 Capitol Street
Augusta, ME 04330
(207) 289-3811

Maryland
Maryland Energy Policy Office
Room 1302, State Office Building
301 West Preston Street
Baltimore, MD 21201
(301) 383-6810

Massachusetts
State Energy Office
73 Tremont Street
Room 700
Boston, MA 02108
(617) 727-1250

Michigan
Michigan Energy Administration
Department of Commerce
P.O. Box 30004
Lansing, MI 48909
(517) 373-0480

Minnesota
Minnesota Energy Agency
American Center Building
150 E. Kellog Blvd.
St. Paul, MN 55101
(612) 296-6720

Mississippi
Mississippi Fuel and Energy
  Management Commission
Suite 228, Barefield Complex
455 North Lamar Street
Jackson, MS 39201
(601) 961-5099

Missouri
Missouri Energy Program
Department of Natural
  Resources
Box 176
Jefferson City, MO 65102
(314) 751-4000

Montana
Energy Division, Department of
  Natural Resources and
  Conservation
32 South Ewing
Helena, MT 59601
(406) 449-3780

Nebraska
Nebraska State Energy Office
State Office Building
P.O. Box 94841
Lincoln, NE 68509
(402) 471-2867

Nevada
Department of Energy
1050 East Williams Street
Carson City, NE 89701
(702) 885-4840

New Hampshire
Governor's Council on Energy
26 Pleasant Street
Concord, NH 03301
(603) 271-2711

New Jersey
New Jersey Department of Energy
101 Commerce Street
Newark, NJ 07102
(201) 648-3290

New Mexico
Energy and Minerals Department
P.O. Box 2770
Santa Fe, NM 87501
(505) 827-2471

New York
New York State Energy Office
Agency Building 2
Empire State Plaza
Albany, NY 12223
(513) 474-2121

North Carolina
Department of Commerce
Energy Division
215 East Lane Street
Raleigh, NC 27611
(919) 733-2230

North Dakota
North Dakota Office of Energy
  Management and Conservation
1533 North 12 Street
Bismarck, ND 58501
(701) 224-2250

Ohio
Ohio Department of Energy
30 E. Broad Street, 14th Floor
Columbus, OH 43215
(614) 466-8476

Oklahoma
Oklahoma Department of Energy
4400 N. Lincoln Blvd.
Oklahoma City, OK 73105
(405) 521-2995

Oregon
Department of Energy, Room 111
Labor and Industry Building
Salem, OR 97310
(503) 378-4128

Pennsylvania
Governor's Energy Council
1625 North Front Street
Harrisburg, PA 17102
(717) 783-8610

Rhode Island
Rhode Island Energy Office
80 Dean Street
Providence, RI 02903
(401) 277-3370, or
(401) 277-3773. Collect

Fig. 3-1. Federal and State energy information addresses. (Continued to page 16.)

Fig. 3-1. Federal and State energy information address. (Continued from page 15.)

get the most up to date information. Incentives are varied, and include the following:

☐ Credits: Amount you may be allowed to deduct directly from tax owed (state credit often related to federal).

☐ Deductions: Amount you may be allowed to deduct from your income prior to being taxed.

☐ Loans: Usually from utility companies or related state agencies that offer low interest rates.

☐ Property Tax Exemptions: Adding energy saving systems to the home, in some states, cannot add to the assessed value of your home for property tax purposes.

☐ Sales Tax Exemptions: Some states do not add sales tax on equipment for energy conservation.

Federal tax incentives (credits) include dollars spent for insulation (storm windows, insulating materials, caulking, weather-stripping), flue dampers, pilotless ignitions added to the furnace, and set back thermostats. The credit is 15 percent of the cost for the first $2000 spent (up to $300 maximum). There is also a 40 percent on amounts up to $10,000 for the cost of any eligible active solar system or wind or geothermal installations purchased between January 1, 1980 to January 1, 1986. For more detail on these tax incentives, check Federal Publication #903. *"Energy Credits for Individuals."* The important thing to remember if you

are deciding whether or not to do an energy saving project (i.e., using CHC to set back your thermostat, or to control an active solar system) is to make sure that you include any appropriate tax incentives when figuring the financial feasibility of your project.

FIGURING THE FINANCES

The following example is a method to calculate the portion of your CHC system used for saving energy and thereby saving money. It can easily be applied to your specific situation. This section is meant to show how CHC can potentially cost justify itself. Though related, it is not a complete methodology for doing an overall cost justification of energy projects in the home; it is merely a method to cost justify the CHC portion of an energy project.

1. First, decide which energy saving and CHC related projects may be appropriate for your particular situation. (Chapter 4 will be helpful in this process.)

2. List the cost of each project. As an example, suppose your house has two heat zones that you wish to control. Let's assume the cost for each thermostat control will be $60.00, and that since a portion of your computer (and equipment) is also involved in this project, $100.00 of computer costs are allocated to this project. The total cost is as follows:

2 Thermostat Controllers @$60.	=	$120
Computer Allocation	=	100
Total............................	.	$220

If you have your equipment installed, such costs should also be added to your figures above.

3. If your project is sizable, you may wish to check for low cost loans for which you may qualify. (Such loans will not be used in this example.)

4. Check any federal or state tax incentive programs for which you may qualify. In this example, the federal incentive would be 15 percent of the first $2000 spent or .15 times $220 or $31.50. Since states vary widely, for simplicity let's assume an equal state tax credit would be allowed.

Federal Incentive	=	$31.50
State Incentive	=	31.50
Total Incentive	=	$63.00

5. Figure your actual costs. In this example, I will keep it simple by not using a loan nor figuring any time costs of money. A simple payback method will be used for the following few steps. Based on this example, your actual cost would be $220 less $63 or $157.

6. Determine the expected savings from the improvements you will make. For example, let's assume your heating bill is $1500 per year, and by having your thermostats controlled independently and religiously every day you are able to save 22.7 percent of your fuel bill. That savings is equal to $341. That's *$341 you will save year after year* for a (one time) actual cost outlay of $157. You can begin to see the dollar advantages of CHC. This one aspect of CHC may pay for all the other advantages and projects that you would like to incorporate into your system.

7. Last, but not least, once you've done your calculations, review them and examine all worthwhile alternatives. Some projects and some methods of performing those projects may make better sense than others.

This calculation is meant purely as an example to provide you with a method to think about saving money with CHC. It is not specific to any one household's situation. However, it should be useful as a roadmap for you to use. Also, remember that CHC has many other advantages and benefits that cannot be dealt with directly in terms of dollars and cents.

CENTRAL HEATING AND COOLING

Saving money on energy costs with Computer Home Control is based on the simple concept that energy consuming equipment should be turned off—or down—when it is not needed. If you are willing to turn down your central heating system's thermostat a few degrees during the night while you are sleeping—and most people find they sleep more comfortably that way—you may be able to save up to 15 percent or more on your heating costs. With CHC, this can be accomplished with no discomfort, since the computer will turn the thermostat down only after you're all in bed, and turn it back up in the morning before anyone gets up. Remember that, except in extreme cases, there is additional savings from each additional degree that you turn down the thermostat.

Further, if your house is empty for a stretch of a few hours or more at a time during the day, you can use CHC to conserve a greater amount of energy and cut your costs even more. If some members of your house are at work, and the others are at school, take a look at how many hours the house is unoccupied. Do things vary on the weekends? When you provide your computer with a rough schedule of the times the house is usually occupied, your CHC system can do the rest to ensure the right amount of heat with no fuel waste.

In some houses, a second floor is predominantly used for sleeping hours. If yours is one of these, you may want to put this floor on a separate heating zone (if not already separate), and control this area according to a different schedule than the first floor. If both parts of your house are rarely used at the same time, then the heat in at least one section can usually be lowered. This type of scheduling would be a nuisance if you tried to remember to handle it manually. Moreover, the house would always be too cold when you came home, or got up, or even went to a different part of the house. It would also stay warmer longer than needed after you left or moved to a different location. But for CHC, these problems can be taken care of as easily as scheduling the computer and forgetting about it!

You will be able to get better control over your energy consuming equipment by controlling it with a computer because the computer can switch things on or off when you cannot—for example, when you're sleeping or away from home. And unlike some of us, the computer doesn't forget, get tired, or put tasks off until another time. If you have set your computer to do a certain task, such as turning your thermostat up before the kids are due home from school, then turning it back down again at midnight, you can rest easy and give it no further thought. It will be done correctly and without reminders from you.

Instructions can be set for each day's schedule. CHC will remember that it's Sunday morning and you don't usually get up until 10 A.M., and therefore, not crank up the heat until 9:30. Of course, on Monday it will start the furnaces at 5:30 AM since you must get up at 6:00. If you have a weekend house which you travel to on Friday evenings, wouldn't it be nice to have the heat ready at 72 degrees just before you arrive? And with CHC, you don't have to worry after you leave on Sunday afternoon that you may not have turned the heat back down.

The savings on central air conditioning systems are just like those from central heating, except, of course, in reverse. The computer will keep things

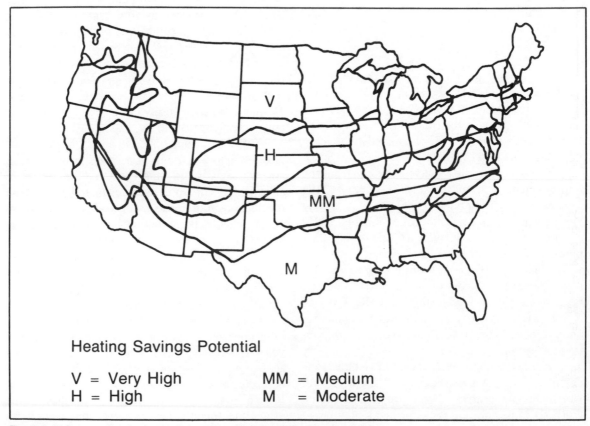

Heating Savings Potential

V = Very High   MM = Medium
H = High   M = Moderate

Fig. 3-2. U.S. map showing potential savings from heating energy projects.

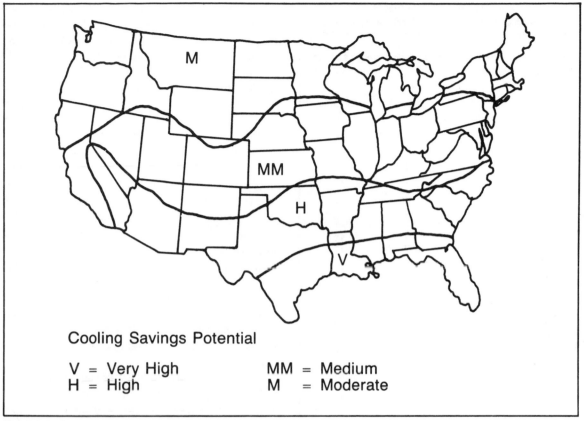

Cooling Savings Potential

V = Very High   MM = Medium
H = High   M = Moderate

Fig. 3-3. U.S. map showing potential savings from home cooling projects.

cool only when the coolness is really needed. Otherwise, CHC will allow things to heat up a bit!

The two maps of the United States should help you locate your potential relative savings (to other parts of the U.S.) for both heating and cooling conservation projects. If you have both central heating and cooling, use both maps (Figs. 3-2 and 3-3). If you have only heating or only cooling, just use the one appropriate map. It's really pretty simple: you'll save much more on heating with CHC if you live in New Hampshire than if you live in Florida!

To help you get more specific, Table 3-1 provides a yearly percentage estimate of the heating fuel savings by lowering the thermostat eight hours each night in major U.S. cities. Table 3-2 provides a rough percentage estimate of your potential savings on air conditioning over the year by raising the thermostat eight hours each day.

Now you're ready to read about a hypothetical family and then use the worksheet which follows to estimate your own potential energy savings. Let's assume that a family known as the Thompsons lives in a house with central heating and air-conditioning in Washington, D.C. Mr. Thompson works for a local bank and on weekdays leaves the house at 7:30 A.M. and returns about 5:00 P.M. Mrs. Thompson is a teacher at an area elementary school, and leaves for work at approximately 8:15 and arrives home at 3:15 to 3:30 each afternoon. In the summer, Mrs. Thompson runs a local day camp and her schedule is fairly similar.

The Thompsons have two sons, one in high school, and one who has recently graduated from college and has taken a job in Boston. The younger son's schedule is similar to Mrs. Thompson's except that he leaves the house approximately a half

Table 3-1. Potential
Heating Fuel Savings in Major U.S. Cities

(Percentage of fuel saved by lowering thermostat eight hours each night.)

City	Lowered 5°F	Lowered 10°F
Atlanta	11	15
Boston	7	11
Buffalo	6	10
Chicago	7	11
Cincinnati	8	12
Cleveland	8	12
Columbus	7	11
Dallas	11	15
Denver	7	11
Des Moines	7	11
Detroit	7	11
Kansas City	8	12
Los Angeles	12	16
Louisville	9	13
Madison	5	9
Miami	12	18
Milwaukee	6	10
Minneapolis	5	9
New York	8	12
Omaha	7	11
Philadelphia	8	12
Pittsburgh	7	11
Portland	9	13
Salt Lake City	7	11
San Francisco	10	14
Seattle	8	12
St. Louis	8	12
Syracuse	7	11
Washington, DC	9	13

hour later, and is usually involved with sports or other recreation after school.

Mrs. Thompson does some family errands on Friday afternoon, and then joins Mr. Thompson for tennis at an indoor club afterwards (winter only). No one is usually around the house on Saturdays between 9 AM and 5 PM, and often everyone has plans for Saturday night as well. Sundays, however, at least one person is usually at the house all during the day.

Recently, the family has decided to have their computer control a number of functions in their home, including the heating, cooling, and hot water systems. They would like their computer to lower their thermostat in winter and raise it in summer by ten degrees when either no one is at home or

when they are all asleep.

According to Figs. 3-2 and 3-3, the Thompsons live in an area of the U.S. where they can expect average results on both projects to save on heating and cooling costs. From looking at their electricity and fuel bills they were able to estimate that last year they spent roughly $1500 for heat and $375 for air conditioning.

The Thompsons feel they can have the heat and air conditioner thermostat adjusted for fuel savings on weekdays usually for about 14 hours, and on Fridays an extra four in the winter. Further, they believe that they can have the thermostat adjusted for savings for 16 hours on Saturday (winter only), and only eight hours (when everyone is asleep) on Sundays. Summer weekends are a bit more unpredictable, and the Thompsons have estimated that there will be only six hours each day where savings can be generated.

The Thompson's heating and cooling system is only a one zone system. If they had a second zone (or installed one), they might be able to receive additional savings.

The formula to calculate savings is similar for both heating and cooling. Simply divide the average hours the thermostat is adjusted for fuel savings (average hours set back in summer or raised in winter) by eight hours (since all information in Tables 3-1 and 3-2 are given for eight hours). Then multiply that figure times the savings percentage

Table 3-2. Potential
Cooling Fuel Savings in Regions of U.S.

(Percentage of fuel saved by raising thermostat eight hours each day.)

Region by Cooling Factor	Raised 5°F	Raised 10°F
M	11	15
MM	9	13
H	7	11
V	5	9

(The symbols M, MM, H, and V refer to the regions diagrammed in Fig. 3-3).

	SAMPLE FIGURES	YOUR FIGURES
1. Heat factor (Fig. 3-2) (for reference only)	MM	
2. Last Year's Heat Cost	$1500.	
3. Thermostat set-back in Degrees	10	
4. Interpolate Savings percentage (from Table 3-1).	13%	

5. Weekly Schedule:
   Winter Heating (hours lowered):

	SAMPLE FIGURES	YOUR FIGURES
Monday	14	
Tuesday	14	
Wednesday	14	
Thursday	14	
Friday	18	
Saturday .	16	
Sunday	8	
Total	98	
Divide by 7 =		
Average Hours set back:	14	

6. (Avg Hrs set back)/(8 Hrs) × (Saving %) × (Heat Cost) = Savings

SAMPLE: 14/8 × .13 × $1500 = $341.
YOURS: ___/8 × ___ × _____ = ____

If no central cooling system then skip to explanation.

	SAMPLE FIGURES	YOUR FIGURES
7. Cool factor (Fig. 3-3). (for reference only)	MM	
8. Last Year's Cooling Cost	$375.	
9. Thermostat set-ahead Degrees	10	
10. Interpolate Savings percentage (from Table 3-2)	13%	

11. Weekly Schedule:
    Summer Cooling (hours raised):

	SAMPLE FIGURES	YOUR FIGURES
Monday	14	
Tuesday	14	
Wednesday	14	
Thursday	14	
Friday	16	
Saturday	6	
Sunday	6	
Total	84	
Divide by 7 =		
Average hours set raised:	12	

12. (Avg Hrs set raised)/(8 Hrs) × (Saving %) × (Cool Cost) = Savings

SAMPLE: 12/8 × .13 × $375. = $73.
YOURS: ___/8 × ___ × $ _____ = ____

Total Heating and Cooling Savings = $414. _____

Fig. 3-4. Heating and cooling savings worksheet showing the Thompsons' estimated savings. Space is available for your figures.

(found in either of the two tables), and multiply again by your yearly heat or cooling costs.

Take a look at Fig. 3-4 where all this information regarding the Thompsons has been summarized. Using this as an example and specifics about your situation, you can estimate your benefits by completing the second column in the figure. The method used to calculate savings throughout this chapter will provide a rough estimate of your expected savings. This method is fairly straightforward and does not require a great deal of measuring various features about you home, nor does it require extensive math. At the same time, it should produce reasonably accurate results for most situations.

According to their figures, the Thompsons can expect to save approximately $341 on their heating costs and $73 on their cooling costs for a total savings of roughly *$414*. With a little careful planning (scheduling), you too can have significant savings using CHC to control central heating and cooling.

ATTIC FANS

One of the best and least expensive ways to cool a home is by use of an attic fan (or any fan that can change the air throughout the house). In later chapters, you will find out how to control these, but for right now it should be noted that Home Control can provide a significant cost savings if you have both an air conditioner and an attic fan.

One of the things that can be implemented fairly easily through your CHC system is tracking the temperature inside and outside your house. By doing so during the summer, CHC can choose whether air conditioning is necessary to cool the house, or whether the outside air is cool enough to be drawn into the house with the attic fan to lower the temperature. Running a fan is much less expensive than running an air conditioner so this can become quite cost effective.

ROOM HEATERS AND ROOM AIR CONDITIONERS

Room heaters and air conditioners can be con-

trolled by CHC with ease. (Care, however, should be used when automatically turning on any appliance that heats up.) Using your Home Control system you can monitor time (and temperature, if you wish) and only have these devices working when a true benefit will be derived. CHC will keep these energy guzzlers off at all other times, again saving you money.

ELECTRIC HOT WATER HEATERS

In this book computer control for only *electric* hot water heaters is discussed. If you have a gas (or other nonelectric) system, you may wish to skip this section and Chapter 8. Like the previous examples, CHC can significantly reduce the cost while providing your family with sufficient hot water for their needs, with little or no reduction in convenience.

The main reason this works is that the need for large amounts of hot water is seldom continuous throughout the day. In many cases, hot water is only needed for a few hours in the morning and, again, in the evening. Even on laundry day only a minimal amount of hot water may be required since many people have switched to cold or warm water washes.

CHC can turn on and off an electric hot water heater so water is hot only when actually needed. Moreover, even when the hot water system has been off for hours, your water will still be warm. Therefore, you rarely will be without warm water, just very hot water (unless you use great quantities of warm water before CHC turns the water heater back on).

In some areas, utility companies allow you to buy off-peak electricity for the purpose of heating hot water (usually at night). The water is stored in the hot water tank of the heater, and although gradually cooling through the day) is used by families as their hot water supply. Obviously, few people would consider such a system unless the water stayed relatively warm. CHC uses a similar principle. Hot water is available in abundance with CHC only when hot water is really needed.

The yearly percentage estimate for hot water electricity savings by turning your hot water off for eight hours a day is roughly 20 percent. Let's go back to the Thompsons again, and then you'll be able to figure what this means to you.

The Thompsons also planned to use their Home Control system to save on their electric hot water costs. They have taken a look at their electricity bills from last year and have estimated that their hot water costs ran about $280. After thinking about their schedule during the week, the Thompsons found that they needed hot water only in the mornings and in the evenings. Therefore, they decided that hot water for about four hours in the morning and another four hours in the evening should be plenty for everyone, with Sunday being the only exception. On Sunday, a few loads of laundry need to be handled, as well as one or two cleaning chores requiring hot water. For these reasons, the hot water would remain on except for nine hours (mostly sleeping time). Figure 3-5 was used by the Thompsons and can help you predict your cost savings.

According to their calculations, the Thompsons expect to save approximately $105 annually on their hot water costs. Added to their heating and cool-

	SAMPLE FIGURES	YOUR FIGURES
1. Last Year's Hot Water Cost	$280	_____
2. Thermostat set-back	100%	_____
3. Savings percentage	20%	_____
4. Weekly Schedule:		
Hours Hot Water system off:		
Monday	16	_____
Tuesday	16	_____
Wednesday	16	_____
Thursday	16	_____
Friday	16	_____
Saturday	16	_____
Sunday	9	_____
Total	105	_____
Divide by 7 =		
Average hours turned off:	15	_____

5. (Avg Hrs set back)/(8 Hrs) × (Saving %) × (Heat Cost) = Savings

SAMPLE: $15/8 \times .20 \times \$280 = \$105.$

YOURS: $\_\_/8 \times \_\_\_ \times \_\_\_\_ = \_\_\_\_$

Fig. 3-5. Electric hot water savings worksheet.

ing savings, that's a total of $519!

Take a few minutes now and consider your family's potential for savings. Working through your own numbers will only take about ten minutes, and your results may be impressive. Appendix C contains a Home Utility Monitoring Program that will help you keep track of your energy costs (savings) year after year.

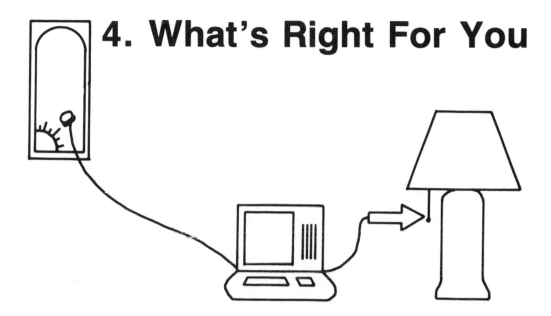

4. What's Right For You

THERE ARE AS MANY RIGHT WAYS TO DEVELOP a Home Control system as there are homes— and no two will be alike. In this chapter, you'll be able to find a plan that's right for you. One suggestion is to keep things flexible, for once you install your system you may very well think of other ideas that you may want to add. This field is growing rapidly, and ideas for enhancements are becoming available at a dynamic pace (just as we have seen in the microcomputer field).

Flexibility can be part of either an expensive or inexpensive system. For example, you could buy a very expensive single purpose burglar alarm system, have it installed, and all it would do is protect you from burglars. And if you move, it might not be able to be separated from your original house. Not very flexible! On the other hand, you could build your own Home Control system from parts, do your own installation, and provide yourself with a system that is inexpensive, yet flexible enough to perform everything cited in this book. Of course, this assumes you know your own limita-

tions in terms of what you can handle and what you should leave to the experts (designing, soldering, wiring, programming, etc.).

This book steers a middle ground, so that the person with little background in computers or electronics can just plug together and then operate a useful system. In any event, don't look at price as the measure of flexibility. Look at product features for flexibility, and look again to make sure you can handle their installation and operation.

STEPS TO SUCCESS

If you can follow these simple guidelines, you'll have a Home Control system that's just right for you!

1. Figure out your particular Home Control needs and desires.
2. Decide what is most important: flexibility, quality, plug-in or techy, price, etc.
3. Evaluate and select appropriate products.

4. If you don't already own one, decide on which computer best suits all your needs.

5. Plan all details.

6. Obtain all necessary parts, materials, and tools.

7. Review installation directions and safety precautions.

8. Install your system from the computer setup to all peripheral apparatus.

9. Load software, set parameters (schedule), and test.

10. Seize control of your home!

Step one, determining your needs, is critical to your success and this chapter will help you with sample home layouts and a checklist of items to include. The second step is to decide what is important for you. You should already be convinced that, whatever else you decide upon, flexibility should be included, as well.

Third, evaluate and select the appropriate products. For each of the operations you plan to control there may be just a few or possibly many options in terms of suitable products. In the component chapters towards the end of the book, suggested products are listed to help you install each component of your system. Also, the Product Directory (Appendix A) should prove useful in selecting specific items for inclusion in your system. The following checklist is useful for evaluating products.

☐ What does it do?
☐ With what can it interface?
☐ How hard is it to install?
☐ Does it require any alterations to the house?
☐ Is it removable if you move?
☐ Could it cause unexpected problems (i.e., combination of a dog and a motion detector)?
☐ Is special programming involved?
☐ What does it cost?
☐ Does anything else need to be purchased, and if so, what does it cost?
☐ Can you handle this product?

If you're not sure if a product meets your specific needs, check with your retailer or manufac-

turer. They'll be happy to explain their product's capabilities.

If you don't already have one, now is the time to decide on which computer. Make sure the one you choose fits into your Home Control needs as well as other uses. The general rule is to decide on the software first and the hardware second.

The next step is to plan all the details of your particular system. Later portions of this chapter should prove helpful in designing the overall framework, and the component chapters will list the steps needed to complete each specific project. Next, obtain the materials to complete each specific project. Although it's best to plan your overall system at one time, you probably will want to build your system a component at a time. This is the time to decide which projects should be installed first and then purchase the necessary supplies.

When installing your system take care that all pieces are correctly mounted. Remember, you want this system to last for many years to come, and a little extra attention to detail will pay off for a long time.

Once your system is installed, it's time to load the software and set all the parameters including linking the sensors to the items to be controlled, and scheduling each controlled item. Be sure to test each aspect of your Home Control system, and finally . . .

Seize control of your home!

TOUR YOUR HOME

This is where Home Control really becomes fun! Everyone in your family should become involved in designing the system since each may have a different idea of what should be included. Don't just sit in one room and try to determine your needs. Walk around the outside of your home and the inside, as well. Make some rough drawings of your house similar to those in this chapter, and note the locations of what should be controlled. Also, think about what the items controlled should be dependent upon. Should the front door light turn on at a certain time of day, should it turn on depending on how dark it is outside, or both?

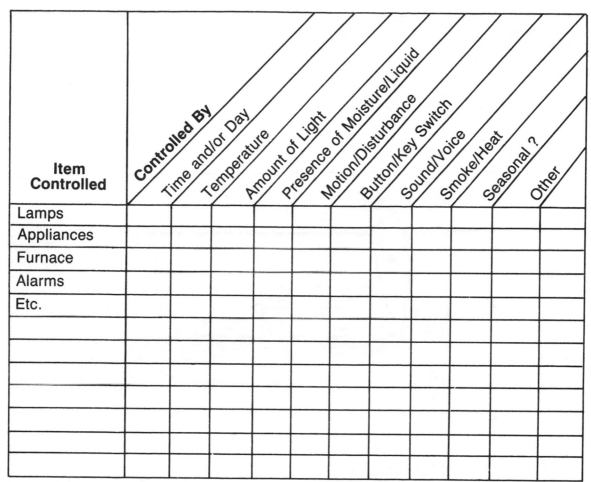

Item Controlled	Controlled By	Time and/or Day	Temperature	Amount of Light	Presence of Moisture/Liquid	Motion/Disturbance	Button/Key Switch	Sound/Voice	Smoke/Heat	Seasonal ?	Other
Lamps											
Appliances											
Furnace											
Alarms											
Etc.											

Fig. 4-1. Sense/signal matrix.

Figure 4-1 shows a partial list of categories of items which can be controlled and suggests things that might be sensed by your Home Control system in order to control each item. Of course, you can use just about any sensing capability (or combination of sensing capabilities) to have your system control whatever you desire. Some, however, will make better sense than others. Who knows! You may wish to have your front lawn sprinkler turn on when your front doorbell is pushed!

Let's start with the outside of your home, and work towards the inside. Figure 4-2 shows the property layout for a sample home. Note at the front of the property there is a walk light, and two more by the front and back doors. Also, there's a flood light for the garage area and two for the backyard. How should these be controlled? By the time of day? By motion at the front door? By how dark it is? By something else? Should any of these continue to be operated manually, but checked by the computer to make sure they have been turned off at a particular time of day? Should some of these be controlled together, or do they all need to be operated separately? These are the types of questions you should be thinking about for each item you wish to control.

Enough about outdoor lighting. What about your lawns and gardens? Are they a little less green than your neighbors? Maybe your Home Control system could help out here by controlling a sprin-

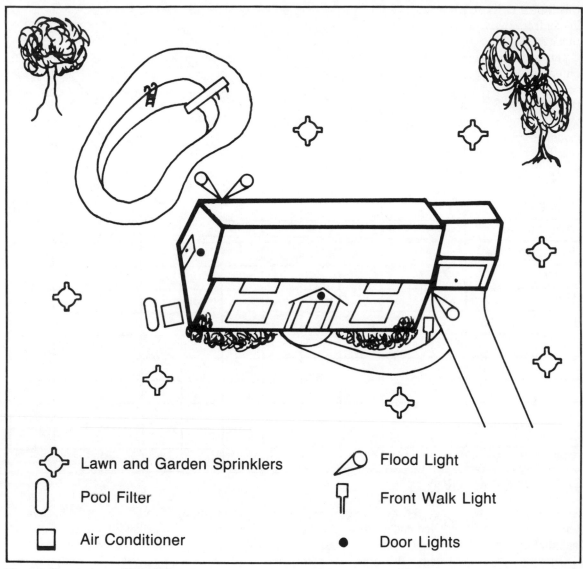

Lawn and Garden Sprinklers

Flood Light

Pool Filter

Front Walk Light

Air Conditioner

Door Lights

Fig. 4-2. Sample home property layout.

kling system. And if you're lucky enough to have a swimming pool, your Home Control system can work hard to operate the filter, check to make sure the water level isn't too low, and/or even control a small robot that will automatically clean your pool!

Before going inside, take a look at your house as if you were a burglar. What would be some likely spots to gain entry into your house? Possibly the basement windows are behind bushes and not easily seen by your neighbors. Maybe a burglar could enter through the garage, or by climbing to a first floor roof and gaining access through a second story window. Or would he just force the front door? These notes can help you decide on what should be included in a burglar alarm system, should you choose to have one become a portion of your system.

Now let's take another view of your home—

this time a cross section which cuts through your house from the attic to the basement. How about those energy ideas that were discussed in Chapter 3. Do you wish to control your furnace, your air conditioning, or your electric hot water? Make a cross sectional drawing of your house and locate any of these items. Also, has your basement ever had a flood during a heavy rain? Could that washing machine hose ever burst? Note the location(s) in your basement or laundry room where water would likely collect first.

Where might smoke (or heat) detectors be located? Likely you will want to have at least one in both the basement and the attic. Use your version of Fig. 4-3 to locate these, and use Fig. 4-4 or Fig. 4-5 to locate these detectors on the main floor(s) of your house. Figure 4-4 shows a two story home and Fig. 4-5 shows a one level or ranch house. Make your own drawing of your house using these figures as a guide. Now walk through your home and make appropriate notes as to the locations of items to be controlled, and what relation(s) they

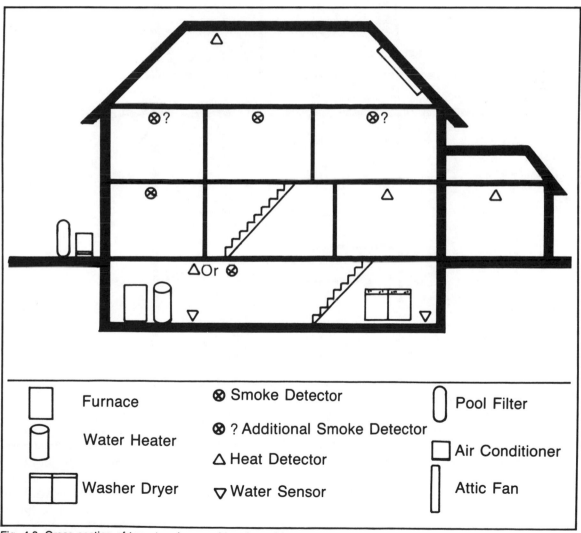

Fig. 4-3. Cross section of two story house with attic and basement.

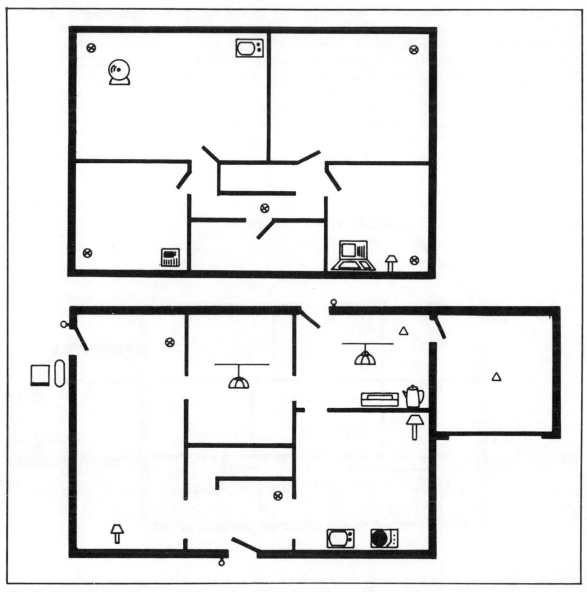

Fig. 4-4. Floor layout of two story home.

should have to time, temperature, amount of available light, etc.

Don't worry about perfection now. Many of the ideas for Home Control will become clearer as you proceed through the remaining chapters. Include in your diagram all lamps, wall or ceiling lights, radios, stereos, room air conditioners and room heaters, fans, televisions, thermostats, humidifiers or dehumidifiers, and appliances such as the coffee pot and toaster oven that you might want controlled automatically. Also be sure to note the location of your computer.

Figure 4-6 is a worksheet to help you. It lists many potential items to be controlled, with space available for others. After each item to be controlled is a line to note its location, the product or module that will be needed, the house and unit code, the "sense" (time, temperature, etc.) that will guide control, and a place for other notes. Also, the worksheet provides spaces for the locations of the sensing side of your Home Control system. Each of the columns will be explained in detail later. For now, it's enough to fill in the locations of the items you have decided to control. As you proceed through the book, you can update the columns as they become clearer.

PRODUCT OVERVIEW

At this point, it may be worthwhile to overview the products currently available for Home Control. These products are listed briefly in the Product Directory (Appendix A) and this section will help you categorize items and make reference much easier. The Product Directory includes the following information. An explanation of each category follows this list.

☐ Sensor interface and signaling devices.
☐ Signaling devices.
☐ Sensor interface devices and individual sensors.
☐ The BSR X-10 product line.
☐ Voice products.
☐ Robots.
☐ Miscellaneous.

Sensor Interface & Signaling Devices. These are more or less complete Home Control devices (they include both sides of the interfaces needed) which can be linked to a computer. These devices include the capability for both analog and/or digital sensing, as well as the control side—usually an X-10 Controller and sometimes a relay (hard-wired) system. Most of the items also include the necessary software. Some of the sensor interface and signaling devices may have additional features—a battery back-up, a hardware or soft-

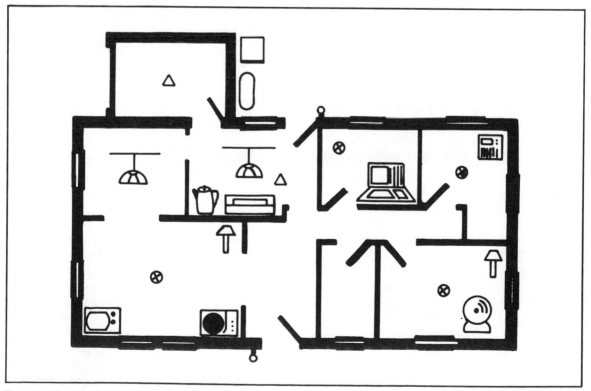

Fig. 4-5. Floor layout of single story home.

Sensor or Controlled Item	Application	Location	Equipment	House or Unit Code	Time or Sensor Link	Notes
Example: lamp	convenience	living rm	lamp module	B/3	5:00pm-11pm	security?

Suggested Items to Include:

Controlled items: lamps and other lighting, appliances, stereo, radios, TV's, central or room air conditioning, fans, room heaters, furnace, hot water heater, humidifier, etc.

Sensors: light, temperature, individual burglar or fire security sensors, moisture or water sensors, etc.

Fig. 4-6. Home Control planning worksheet.

ware clock, and even voice synthesizing or recognition capabilities.

Signaling Devices. The items listed under this category are those that the computer can use to control external events. Usually these devices cannot sense any real world conditions, except, in some cases, time. For the most part these are computer linked X-10 Controllers used to control the X-10 Lamp or Appliance Modules. With some care, signaling devices can be linked with those from the next category (sensor interface devices) to provide a complete Home Control system.

Sensor Interface Devices and Individual Sensors. The sensor interface device category includes those items that can help your computer understand or interpret the outside world. These, therefore, can convert information from the sensors for the computer. (Although some of these have output capabilities to control external events, a complete Home Control application would be simplified if combined with an X-10 Controller.) Also included in this category are a few actual sensors that can be located around the house and interpret the real world. They can be linked with the sensor interface devices in this category (or the first category) and together provide the raw input necessary to help your computer understand what's going on.

BSR X-10 Product Line. Since many of the items in the first two categories use the X-10 Control system, an entire section of the Product Directory is devoted to the controlled modules and some stand-alone (noncomputer linked) X-10 Controllers. One of the widest lines is available through BSR (USA) Ltd., and a substantial overview of their X-10 product line is provided in Appendix A. Included are the various Modules that you can control with your Home Control system as well as some stand-alone controllers which may support your overall design by providing additional flexibility.

Voice Products. Included here are devices that can perform voice synthesis (the capability to speak), and voice recognition (the capability to recognize the spoken word). With some care, these voice products can be used in conjunction with the products in the previous categories to provide voice characteristics in your Home Control system. (Note: Make sure that you have obtained enough information about a particular voice product and its compatibility with other products before purchasing.)

Robots. Although many would say that robots currently offer little in terms of practical, cost effective features, they are fun and may be of interest to you. Even today in particular situations, there are certainly some practical applications, and advances are occurring rapidly in this area which will make them more desirable. Therefore, a listing of available products has been included in the Product Directory.

Miscellaneous. This section includes some interesting products that just didn't fit neatly into the other categories.

Take a few minutes and look through the various products included in the directory. Many of the product applications and terms used will become clearer as you continue through the book, and you'll find the Product Directory to be a good source for ideas as you develop each aspect of your Home Control system.

5. Setting Up Home Base

THIS CHAPTER WILL DISCUSS HOW TO SET UP your home with the control devices directly connected to your computer—the sensor interface and signaling devices. Sometimes both devices are in one unit. The Product Directory includes a wide variety of Home Control sensor interface and/or signaling devices from which to choose.

Unfortunately, it would be near impossible to describe each available product in great detail. However, so that you can better understand this equipment in general, this chapter will fully describe a few representative products that have a wide variety of features and can handle many different types of applications. These products have been specifically chosen to show the variety of Home Control Products in the market today.

☐ The RS-232-to-X-10 Interface from Heathkit.
☐ The HomeBrain from HyperTek.
☐ The Master System from Anova Electronics.

Keep in mind that there are many excellent products on the market. One product may be much more suitable to your specific needs than another. I suggest that you first contact the manufacturer or distributor of a product and request full details before you purchase it. Be assured that you won't be the first to call or write to get some questions answered. The products described in this chapter, however, should provide you with a good feel for the basics of a Home Control system and what will be involved in setting up your home base.

RS-232-TO-X-10 INTERFACE

One of the most practical ways of starting a Home Control system is with Heathkit's RS-232-to-X-10 Interface at $129.95 (Fig. 5-1). In terms of our definitions, this is only a signalling (controller) device; yet when tied to your computer, it puts a lot of Home Control at your fingertips. This unit can actually control up to X-10 Lamp and Appliance Modules independently by sending signals through your house wiring.

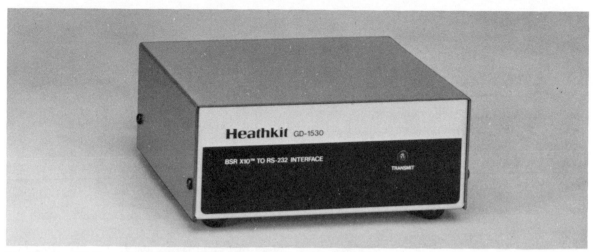

Fig. 5-1. The "X-10 to RS-232 Interface" (courtesy of the Heath Company).

In general, there appears to be no real standard method for connecting Home Control items to a computer. This is largely due to computers themselves being quite different from one another and the fact that Home Control sensing interfaces and signaling devices are often developed to be attached to a particular computer. The RS-232-to X-10 Interface was developed, however, to use a standard interfacing (connection) port which many computers have either as standard equipment or as a fairly standard option. This interfacing port is the serial (RS-232) port which is generally used for computer communications (through modems) and can be used to connect printers and other devices.

One particularly nice benefit of taking this approach is that Home Control devices that connect in this way are likely to be adaptable should you ever decide to buy a different computer. Another feature is that it is completely plug-in ready. In other words, there is no need to open your computer, and insert computer cards (special function boards) or make any other kinds of internal connections.

The Heathkit X-10 Controller weighs less than three pounds and comes complete with documentation describing the necessary hookup and explaining how to control it using BASIC programming (sample programs included). For those of you who

are comfortable with BASIC programming, you can use a timer function in your computer (if available), or build a simple software clock using FOR-NEXT loops to provide timed control of your X-10 Modules. And later, if you wish to be able to sense the outside world as part of your Home Control system, you can add a sensor interface to your system for more complete Home Control.

But before deciding that this system alone just can't be sophisticated enough as a Home Controller, keep in mind that as you progress through later chapters, this X-10 Controller and your computer can provide timed control of the following items, and this is not an exhaustive list:

☐ Lamps and appliances.
☐ Central heating and air conditioning.
☐ An electric hot water system.
☐ A simple lawn and garden watering system.

Not bad for a simple and inexpensive alternative!

HOMEBRAIN

The HomeBrain is a combined sensor interface and signaling device. Also sold by HyperTek (the manufacturer of the HomeBrain) are many of the devices that you might want in order to complete a Home Control system (actual sensors, X-10

Modules, etc.). The HomeBrain (pictured in Fig. 5-2) is a full featured system that can control any and all of the functions found in Chapter 6 through 16. It includes an X-10 signaling capability which can command up to 256 separately controlled X-10 Modules. Further, the HomeBrain can also control items around the house using eight relays (expandable to 16). The standard sensor interface includes 16 digital inputs (expandable to 48), and 16 analog inputs. (If you're unclear about any of the terms used above, review Chapter 2.)

The HomeBrain has its own built-in microprocessor. This means that once the unit is programmed, your computer is free to do something else. You can even disconnect your computer completely, and the HomeBrain will keep right on taking care of its household duties. Also included in the HomeBrain is a sophisticated clock that keeps track of the date (e.g., Jan. 1, 1985), the day (Monday, Tuesday, etc.), and the time of day as well.

If there is a brownout, the equipment will keep on running indefinitely, and if power is interrupted completely, the HomeBrain can still function for about three hours. (Of course, things that operate via normal household current will not work, but the HomeBrain can keep such functions as a burglar or fire alarm system working on battery power.) After three hours, if power has still not returned, then the HomeBrain goes into a sleep mode where, although it ceases functioning, it retains its memory (the software and schedule instructions) for a one month period.

The HomeBrain can even be linked with a *modem*—a device to send or receive computer data over the telephone. This can be used to program the unit from remote locations, or in the event of a break-in, a basement flood, or a fire, the modem can be used to notify the appropriate authority.

The HomeBrain unit is roughly the size of an ordinary electrical junction (fuse) box located in the basement or utility area of most homes. Its dimensions are 18 by 15 by 4 inches and it can be located either with your computer, or in virtually any other location in your house. HyperTek suggests that it be placed in the basement or utility area, since this is usually least obtrusive, and any wiring that needs to be done is often easier.

Included with the HomeBrain is a 57-page manual that includes the following:

☐ An overview of the product.
☐ Details on how to set it up.
☐ Details on how to connect any necessary wiring.
☐ The HomeBrain's internal features.
☐ Information how to use their software (complete with examples).

With the HomeBrain you can obtain the appropriate software for many different home computers including the Apple II line, the IBM PC, Commodore computers, and most any computer that operates under the CP/M operating system. (The operating systems used with the Apple, IBM and Commodore are their standard operating systems, or in otherwords there need not be anything special about your computer if you own one of these.)

The software that is available for the HomeBrain is extensive. The simplest version is a standard, yet flexible package which does not require any programming. However, for anyone who wants to get involved with the nuts and bolts of the system, HyperTek makes available a Toolkit which is really a programming language (like BASIC, Fortran, or Pascal) specifically designed for the HomeBrain and Home Control. With the Toolkit, those who have a flair for doing their own can develop special application programs. But for most, the standard package is more than adequate since it offers a great deal of flexibility.

Setting Up the Brain

The HomeBrain is relatively easy to install. Though this sounds overly simplistic, before you start setting up any Home Control System, take the time to **completely read the documentation**. Although most Home Control products are carefully thought out by their manufacturers, they can be sensitive. A little extra time with the instructions can save a lot of frustration later.

Fig. 5-2. The "HomeBrain" (courtesy of HyperTek Inc.).

Setup of the HomeBrain requires basically three things—mounting the unit, connecting the battery, and connecting the HomeBrain to your computer. Both the mounting and battery installation are straight forward, and require a total of a few minutes effort. Connecting the HomeBrain to your computer is also quite simple. HomeBrain connects to your computer using its RS-232 port, just as the Heathkit product does.

The HomeBrain can use either a commercially available RS-232 interface cable, or a simplified three wire cable. When you buy the HomeBrain or any other Home Control item, be sure to check with the retailer to make sure you have all necessary and appropriate cables. Once the cable is connected, the computer link is complete and you're ready to connect the various sensors, and items to be controlled.

Sensing with the Brain

As mentioned earlier, HomeBrain has 32 discrete sets of terminals used to sense conditions around the house. (The term "terminals" might best be thought of as similar to the two screw type connections on the back of a stereo amplifier. On most products, two such screw connections are available for each sensor, just like two screw connections are available for each speaker on a stereo.) The terminals found on the HomeBrain are similar to those found on other manufacturer's products, and are used for connecting sensors that sense light, temperature, and other things. Sixteen of these are analog sensor terminals (able to measure how hot, how light, etc., by determining different voltage levels) and sixteen are digital sensor terminals (able to sense on or off conditions). The analog sensor terminals have the ability to work as digital sensor terminals, if so desired. The locations of the terminals are shown in Fig. 5-3. These 32 terminals, a very generous supply, are probably more than most people would ever use.

Note on the top of Fig. 5-3 the word "knockouts" with three arrows pointing towards the top of the unit. These knockouts (pieces of metal that can be easily "knocked" out) are provided so that wires can enter the HomeBrain and be attached to the terminals.

Signaling with the Brain

The HomeBrain also has two types of control or signaling methods—relays and the X-10 method. Only the relays are easily recognizable and their location can be seen in Fig. 5-3. HomeBrain comes equipped with eight relays and can be expanded to as many as sixteen. Relays are rarely available on Home Control products, and they are one of the features of the HomeBrain that makes it particularly flexible. As an example, these are useful during power outages to ensure that a burglar, fire, or flood condition alarm system is still operable. Those systems that just make use of the X-10 controller method will be of little use under power outage conditions. (However, this might not be of particular concern to you, and besides, the relay system is not wireless as is the X-10 system.)

On the HomeBrain each relay system can be wired in two different ways. The first, called *normally open* , means that whatever is being operated is generally off—such as an alarm or siren. The second, called *normally closed*, means the opposite: the item being controlled is usually on. An extra terminal screw is provided for each relay for this purpose.

The HomeBrain's X-10 System can control up to 256 individually controlled items throughout your house by sending electronic messages through your home's electrical system.

Making the Brain Think

Most manufacturers of Home Control products offer software (usually on diskettes). Others may provide only documentation that shows how to incorporate their product's functions into software that you must write. However, available software is usually more different than similar which suggest two things:

☐ The HomeBrain's software, as described here, will not necessarily be similar to another package you may consider.

☐ Be sure you find out the specifics about the software included with any package before making a purchase. This is especially true if you are

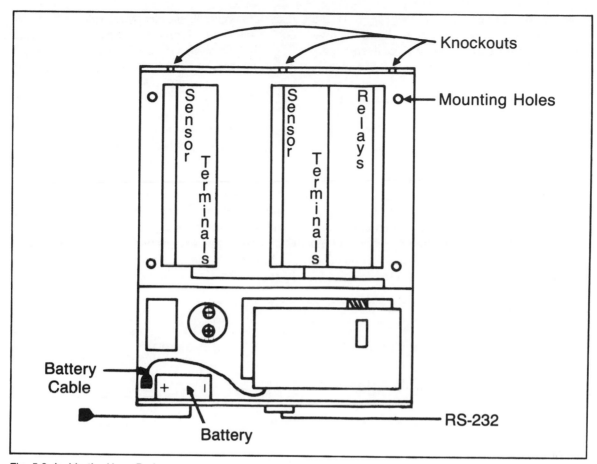

Fig. 5-3. Inside the HomeBrain.

not a programmer. Make sure that you are getting simple, user friendly software!

However, information on a specific products software—in this case, HomeBrain—will at least give you a basis for comparison shopping among other packages.

The variations in available software and control equipment reflect the very different types of people interested in this subject. Purchasers can be classified into three different groups:

☐ Group I is only interested in the benefits of Home Control, and don't care if they ever get involved with a computer.

☐ Group II is only interested in the benefits of Home Control and wish to have software that

does not require programming knowledge, but that allows them to make scheduling changes and modify the operation of the system at will.

☐ Group II is only interested in programming and the design of computer and Home Control systems. This group likes full control so that they can design any type of Home Control strategy.

The HomeBrain is a good example since it has different packages available for the three types of purchasers. Many of the other products target software exclusively against one particular group. Here's how it works for the HomeBrain.

Group I. For those with no interest in computers themselves, HomeBrain can be programmed by the retailer at the time of installation. Different schedules for various times of the year are stored in the memory in the HomeBrain's own microprocessor. A computer need not even remain in the home after the initial set-up and is only necessary to make a change to the schedules, or if you later want to change or add a feature to the system. In this event, reprogramming is done by the retailer returning with his computer or, in some cases, the retailer can even reprogram the HomeBrain over the phone lines.

Group II. A standard software package is available for this group. The package assumes that the HomeBrain has been installed according to more strict specifications. (i.e., particular sensors, when included in the system, are wired to specific terminals, and particular items to be controlled, again—when included, are connected to specific relays). However, these equipment standardizations don't have any real impact in terms of scheduling flexibility. This software is friendly and allows the nonprogrammer to accomplish his desires, and to change those schedules at will. As an example, say you originally had your front door light turn on at different times depending on the time of year, but then decided that on cloudy days it should turn on a bit earlier. The standard program would allow you to add your light sensor (to the time factor) as a means of controlling your front light.

Also for nonprogrammers are two software packages called Display and Create. The Display package is used to display and control the functions of a house using a diagram of the house produced on the Create package. This allows family members to control particular functions which have been

ENANET - enables network (short control linking program).
DISNET - disables network.
SKPNET - conditional break from network.

INPUT - push status of register to stack.
TRUP - checks for transition of off to on.
TRDN - checks for transition of on to off.
TRCH - checks for transition either way.

OUTPUT - turns register on or off.
OUTCC - X-10 Module command.

Logic commands: AND, OR, XOR, and NOT.

Other commands include counter and timer functions. For example:

SETCNT - sets counter to new value.
ENATMR - enables a timer.
DISALM - disables internal alarm clock.

Fig. 5-4. Abbreviated list of HomeBrain Toolkit commands.

```
DEFNET 1
TRUP 3
OUTPUT 64
INPUT 1
AND
ONREG 128
ONREG 129
SETTMR 1,300
TRUP 91
OFFREG 128
OFFREG 129
END
```

Using a motion detector and light sensor, this program controls the front door bell, front door light, and driveway light.

Theory of operation: When presence is sensed, the front door bell will be rung briefly, and if dark outside, the front door and driveway lights will be turned on for five minutes. After the five minutes the lights are turned back off.

Fig. 5-5. A frontdoor arrival routine.

predetermined while using the Create package. Both are designed for nonprogrammers and are user friendly.

Group III. For those who enjoy programming and want to be able to wire and operate the HomeBrain in any way possible, a complete programming language is available called the Toolkit. Many of the commands in this language are summarized in Fig. 5-4, and by reviewing this summary you programmers out there can begin to see that just about anything is possible using this language.

Many of the commands can be better understood if they are divided in half. For example, DISALM stands for DISable ALarM: it actually disables one of 16 alarm clocks built into the HomeBrain. ENAPAS is an abbreviation for ENAble PASsword: to operate the HomeBrain a password must be supplied.

Although this chapter's intent is not to be a programming guide, a simple sample program for the HomeBrain (using the Toolkit) is provided in Fig. 5-5.

MASTER SYSTEM

After you have completed reading this book, you may decide that having your computer tied to your Home Control system is not for you. And although there are a number of Home Control products that can operate after being programmed by a computer and then disconnected, the particular features of the products you find may not suit you for one reason or another. An alternative for you might be the Anova Master System shown in Fig. 5-6.

Actually, depending on your definition of a computer, most would probably consider the Master System a computer itself, although a little unconventional! It certainly has the input, output, and logic functions, and in terms of Home Control, it's quite sophisticated. The Master System is actually made up of three subsystems that all cooperate with each other.

☐ The Anova Telephone Center (Model 7000).
☐ The Anova Control Center (Model 8000).
☐ The Anova Protection Center (Model 9000).

Let me describe each component of the Master System.

Protection Center

The Protection Center can be thought of as a Sen-

Fig. 5-6. The Master System (courtesy of Anova Electronics, Inc.).

sor Interface in that it can sense and interpret signals for emergency conditions including intrusion/burglar attempts, fire and smoke conditions, utility failure, and medical or personal emergency (panic) conditions. The Protection Center is a wireless system using RF (radio frequency) detection transmitters that are part of the various sensors. The sensor/transmitter devices available include a Door/Window Intrusion Transmitter (#9010), a Smoke Alarm/Transmitter (#9030), a Water Detection Transmitter (#9040), and a handheld Personal Emergency Transmitter (#9020).

The Protection Center is more than just a Sensor Interface because it also includes both the logic and signaling capabilities needed for a stand-alone protection device. If an emergency condition is sensed, the protection center can react with four different alarm sounds and the console will display the particular condition sensed. To notify you further about an emergency, the Anova Protection Center can signal remote alarms to sound, and turn on lights and/or appliances. With the Telephone Center, the Protection Center can even call for help. Other features of this unit include a battery back-up for full operation during power failures, a low battery indicator, a key lock on the panel, and a constant checking capability on the system's status.

Control Center

The Control Center offers remote control (by sending signals over normal house wiring) of up to 16 lights and appliances. This control can be either instant or timed (through a seven-day clock), and the console provides a constant status of each item controlled. Special applications can be controlled at the console including dimming of lights, the ability to turn all lights on at once, the ability to turn all lights and appliances off at once, a feature that immediately turns selected items on and, after a predetermined time interval, the same items off, and a programmable snooze alarm.

The Control Center has a battery back-up that maintains its memory in the event of a power failure (although lights and appliances will not work during the failure). The actual remote Light and Appliance Modules used by the Anova Control Center feature local on/off (dimming for lights) control capabilities, and have two way communications with the Control Center (thus the Control Center actually knows if a light or appliance is on or off). A security switch is provided on the modules so that any particular lamp or appliance can be linked to the Protection Center.

Telephone Center

The Telephone Center is a very sophisticated telephone system which includes an answering machine, an automatic dialer, a speaker phone, and the capability to link to the Protection Center in case of an emergency.

The answering machine can record up to 60 minutes of incoming calls and only records when it senses the caller is actually speaking. Further, it has a seven channel outgoing message tape, a time logging function for incoming messages, a digital message counter, and a beeper that allows you to listen to your messages from any phone anywhere.

The automatic dialer offers one-button dialing of up to 16 numbers. It has a battery back-up to retain its memory during power failures.

The speaker phone allows hands-free and group conversation. Other features of the Telephone Center include 'Call screening' (for those of you who receive calls from your least favorite relative or unwanted solicitations), automatic redial of busy numbers, a call timer, call holding, and a time and date clock.

The Master System incorporates all these functions into a contemporary styled three piece unit that all looks like it belongs together and therefore could be located in any room of your house. With all the features of this product, it truly is a worthwhile alternative for your Home Control system.

alternative for your Home Control system.

PRODUCT SUMMARY

This chapter has provided an overview of a few products which show a wide variety of types of Home Control systems in today's market. There are many other fine products that can be used for Home Control, and now that you have a reasonably good idea of these few, you should be in a better position to compare the products available and pick the one best suited to you and your family.

The following 11 chapters will help you in making that choice. These chapters may be thought of as the component chapters, for each takes a specific component or application of Home Control and describes it in detail. By reading and then building these components, at last, Home Control can be actually implemented in your home!

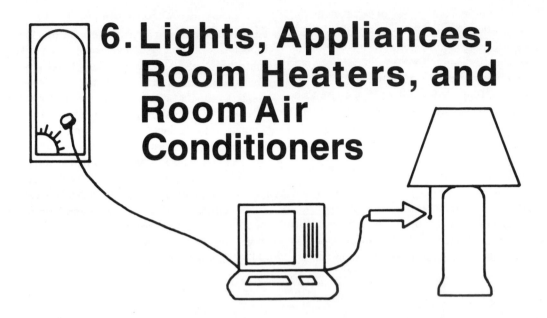

6. Lights, Appliances, Room Heaters, and Room Air Conditioners

THE COMPUTER HOME CONTROLS THAT ARE the easiest to install are described in this chapter. These include lights, lamps, radios, TVs, coffee pots, room heaters, room air conditioners, attic fans—in short, any electrical device or appliance that you want to control according to the time of day or the day of the week or both.

All have certain features in common which make them easy to install and use.

1. Only standard plug-in parts are used.

2. No additional wiring of any kind is necessary.

3. The computer clock is continually checked to see if it's the time and day to do what you want. For example, you might want an outside light on your house turned on at 6 P.M., but only on Friday and Saturday nights.

4. All applications discussed will use an X-10 Controller and standard X-10 Modules connected to whatever is being controlled.

There are five simple steps that you must follow:

1. Select the item or items you wish to control (lamps, appliances, etc.).

2. Obtain and set up the X-10 Controller (see Chapters 2 and 5).

3. Obtain an X-10 Module for each item you wish to control.

4. Using your control software (described in Chapters 2 and 5), enter the schedule for each device or appliance.

5. Plug each lamp and/or appliance to be controlled into its module, and then plug the module unit into a wall outlet.

That's it!

If you wish to get going immediately, you might want to start with the house survey you completed in Chapter 4. Look down your list and note those items which you wish to have controlled only by the clock or by the calendar.

Safety Note. Appliances that heat up (such as electric room heaters, coffee pots, toasters, ovens) **can be dangerous if turned on at the**

wrong time or if they remain on for extended periods.

To control heat-generating appliances safely, it is suggested that your computer turn such appliances on only when you also have the computer check that they are off a short time later. Here's a simple example of three ways to accomplish the same thing with varying degrees of safety. Suppose you want your coffee ready and waiting in the kitchen each weekday when you get up in the morning. One way—not the safest, and hence not recommended—is to set your computer to turn the coffee pot on each morning at 6 A.M. (Of course, to work properly, any of these methods require that the water and coffee have been placed in the pot the night before!)

But what about the time you forget to turn the pot off before leaving for work? It stays on all day and becomes a potentially serious hazard.

The second method is simple and safer. Have the computer also check to make sure the coffee pot is turned off at 9 A.M. But now what about the morning you forgot to put the water and coffee into the pot the night before? Or the morning you're away from home?

Here is the third and safest way. Have a stand-alone X-10 Controller (i.e., one that is not connected to your computer—various types are described in the Product Directory) in your bedroom. Then you can signal the coffee to go on as soon as you wake up. By the time you make it to the kitchen, the coffee will probably be ready. You should still set your computer to check every day at 9 A.M. to make sure that the pot is off. This will happen whether or not you actually make coffee that day, and you don't have to worry about leaving a heat-generating appliance on when you are away from home.

This warning discussion was included because it's important. But don't be scared off from using CHC; just make sure that you do so safely. And not all the appliances you want to control by the clock will require such precautions. A look on the brighter side shows all the advantages to controlling lights and appliances.

You could have your house brightly lit up prior to your arrival home from work on a cold, dark night. Your Computer-based Home Control system can also warm the house up for your arrival after saving on fuel costs all day if you follow the procedures in Chapter 8 for controlling your furnace. The radio could start playing your favorite station as you walk in the door. And in the summer, it might be nice to have the attic fan begin working, or a room air conditioner start before your arrival.

A realistic but varied (and with some software—random) pattern of lights going on and off in different parts of the house when no one is at home can be a deterrent to would-be burglars, and these, together with radios in one or more rooms similarly programmed, give your home a lived-in look.

HOW DOES IT WORK?

Chapter 2 and 5 described the basic parts and connections. To review, these are an X-10 Controller connected to your computer and the appropriate control software to make the system run. For each item to be controlled, you will need the appropriate X-10 Control Module. Note that there are different X-10 Control Modules for different devices. Make sure that the specifications of the modules you are going to buy fit the application for which they are to be used. A list of X-10 Control Modules appears in Fig. 6-1.

Let's assume that you have already hooked up your X-10 Controller to your computer. Suppose you want to control a lamp in your living room. You want to have the lamp turn on prior to your arrival home from work on weekdays. Usually, you arrive home at 5:45 P.M. so you want the lamp to turn on at 5:30. On weekends you want to turn the lamp on a little earlier—at, say, 5:00. In addition, since you usually entertain on Saturday evenings, you'd like the living room to have a softer effect. In order to accomplish this you may want the lamp to dim to half of its normal brightness.

First, you'll need to obtain the correct module for this purpose. Since your lamp (we'll assume) uses a regular incandescent bulb and the bulb used is rated at 150 watts, the Lamp Module fits this application perfectly. This module can handle

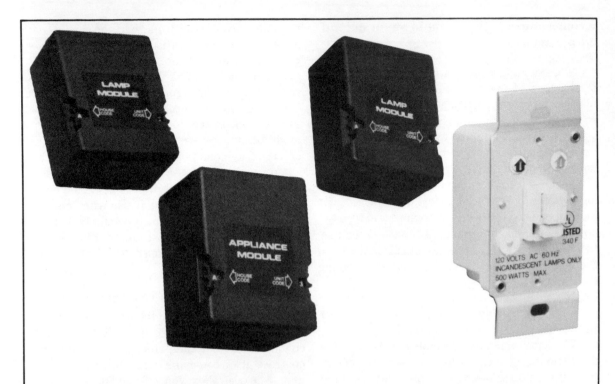

Lamp Module: Allows you to turn lamps on and off anywhere in the house by remote control. Responds to ALL LIGHTS ON, BRIGHTEN, and DIM commands.

Appliance Module: Allows you to turn appliances on and off anywhere in the house by remote control. Will not respond to ALL LIGHTS ON, BRIGHTEN, or DIM commands. Available in either two or three (grounded) prong models.

Wall Switch Module: Fits where existing wall switches fit and allows you to turn any wall switch operated lights on or off (inside or outside the house). Responds to ALL LIGHTS ON, BRIGHTEN, and DIM commands.

Wall Receptacle Module: Fits where existing wall outlets fit and allows you to turn any lamp or appliance on and off by remote control. Does not respond to ALL LIGHTS ON, BRIGHTEN, or DIM commands (not shown).

Heavy Duty Appliance Modules: These operate like other Appliance modules, but are specifically constructed to be used only with 220/240 volt split phase systems. These can control heavy duty room air conditioners, and similar appliances which use 220/240 volts and are within a maximum rating of 15 or 20 Amps (not shown).

Fig. 6-1. X-10 Modules (courtesy of BSR (USA) Ltd.).

a light bulb (or set of bulbs) up to 300 watts—more than enough for our purpose. The Lamp Module also has the ability to dim or brighten your lamp. This is the piece of equipment needed.

Next, set the appropriate HOUSE code (red dial) and UNIT code (black dial) on the module, plug the lamp into the module, and plug the module into the wall outlet.

Now you must adjust your software schedule on your computer to make the right things happen at the appropriate times. Each manufacturer's software will be a little different. Basically, however, you want to load the software into the computer and either create or update the schedule by entering the individual pieces of information. These will include the following:

☐ Module HOUSE CODE: Usually a letter from A to P.

☐ Module UNIT CODE: Usually a number from 1 to 16.

☐ CONTROL CODE: Codes such as ON, OFF, CLEAR (turns everything OFF), ALL (all lights on), DIM(0-9), or BRIGHTEN(0-9).

☐ TIME: Military time (24 hour clock; e.g., 7 A.M. would equal 7:00, 12 Noon would equal 12:00, and 6 P.M. would equal 18:00).

☐ DAY: Day of the week (likely abbreviated).

Based on the proposed schedule above, and assuming that the HOUSE CODE used is B, the UNIT CODE is 3, and the living room lamp should turn off at 11:30 P.M. each night; a computer printout of this schedule might look as shown in Fig. 6-2.

The first line of the schedule turns the lamp on every day at 5:30 P.M. (assuming the lamp is not already on). The next two lines turn the lamp on at 5:00 P.M. on the weekends. The next line dims the lamp to create the appropriate mood for entertaining on Saturday evening, and the last line turns the lamp off every day of the week at 11:30 P.M.

By plugging in a lamp to an X-10 Module, and setting the appropriate schedule at the computer, it easily becomes controlled by the Home Control system.

CONTROL SCHEDULE

FILE NAME: LAMP

HSE CDE	UNT CDE	CMND CDE	TIME HR:MN	DAY CDE
B	3	ON	17:30	ALL
B	3	ON	17:00	SAT
B	3	ON	17:00	SUN
B	3	DIM5	17:01	SAT
B	3	OFF	23:30	ALL

Fig. 6-2. Printout of a schedule for a lamp controlled by the X-10 System.

WHAT MUST I BUY?

The modules can be purchased at various electronic and department stores, including Sears, AT&T Phone Stores, and Radio Shack. Some Modules are sold under the store's own brand name, but all X-10 Systems will work together without difficulty. The following is a full cost retail price list, but often you can find the modules discounted.

Lamp Module	$22.50
3 Prong Appliance Module	$22.50
2 Prong Appliance Module	$22.50
Wall Switch Module—push button control	$22.50
Wall Switch Module—switch control	$16.99
3 Way Wall Switch Set	$29.99
Wall Receptacle Module	$29.99
Heavy Duty 220 volt Appliance Module (15 Amp Prong Configuration)	$44.99
Heavy Duty 220 volt Appliance Module (20 Amp Prong Configuration)	$49.99

WHAT MUST I DO?

Choose the appropriate modules (referring to Fig.

6-1) whose amps or watts match or are greater than those on the appliance you wish to control. The watts are found on the tops of light bulbs. The Amps are usually found on the sides or bottoms of appliances, or on the appliance motors. Now purchase the appropriate modules.

Important Note: Watts and Amps of the items to be controlled should never exceed the rating of the module. All of the modules, unless otherwise noted, work on standard house current, defined as 110-120 volts. The Heavy Duty Modules are exceptions to this and are rated for 220-240 volts. **Check ratings carefully.**

Once you have purchased your modules, connect them to the items to be controlled. Now adjust your control software to reflect your scheduling requirements. That's all there is to it. Enjoy!

HOW LONG WILL IT TAKE?

As noted, these applications in Computer Home Control are the simplest and quickest to install. Once you have purchased the modules, you need only adjust each for the HOUSE and UNIT CODE, plug the lamp or appliance into the module, plug the module into the wall outlet, and adjust your software. A few minutes should cover this process!

Special Note on Wall Switch Modules. The Wall Switch module works on the same principle as all the other modules noted above, except for one feature: unlike most others, the Wall Switch Module is not plugged into a wall outlet, but instead replaces a normal wall switch found in your home. It is relatively easy to install by following the directions included and as described below. **Be sure to turn off your electricity first before installing one of these.**

1. Set the HOUSE CODE (red dial) to the desired setting (use small screwdriver).
2. Set the UNIT CODE (black dial) to the desired setting.
3. **Make sure electricity is turned off at circuit breaker or fuse box.**

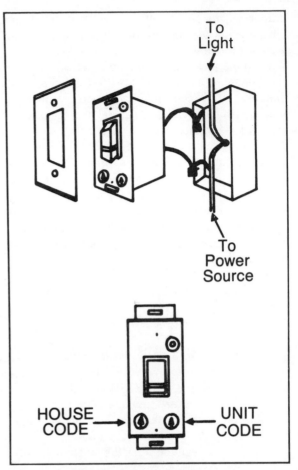

Fig. 6-3. Wall Switch Module installation.

4. Remove wall plate and old switch.
5. Connect leads as shown in Fig. 6-3, blue lead from the Wall Switch module to white wire and black lead to the black wire. Be sure to use wire nuts (provided) for insulation.
6. Mount the Wall Switch module, making sure the code dials are at the bottom.
7. Replace the wall plate, and turn the on-off switch to the on (up) position.
8. Turn the power on at the circuit breaker or fuse box.

Each of these takes approximately 10 to 15 minutes to install.

Note that in addition to controlling your lights via computer, when you install one of these Wall

Switch Modules the lights can also be manually controlled at the switch locations as with a normal wall switch. This feature allows the convenience of both manual and computer control. (Other modules can be manually controlled to a certain extent. However, the computer cannot always undo what you have done manually. For example, suppose you have a lamp connected to your CHC system, and your system is set to turn the lamp off at a certain time and then back on again later. If, before the computer turns the lamp off, you do so manually, then the computer X-10 Controller will not be able to turn it back on. If, however, the computer turns your lamp (or appliance) off, you can manually turn the lamp on at the lamp on/off switch.)

The Wall Switch Modules are meant to be used with incandescent lighting and include the dim and brighten features.

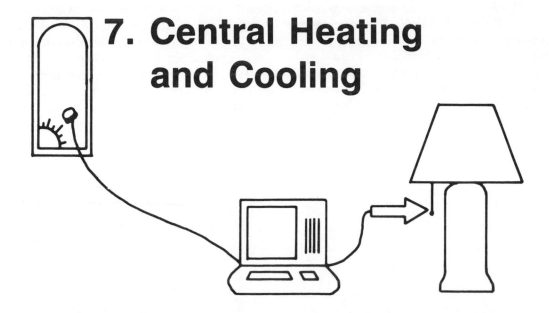

7. Central Heating and Cooling

CENTRAL HEATING AND COOLING (AIR CONditioning) control are likely the most cost effective ways to reduce the expenses of running your home. As related in Chapter 3, a single 10 degree nightly reduction in heat can save a home owner in some areas more than 15 percent. On a fuel bill of $1500 dollars a year, 15 percent represents a $225.00 savings. This alone, in a few years, may pay for your Home Control system (and possibly your computer!). And don't forget the federal (and in some areas, state) tax advantages. Your entire heat related Home Control expenses (and possibly a percentage of your computer) may wind up as a credit on page two of your 1040!

To continue with the heat example, why have only one reduction at night? In many households, including families with school-age children, a second reduction in heat will yield additional savings. Think about your weekday schedule. How many hours on average is everyone away from home during the day? And do you make use of that second heat zone in your house? Or if you don't have one, would one be worthwhile to add?

Weekend scheduling, in particular, is where a Home Control system can really pay off both in terms of convenience as well as in cost. A computer control system provides great flexibility since you can program weekends differently from weekdays. Actually, you can schedule each day differently, if that's what's needed to suit your life-style. The advantage of computer operation is that once programmed for your unique circumstances, you can forget about it.

Now let's switch to Central Air. (To control room air conditioners, see the previous chapter.) In general, the basic advantage is the same as described for home heating. Computer control allows you to only air condition your home when it is really needed for comfort and you save money in a similar fashion to controlling your furnace. A single eight hour increase of 10 degrees in the Washington, DC, area can save a homeowner with an annual air conditioning bill of $400 about 13 percent or $52. A dual shutdown of your air conditioner can save even more!

By using your Home Control system you can

easily see how you could save money and at the same time keep cool all summer long.

HOW DOES IT WORK?

Most home furnaces—whether gas, oil, or electric—and most central cooling systems use basically the same method of regulation. Whatever type of system, the only piece of apparatus necessary to alter is the thermostat. Basically, as shown in Fig. 7-1, the thermostat is a temperature sensing device. Once a preset temperature is ed (in the case of furnace control, when the temperature drops below a certain level), the thermostat allows an electric signal (switch) to turn on. This signal turns the furnace on and the house begins to warm. Once the house reaches the desired temperature, the signal shuts off and so does the furnace. The thermostat senses temperature and allows the switch to be either on or off.

Many methods could be used for computer con-trol of the furnace, though some are better than others. For example, one would be to have the computer directly control the signal to the furnace as in Fig. 7-2.

This method will certainly turn your furnace on and off, but the problem is that it has no way to sense temperature. Once the furnace turns on it will stay on no matter how hot your house gets. And, once the furnace goes off it will stay off, no matter how cold it becomes. Figure 7-3 shows how to take care of this particular problem.

Method number two resolves the problem by sensing temperature (through a thermistor—a temperature sensing device, connected to the computer) so that the computer knows when the house has become too cold or too hot. Theoretically, various temperatures could be maintained throughout the day and throughout the week. This sounds like an optimal heat control system. The problem arises when there is a power outage, or

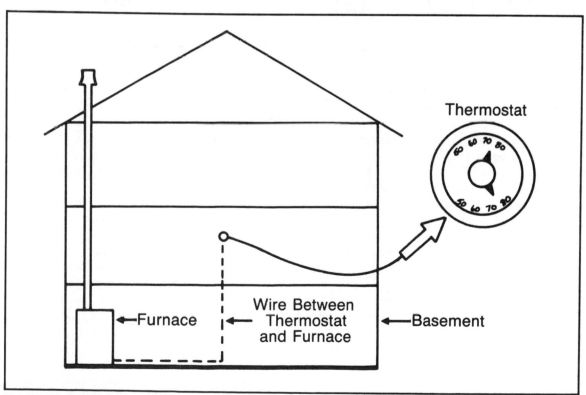

Fig. 7-1. Thermostat control of furnace. Electrical contact made at the thermostat when temperature dips.

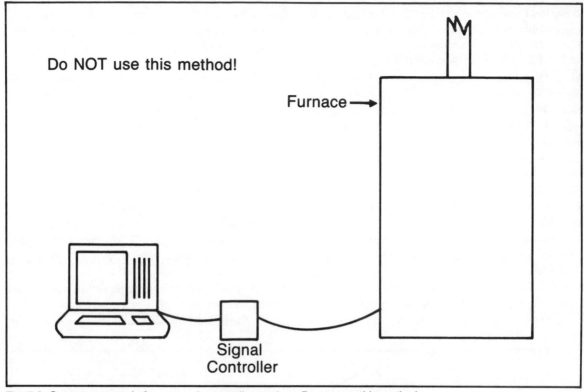

Do NOT use this method!

Furnace →

Signal
Controller

Fig. 7-2. Computer controls furnace only according to time. Do not use this method.

for some other reason your computer fails (such as your son Billy decides he wants to play SPACE PIRATE BLASTERS on the computer after coming home from school). Again, the furnace may stay on or stay off depending on how it was set when the computer went off. This could lead to either a very hot or very cold house! These methods are not recommended for Central Cooling for the same reasons.

The better alternative relies on tried and true technology—the kind that controls your home now, but with a few minor adjustments. Two are described in this book, one in this chapter and one in Appendix B. By far the easiest method is found here. However, the one described in the appendix is somewhat more exacting in terms of both timing (having the furnace or air conditioning system turn on as soon as the appropriate temperature is sensed), and also in terms of regulating to an exact temperature. For most pur-

poses, however, the method described in this chapter will offer the advantages you're looking for, and at the same time be easy to implement.

Remember the explanation of how a thermostat controls either the furnace or cooling system? The simple CHC method as shown in Fig. 7-4 works, in effect, by fooling the thermostat. This is done by turning on and off (via computer control) a very small local heater placed right below the thermostat. The local heater, as shown in the diagram, is roughly the size of a hockey puck and is controlled by one of the X-10 Appliance Modules. The local heater uses only a small amount of current, and therefore, a small voltage reducing box (transformer) is connected to the X-10 module. This cuts the voltage from normal house current (120 volts) to a much lower current (20 volts). A double strand wire connects the voltage reducer to the small local heater. No actual connection of any kind is directly made to your furnace, your cooling system, or even your thermostat.

Let's look at heating first. You may decide to keep your house at 72 degrees when you are awake, and at 62 degrees when you are asleep or away. The first step is to set up the computerized thermostat controller and then set your thermostat to 72 degrees. When you want the house at the lower temperature, you will have the small localized heater turn on under your thermostat and raise the temperature 10 degrees. This fools the thermostat into thinking the house is warmer than it actually is; the furnace will shut down and the house will be allowed to cool until it reaches approximately 62 degrees. At that point, the thermostat will think that the house is heading below 72 degrees, and will allow the furnace to turn on (maintaining the heat at 62 degrees). When you are awake and at home, your control system will be scheduled to have the

small localized heater in the off position, and your house will be at a comfortable 72 degrees.

To control the air conditioning, you would first set your thermostat at the maximum temperature that you would be willing to have your house reach (possibly at those times when no one will be at home). Now the localized heater should be scheduled to turn on when you are at home and when you want the house to be cooler. The localized heater will raise the temperature by 10 degrees at the thermostat and the central air system will remain on until your house has reached approximately 72 degrees. (The thermostat believes the house has reached 82 degrees, though in fact the house is at 72 degrees.)

WHAT MUST I BUY?

Obtaining the necessary parts is simple because

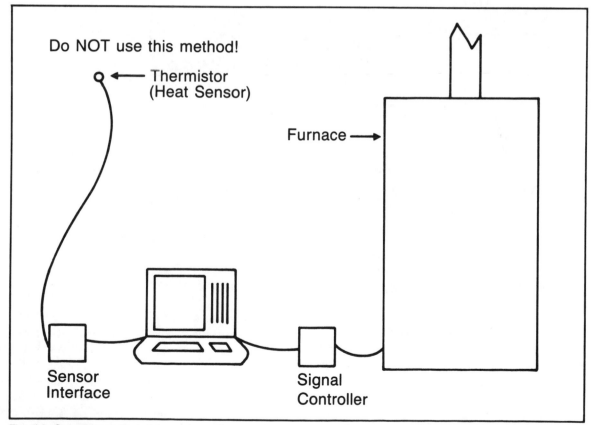

Fig. 7-3. Computer controls furnace according to time and temperature. Do not use this method.

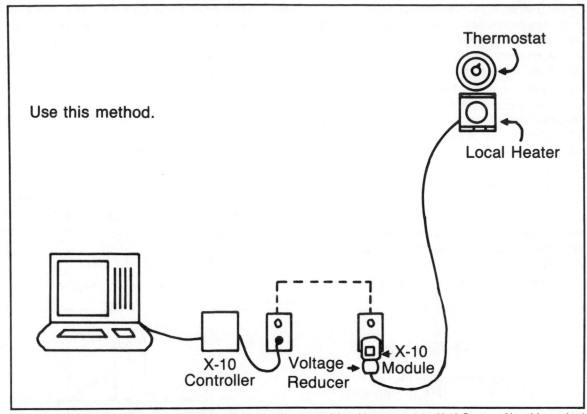

Use this method.

Thermostat

Local Heater

X-10 Controller

Voltage Reducer

X-10 Module

Fig. 7-4. Furnace controlled by time and temperature using a small local heater and the X-10 System. Use this method.

they are all provided in one package sold by BSR (USA) Ltd. The package is #TH2867 and is labeled SAVE ENERGY. Included is a Thermostat Set-Back Controller (the localized heater), the voltage reducer (called a *power supply* by BSR), an X-10 Appliance Module, the necessary wire, and complete instructions. The recommended retail price for the set is roughly $79.99. The same package without the Appliance Module (#TH2807) sells for $59.99 and is shown in Fig. 7-5.

WHAT MUST I DO?

Set-up is fairly straight forward. Be sure to follow the directions provided by the manufacturer. The localized heater can be attached to the wall by either small screws or by adhesive strips provided on the back of the housing. The location of this device should be one fourth of an inch directly

below your thermostat. Run the double stranded wire from the localized heater down your wall and along the baseboard to the nearest wall outlet. The wire is supplied with an adhesive backing, or you may prefer to carefully tack the wire to the wall as you go. Once you determine the length of wire you will need, cut off the remainder and strip the two leads at the voltage reducer end of the wire. Connect the leads to voltage reducer as shown in the wiring diagram in Fig. 7-6.

As mentioned, an Appliance Module is provided with one of the two packages from BSR. If you are interested, a cleaner look is possible using a Wall Receptacle Module (BSR CAT. NO. SR227) which replaces the standard two socket wall outlet. After the wires have been attached to the voltage reducer, it should be plugged into the Appliance Module (or Wall Module if preferred).

The Thermostat Set-Back Controller has four convenient settings. When not in use, it can be turned off; or when in use, it can be set to raise the temperature at the thermostat either approximately 5, 10, or 15 degrees. Use the setting which best suits your particular conditions.

The last item left to do is to establish your software schedule. Since you are sensing only time and signaling an X-10 Module, control is now as easy as controlling a lamp or appliance as described in Chapter 6.

Note: The BSR instructions state that "Command signals from the Timer . . . turn your central heating or air conditioning on and off up to twice a day . . . " This twice a day function is strictly a limitation of the timer they are describing and your limitation is only dictated by your software. More than likely, your computer control system will allow you to turn the unit on or off as often as you would

like. Further, with the capability of a seven day clock in your system, you can program every day of the week differently. The particular stand-alone timer BSR describes is limited to a 24 hour control cycle.

HOW LONG WILL IT TAKE?

Setup of the localized heater, the wiring to the voltage reducer, and plugging the voltage reducer into an Appliance Module should take no more than fifteen to twenty minutes. If a Wall Receptacle Module is used, add another fifteen minutes.

Special Note on Wall Receptacle Modules. The Wall Receptacle Module works on the same principle as all the other modules noted in the last chapter. However, like the Wall Switch Module, the Wall Receptacle Module is not

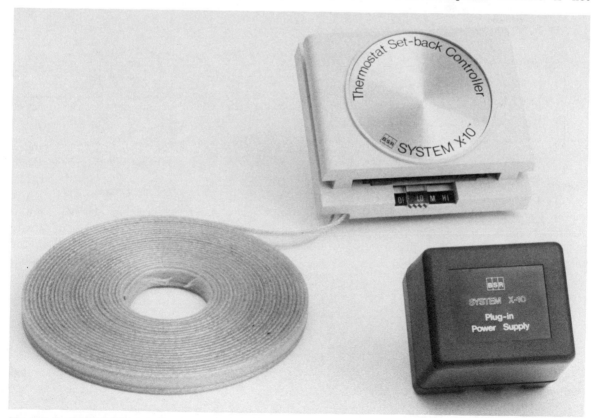

Fig. 7-5. X-10 thermostat control system (courtesy of BSR (USA) Ltd.).

plugged into a wall outlet. Instead, it is used to replace a normal wall outlet found in your home. Since most home outlets have two places for plugs, so does the Wall Receptacle Module. However, only one of the two plug positions is controlled by the X-10 System. The other is just like any ordinary outlet.

It is relatively easy to install the Wall Receptacle Module by following the directions included with these modules and as described below. **Be sure to turn off your electricity first before installing one of these.**

1. Set the HOUSE CODE (red dial) to the desired setting (use small screwdriver).

2. Set the UNIT CODE (black dial) to the desired setting.

3. **Make sure the electricity is turned off at circuit breaker or fuse box.**

4. Remove wall plate and old receptacle.

5. Connect leads as shown in Fig. 7-7, blue (or white) lead from the Wall Receptacle Module to white wire and black lead to the black wire. Also, connect the green wire from the module to the

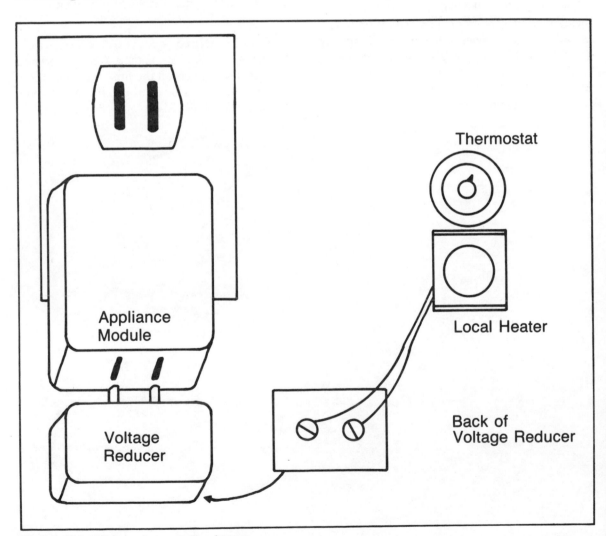

Fig. 7-6. Wiring diagram for controlling furnace.

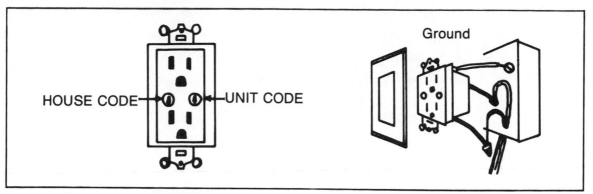

HOUSE CODE — UNIT CODE

Ground

Fig. 7-7. Wall Receptacle Module Installation.

ground wire (green) or to a grounded junction box. Be sure to use wire nuts (provided) for insulation.

6. Mount the Wall Receptacle Module.
7. Replace the wall plate.
8. Turn the power on at the circuit breaker

or fuse box.

Each of these takes approximately 10 to 15 minutes to install. The Wall Receptacle Modules are meant to be used like any other Appliance Module. They will not respond to ALL LIGHTS ON, BRIGHTEN, or DIM commands.

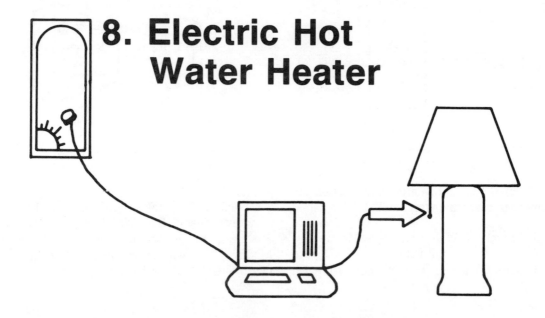

8. Electric Hot Water Heater

FOR MANY, THE HOT WATER HEATER IS THE most expensive appliance in the house. It's not uncommon for the yearly bill to exceed $500 to $600. According to the United States Department of Energy, in 1981 the average household using an electric hot water heater spent an average of $323 based on a cost of .0564 per kilowatt hour (kwh). Compare this cost to your current electric bill, and many of you will find that a bargain by today's rates!

Before moving ahead to how your electric hot water heater can be regulated by your Home Control system, a few general conservation ideas on your hot water system are provided. Anyone who is interested in this particular aspect of Home Control is interested for one reason—saving money—and these tips can help as well.

First, let's take a look at how much hot water is needed around the house. The list on this page is based on average usage.

You will readily see that your requirements likely are low compared with the 40 to 60 gallons of hot water most systems have available 24 hours

a day, every day of the year. That's a lot of energy dollars out the window!

	Gallons
Meal preparation	3 to 5
Meal Clean-up:	
by hand	3 to 5
dishwasher	8 to 14
Clothes washer	7 to 18
Bath (tub)	10 to 16
Shower	6 to 12
Personal care and shaving	1/4 to 2

Another common energy waster is to have the hot water heater turned up higher than necessary. This, at times, is down-right dangerous. For most purposes, hot water should be around 120 degrees. Commonly, however, hot water heaters are adjusted for 160 or even 180 degrees. At those temperatures, the water is not tolerable to work or bathe in, so cold water is then used to reduce the heat. Thus, a lot of energy has been expended to first heat the water, which later is wasted as it is cooled to a reasonable temperature. The first money saving step is to make sure the water is not being overheated.

A second way to cut down on energy loss is to insulate hot water pipes. Each time hot water is used, it leaves the tank to get to the location where needed. If you wash your face on the second floor and your tank is in the basement, once you shut your water off, the whole length of the pipe allows the heat to escape. With insulation, this heat loss can be slowed greatly.

Other general maintenance tips include the following:

☐ Check burners (gas or oil), or coils or heating elements (electric) to make sure they are clean and adjusted.

☐ Periodically drain the hot water heater (if done reasonably often only a pail or two is necessary) to get rid of the sediment which collects at the bottom of the tank.

☐ Inspect pipes closely, and repair if leaking, insulate as necessary, and repair or replace leaking faucets.

☐ Check any valves and the heater's thermostat for proper operation.

Incidentally, some older dishwasher models do require hotter water (140 to 150 degrees) to operate satisfactorily. One effective method to circumvent this problem and still allow your hot water system to operate at 120 degrees is to install a booster heater near the dishwasher. A booster will take your hot water (now at 120 degrees) and raise it the 20 or 30 degrees needed for optimal dishwasher performance. A booster is particularly efficient because it only operates when water is running through it; and uses no energy the rest of the time. Boosters come in all different sizes, but are often small enough to fit in the cabinet under your kitchen sink (usually located next to the dishwasher) and still leave room for storage. The payback for these boosters is often less than a couple of years.

Another type of device is a local water heater. These are small electric water heaters that are placed at or near the point of usage. Some are tankless hot water heaters, and are usually best where medium to large suppliers are not needed quickly. Others are small electric tanks that must be switched on about a half hour before the water is needed. The latter are particularly adaptable to a Home Control system since you can use your system to turn them on or off (just like any other appliance) according to a schedule, or other events in your home.

Getting back to the main hot water heater, this type of scheduling was discussed in Chapter 3 when the subject was saving money. Here's how it operates:

HOW DOES IT WORK?

Control of an electric hot water heater uses the method described in the Chapter 6. Basically, think of your electric hot water heater as just an overgrown appliance! Your Computer Home Control system can be used to turn it on and off according to when hot water will be needed. Begin to develop a schedule when you will and when you won't need hot water. Be sure to remember, though, that if you decide you want a hot shower at 3:00 A.M., and your hot water heater has been off from 6:00 the night before, it will take more than just a few minutes before you can have your steamy shower. Depending on your particular heating system, you could be shivering for a half hour!

WHAT MUST I BUY?

Check the ratings on your hot water heater. Most run via 220 to 240 volts. Also check the amperage rating—maximum ratings should not exceed 20 amps. If they do, have a qualified electrician install a simple relay system so that an X-10 Appliance Module can be used to control a switch that will turn on or off the current to the hot water heater.

Take a look, also, at how your system connects to the electricity in your house. Is it wired directly (often the case) or does it plug into a wall outlet? If your system plugs in, you're in luck and you should be able to just plug in one or the other of the two 240 volt Appliance Modules. If not, an elec-

Fig. 8-1. 240 volt heavy duty Appliance Modules (courtesy BSR (USA) Ltd.). The module on the left is rated at 15 amps and the module on the right is rated at 20 amps. Note the different socket shape.

trician can put in the appropriate plug and outlet. One of the two 240 volt Appliance Modules is rated at 15 amps and the other is rated at 20 amps. These can be differentiated by their socket configurations as shown in Fig. 8-1. Both 240 volt X-10 Modules are available from either BSR or HeathKit.

WHAT MUST I DO?

Before doing anything, turn off the power. At these voltages, power should be off even if you are only unplugging and replugging equipment. If your system is directly wired to the electricity, have an electrician make the necessary plug and outlet arrangement. If your hot water heater simply plugs into a wall outlet, then follow these instructions:

1. Again, **make sure the power is off**.
2. Unplug the hot water heater from the outlet.
3. Set the HOUSE and UNIT CODES on the appropriate 240 volt Appliance Module.

4. Plug the Appliance Module into the wall outlet.
5. Plug the water heater into the Appliance Module.
6. Turn the power back on.

Your hot water heater is now under the control of your computer. The last thing required is to adjust the software to suit your schedule. Your seven day clock can ensure that you have hot water when you need it, and savings the rest of the time!

HOW LONG WILL IT TAKE?

Whether your hot water system plugs into a wall outlet or is hard-wired and, hence, an electrician adapts it, your part of the entire process should take about 15 to 20 minutes including the adjustments to your software.

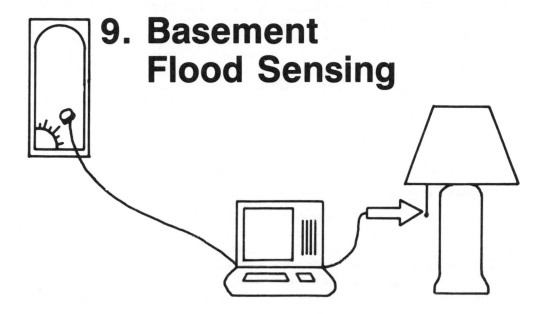

9. Basement Flood Sensing

IF YOU'VE EVER HAD A BASEMENT FLOOD, YOU know all too well the mess it causes and the damage it can do. And if you haven't had this occur, take it from me—you never want to chance it! A basement can flood for a number of reasons: leakage through the wall of the basement after a heavy rainfall, a broken water pipe, a washing machine that overflows, a cracked hot water tank, or even a dehumidifier that is not emptied properly. The flood control system described here won't stop the cause of your flooding problem, but it will warn you early enough to prevent any real damage.

HOW DOES IT WORK?

This flood control system is very easy to implement. It uses a water sensor connected to your Home Control system, with a signal of some sort to alert you that a flood condition exists. You may wish to use more than one water sensor strategically placed in your basement. These locations should be at low level points on the floor near the possible hazard conditions—a wall that has previously leak-

ed or a washing machine that potentially could overflow. Each sensor will be connected via a double stranded wire to a set of terminals on your sensing interface unit.

When a flood condition is sensed, your computer will take the appropriate action to let you know of the problem. This action could be flashing lights or turning a radio on and off, repeatedly. You may also wish to have a bell or siren go off as explained in the next chapter, and you can even send a signal through the phone lines as explained in Chapter 12. Notifying the Outside World. The latter is especially desirable if no one is usually home during the daytime, when you are away on vacation, or for a summer or weekend house. In this chapter, however, a simple signaling method using the X-10 system will be discussed.

WHAT MUST I BUY?

This is one of the least expensive projects you will find. If you wish, you can build the water sensors from a few odds and ends that you already have around the house. Or if you prefer, you can buy commercially available water sensors from stores that specialize in security systems or the like, or possibly from your Home Control equipment manufacturer. One easy to find water sensor is sold by Sears (catalog #9 H 57045) for $39.95.

The only equipment necessary for signaling will be the same light and Appliance Modules that you used in Chapter 6. This multiple use of Home Control components is one of the key benefits of an integrated system. Many of the projects in this book can make use of equipment (both sensor and signal) for other things as well.

WHAT MUST I DO?

First, decide whether you wish to purchase or build your water sensors. To build a water sensor, you will need a small plastic planting pot, some potting soil, a pencil or wood dowel, and the necessary wire (22-24 gauge). (If you are planning to use your Home Control system to water your lawn or garden(s) as discussed in Chapter 14, you may wish to build one extra water sensor for this purpose. Use heavier wire (18 or 20 gauge) that is approved for burial.

Figure 9-1 shows that you poke or drill some holes in the bottom of the planting pot to allow water to seep in if a flood occurs. Also, drill two holes on either side of the pot (towards the bottom) so that the pencil or dowel can snugly slide through the pot. Cut two one foot lengths of wire, and strip the insulation off on both ends on each—about one inch on one end and three inches on the other. After inserting the dowel into the planting pot, wrap each wire (using the three inch stripped end) around the dowel so that the two wires do not touch and are roughly one half to one quarter inch away from each other at their nearest point. Now fill the planting pot with about two inches of soil. For ballast, you may want to place a few small rocks on top. Your water sensor is now complete.

Place each water sensor in the locations where

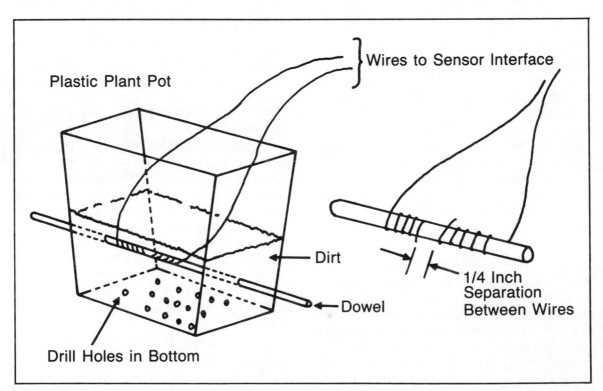

Fig. 9-1. Construction diagram for water sensor.

a flood is most likely to occur, and wire to a pair of analog terminals on your sensor interface. (If you purchased your water sensors, check to make sure whether they should be wired to analog or digital terminals.)

When dry, the water sensors will allow little or no current to pass between the two wires in the potting soil. However, when moist or wet, electricity will be conducted through the soil and your computer will show an increase in the analog reading. Test your sensors by first checking the readings when they are dry. Then simulate a flood condition (add a little water to the soil) and check the readings again.

Now adjust your software to reflect the difference in the two readings. Normally, the analog current reading will be low. When the analog reading increases—a flood is present and your software should start some lights flashing and possibly a radio should go on and off repeatedly.

Important: If you decide to use a siren or bell to signal a flood condition, be sure to set the software so that the siren can be turned off even though the flood condition has not been corrected. Otherwise, the siren or bell will stay on until either the flood sensor is disconnected or dries out, or the alarm is disconnected. Some audible alarms are extremely loud and it may be very unpleasant if you can't easily turn them off once you're aware of the flood condition.

HOW LONG WILL IT TAKE?

Once you have all the necessary materials, this is a fairly quick project. Building the moisture sensor, including testing, wiring, and software adjustments, should take about thirty minutes. If you are using lights and a radio as your alarm, you will probably already have them in place from setting up the control of lights and appliances in Chapter 6.

10. Burglar Alarm System

IMAGINE THAT YOU ARRIVED HOME TODAY AND your new TV, your VCR, the family jewels, the silver, and your collection of whatever was gone. Worse yet, imagine someone in your family arrived home before you-know-who finished packing! Unfortunately, people don't do enough imagining until after they have been victimized. According to industry experts, usually only people who were actually "hit" by a robbery, or saw it happen to a relative or neighbor, seriously investigate protecting their home. However, recent FBI figures show that one out of every six U.S. homes will be the victim of crime this year. These range from childlike pranks to serious vandalism, outright burglaries, all the way to actual personal tragedies.

Although statistics vary greatly, estimates of the growth of home protection schemes (including burglar alarm systems) average around thirty percent annually. In 1978, less than two percent of the homes in the U.S. had such protection; in 1983, it is estimated that from six to over nine percent do. (Even of these "protected" homes, very few are linked to a central monitoring system and thus have only internal alarm systems on which to rely.) Actually, according to the experts, the increase in security systems has not resulted from an increase in crime over this time period, but because of the following reasons:

☐ Micro chips used in alarm systems (including regular stand-alone systems) have made these much more within reach of the less affluent homeowner,

☐ More women have joined the workforce, and many more houses each year are not occupied during the day, and

☐ Many homes have much more in the way of valuables—expensive stereos, 35 mm cameras, jewelry, VCR's, and of course, home computers—and the owners feel a greater need to protect these items.

Although generally people think that burglaries happen in the dead of night, just the opposite is true. Most occur during the day. Burglars generally use a door to gain entrance, and if a door is not particularly convenient, they choose a window. Also, most people have their houses ill equipped with even the most rudimentary protection devices such as good locks for doors and windows. Therefore, if you have decided to include a burglar alarm system in your Home Control plans, it is recommended that you first take some steps to ensure you've covered the basics. This may require a little homework on your part, but it should make your overall protection plan much stronger.

The first thing to consider is contacting your local police department to find out whether they can help you. Many police departments offer, free of charge, a home visit where an officer will actually tour your home with you and make recommendations to help ward off burglars. These visits are part of the police department's Crime Avoidance or Crime Prevention program. If such a program is unavailable, your home insurer, a security (burglar alarm) company, or your public library may be able to offer additional information. By the way, many insurance companies will discount the rate you are charged by as much as 15% if you install an alarm system that meets their standards, so you should check with your insurer to find out their standards prior to installing anything. Security companies are a good source for advice and ideas for your home's protection and many have a wide selection of sensors and alarms for your Home Control system.

The following is a brief security checklist which should be covered as you go through your home. These are the basics. However, don't forget that each home is different and may have special requirements.

☐ Check all doors and windows for proper locks. A reputable locksmith can provide advice, if needed. Also, make sure the frames around the doors and windows are sturdy, and the same goes for the doors and windows themselves.

☐ Consider yard lights near all exterior entrances, including your garage.

☐ Have your house look and sound lived-in when you're away. Use lights and a radio for this purpose.

☐ Make a detailed inventory of our valuables (photograph expensive items) and place the inventory (and pictures) in a safe deposit box. Use an "electric pencil" (etching device) to identify your belongings.

☐ When landscaping, care should be taken with the placement of trees and bushes which could provide cover for a burglar attempting to get inside your house.

☐ If you're going away for a day or more, make sure all deliveries (mail, newspapers, etc.) are stopped. If you will be away for an extended period, make arrangements to have your lawn cut.

☐ Help your neighbors by watching their houses, and ask them to check on yours. Instead of hiding a key outside your house, leave it with a trusted neighbor.

This list can be used as a minimum guide for your thoughts about the security of your home. However, each home has unique features such as sky lights or a coal chute, so be sure to consider any special cases that may impact your protection scheme.

Take another look at the list above in terms of Computer Home Control. Your computer can be invaluable in terms of giving your house that lived-in look when you're away. Consider what has already been covered in Chapter 6. With your computer, it's easy to have both interior and exterior lights turn on and off at appropriate times. Further, you can vary their schedule from day to day by using a seven day clock. From the outside of your house, you can even have the lights appear to be turning on and off as if someone was walking from room to room! And don't forget about your radio or TV. Your computer can make your house sound as if you were home, too.

The focus of this chapter, however, is to show you how to develop computer sensing and signaling devices to do two things:

1. Let you know if someone is trying to break into your home.
2. Discourage the burglar from going any further with his or her efforts.

No security scheme gives 100 percent protection. However, actual surveys have been done with burglars, and by and large they agree that a home protected by a burglar alarm system is the best deterrent. Also, if a burglary does occur, a security system can be decisive when many people can't be.

One nice thing about Computer Home Control is that it can be a relatively inexpensive way to protect your home. This assumes, of course, that you bought your computer for more than just home security so that the cost of the computer itself is allocated against all of its uses. Also, if you bought your main signal and sensor interface devices for multiple purposes, these too should be discounted accordingly. The discounted portion of this equipment, added to the cost of the door and window sensors, possibly a motion detector or two, and the cost of a buzzer, bell, and/or siren is relatively modest compared to the expense of a standard burglar alarm system. Most of these range between $1500 and $3500, while the actual sensors and alarms for your system should range from $100 to $400. Once you plan your system, you can perform your own comparison between a Computer Home Controlled system and a stand-alone system feature by feature. However, prior to planning your burglar alarm system, there are a few things which you should consider.

First, do you want your burglar alarm system to be able to run while you are using your computer for other things? In other words, if you are working on a spreadsheet or word processing application in your den, is it important to you to know if someone is climbing in through your basement window? Many people are primarily concerned about protection at night or when they're away from home. Others feel that if they're going to go to the trouble of having a burglar alarm system, it should be operable 100 percent of the time. If you decide you want your system to work all the time, your Home Control system must be able to operate independently of your computer. Some of the more sophisticated products in the Product Directory have this capability.

Do you want to include a battery backup in case of a power failure? Again, some people won't really care and others will see it as a basic necessity. Although this is covered more thoroughly in Chapter 17, it's important to note that there are different types of battery backups. A battery backup capability may only mean that a product is able to maintain its clock at the correct time until the power returns or it may mean that the product is able to operate a complete system during a power outage. If you want this capability, be sure to doublecheck the manufacturer's definition of battery backup.

If someone is attempting to break in to your house, should your system be capable of notifying the police? This is a subject covered in Chapter 12, Notifying the Outside World. If you desire this capability be sure to read that chapter before finishing the design of your burglar alarm system.

Should your system be capable of letting you know exactly which door or window has been tampered with by displaying such information on your monitor or printer? (What's the likelihood during a break-in that you'll run to your computer, turn on your monitor, and take a curious moment to find out exactly where the burglar is?) This much sophistication is probably not necessary, and besides, it does make wiring more complicated. The one advantage to this capability is that if you had a sensor that was malfunctioning, it could be identified more quickly.

Since we're on the subject of wiring, should you consider using a wireless system (a system where the sensors send messages to the sensor interface via radio frequencies)? The advantage of a wireless system is that it is definitely easier to install since you don't have to run wires between your sensors and your computer. However, since each wired sensor does not need to be wired independently (as you will see), a wired system is not really that complicated. Further, many experts contend that wireless systems are not as dependable as wired systems for the following reasons:

☐ Stray broadcasts have been known to cause false alarms (e.g., when your neighbor opens his garage door with a remote control unit).

☐ Each sensor requires a signaling capability that is dependent on a battery. If the battery wears out, you have a door or window unprotected and usually no way of knowing until you check the battery.

☐ Similarly, if the wireless sensor itself becomes defective you have no way of knowing except by thorough checking and testing.

Some wireless systems are better than others, and if you plan to use one, be sure to check on the three points above.

Should you locate a bell or siren on the outside of the house where a burglar is likely to notice it? Although this shows the burglar at least one aspect of what he's up against (so that he may first try to defeat the alarm), experts say this is a good deterrent to convince the burglar to choose another house. Be sure that when you install your bell or siren that you attach it in a location that is particularly hard to get to, such as on the side wall of your house a few feet below the peak of the roof. To further protect it you can place it in an enclosure that has an anti-tamper switch attached. This tamper switch will set off the alarm if someone tries to disarm it. You may also want to include a high intensity flashing light near the alarm to help police locate your house quickly.

Another point that experts agree on is that stickers should be placed on doors and/or windows to let would-be burglars know that the house is protected.

Should you also include an inside alarm in your system? Probably two! The first alarm is to make sure you (and your burglar) know that a break-in has been detected. Although an outdoor alarm may be plenty loud outside the house, often if you are inside and at the other end of the house, it may not be loud enough to get your attention. Make sure your inside alarm is loud enough to wake even heavy sleepers. The other alarm should be buzzer or beeper to remind you to disarm the system upon arriving home. Letting your system know that it's the "good guys" can be accomplished by way of a well hidden button switch, a key switch, or a digital key-pad.

Should you use perimeter or interior protection?

Perimeter protection means having sensors at doors and windows that detect any tampering, while interior protection involves using motion detectors or floor mats under carpeting to detect a burglar once inside. Perimeter protection is definitely the preferred method since it's designed to prevent the burglar from getting inside the house. However, some experts believe that it's wise to have dual protection, just in case a burglar manages to get past the perimeter safeguards.

HOW DOES IT WORK?

A basic burglar alarm system works reasonably simply and this chapter will demonstrate fairly standard, readily accessible, and inexpensive sensors and signaling devices.

For simplicity, Fig. 10-1 shows a relatively modest one story house, with three doors, a garage, and a few windows. Looking closely at the diagram, you can see dotted lines that lead from the house entrances and windows to the computer in the bedroom. These represent the sensor connection wires leading to the computer. Unfortunately, this project does have a few wires running around your house, but these can be relatively thin, since they are carrying fairly low voltages (probably 5 to 24 volts). Also, several doors and/or windows can be connected using the same dual strand of wire, which cuts down on the wiring. Make sure the wires are well concealed from view. Home electrical wiring books at your local bookstore or library are full of suggestions on how to do through the wall wiring. However, neat wiring along moldings will suffice in most cases.

Based on digital (on or off) sensing devices, your Computer Home Control system can easily tell if a door is opened, if a window is disturbed, or if there is motion inside (or outside) the house. As noted in Fig. 10-1 there are sensors located at the potential entry points (windows or doors) and a motion detector has been installed as an extra interior precaution. A key switch has been used as a sensor inside the house. The purpose of the key switch (or hidden switch button or digital key-pad) is to allow you to enter or leave your house through

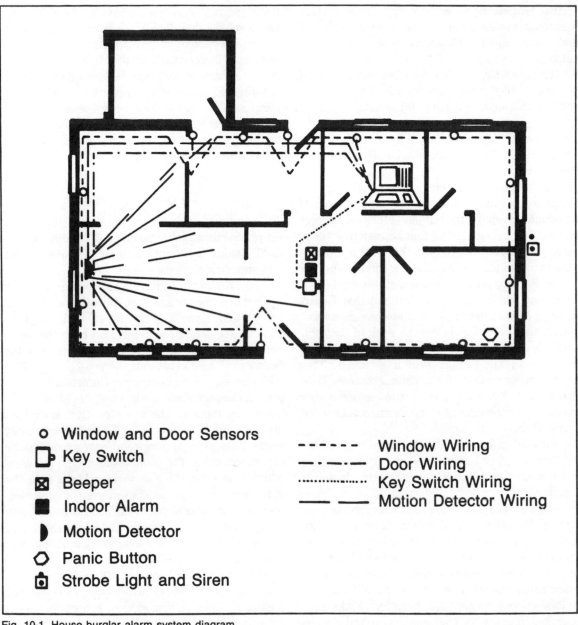

Window and Door Sensors
o

Key Switch

Beeper

Indoor Alarm

Motion Detector

Panic Button

Strobe Light and Siren

- - - - - **Window Wiring**
- · - · - **Door Wiring**
·············· **Key Switch Wiring**
—— —— **Motion Detector Wiring**

Fig. 10-1. House burglar alarm system diagram.

a door that is part of the security system—without setting off the alarms. You will need to adjust your software to allow you a few seconds to enter the house and turn the key switch in order to de-activate the alarms from sounding. Also, using the key switch prior to leaving should provide you with

30 to 60 seconds before the burglar alarm system re-arms.

One important thing not to forget is that if you are installing more than one safety component to your Home Control system, you must be able to distinguish whether you have a burglar, a flood, or, a subject for the next chapter, a fire. For multiple safety components, you could use different types of alarms or alarms with multiple sounds. As an example, you could have the lights and radio turn on and off for a flood in the basement and use a siren to signal a break-in attempt.

WHAT MUST I BUY?

Take a few minutes and review the drawings of your house which you made in Chapter 4. Using the house in Fig. 10-1 as an example, adjust your sketch accordingly.

There are many different types of sensors for various purposes which can be purchased for just a few dollars. From your drawings, decide what devices (sensors, alarms, etc.) need to be connected to your system. Should only your first floor be protected, or would you prefer to have the upper floor(s) covered, too? How about basement windows? What type of sirens, bells, or buzzers do you need? Would you prefer to have both a siren or bell inside as well as outside the house?

What about interior protection using floor mats or motion detectors? If you have a large dog that has the run of the house, floor mats may not be your best alternative for interior protection. Also, there are different types of motion detectors to consider. Ultrasonic or microwave detectors send emissions throughout a room and sense if the reflected emission patterns change. If not adjusted properly, pets or even curtains blown by the air can cause false alarms. These detectors can be tricky to adjust properly. A second type, infrared motion detectors, usually send an invisible beam across a room to a receiver on the opposite wall. If a burglar is aware of the presence of this equipment, he or she may be able to avoid the beams.

Thermal sensors (a third type) are able to sense the presence of individuals entering a room by their body temperature—roughly 98.6 degrees compared to other things in the room which average 62 to 78 degrees. These detectors are not particularly sensitive to hot air systems, and will not sense movement or radio frequencies. Therefore, they are unlikely to signal false alarms.

After deciding what should be included in your system, you may wish to visit a store that specializes in security systems, or a hardware or electronics store that carries security equipment. When purchasing equipment, be sure that you buy quality items. You may be able to save a few dollars with an inferior grade at a discount department store, but remember—you may be depending on this equipment during an emergency. One national outlet for equipment for your system is Radio Shack. Both their quality and selection is good. Some of the items they have available include the following:

☐ Door and window sensors in different sizes and types. Some are made to be completely concealed from view. (Sensors should be difficult to see). Prices run from $3.49 to $3.99.
☐ Glass alarm foil (for sensing breakage)—$5.99 for 120 feet.
☐ Glass breakage detector—$7.95.
☐ Vibration detector which can sense disturbances on most any surface—$3.95.
☐ Panic button—$1.49.
☐ Tamper switch—$1.39.
☐ Floor pressure mat—$10.95.
☐ 2-conductor twisted wire—$5.49 for 100 ft.
☐ Warning decals—$.99 for 5.
☐ High security key switch—$9.95.
☐ Key switch plate with status indicator lights—$5.95.
☐ 8″ alarm bell—$19.95.
☐ Electronic siren—$16.95.
☐ Security strobe light—$19.95.
☐ Buzzers from $.99 to $6.95
☐ Infrared motion detector—$69.95.
☐ 12 Vdc voltage reducers from $9.95 to $34.95.

This list should not be considered exhaustive, but it will give you an idea of the great variety of equipment that is available for your alarm system. As always, when choosing specific products for your system, make sure that voltage requirements, etc., are appropriate. Store sales personnel can often be very helpful in this regard.

Before making any purchases, be sure to read the fine print about the devices you choose. One very important thing to look for is whether the item says it operates as a *normally open* or as a *normally closed* sensor. Normally open means that, unless tampered with, electricity will not pass through the sensor. Normally closed means that, unless tampered with, electricity will pass through the sensor. (Think of electricity as making a loop from one terminal (connecting screw) of the sensor interface device through the sensor, and back to the other terminal. Open means there is a gap, and electricity cannot normally go round the loop. Closed means no gap, and electricity can normally travel the entire loop.) More than one sensor can be attached to each loop on your Home Control Sensor Interface if the following two conditions are met:

1. The alarm system should act the same way to all the sensors connected to that terminal pair.

2. All sensors connected to the same terminal pair are the same type: either normally open or normally closed.

Make sure, therefore, that all sensor equipment purchased for any given set of terminals is all of the same type. In general, normally closed systems are preferable since in a normally open circuit, the burglar alarm system cannot tell if something has become disconnected by mistake. If, for example, a wire comes loose, you may have an unprotected door or window without knowing it. In a normally closed circuit, your alarm system would quickly let you know of any loose wires!

WHAT MUST I DO?

Once you have your sensor and siren equipment, review the diagrams you made of your house once more. Plan exactly where the wires should run in order to connect the sensors correctly, and so that the wires are fairly unobtrusive. Now look at the wiring diagrams for both normally open or normally closed sensors in Figs. 10-2 and 10-3.

Normally open (normally off) sensors are wired in parallel so that if any one sensor is tampered with, the Home Control Sensor Interface will sense an on condition. Only one sensor triggered will complete the loop as shown in the diagram, and change the condition from off to on.

Normally closed (normally on) sensors are wired in series so that if any one sensor is tampered with, the Home Control Sensor Interface will sense an off condition. Only one sensor triggered will break the loop as shown in the diagram, and change the condition from on to off.

Be sure that all sensors (whether magnetic switches, motion detectors, or combinations) connected to one set of terminals follow one or the other diagram above. Momentary contact key switches and button switches can be wired (if more than one) similarly to either example above, again according to whether they are used as normally open or normally closed. Key switches should not be wired to the same terminals as the doors with which they are linked. Figure 10-4 shows a simple wiring diagram for the house in Fig. 10-1.

If your Home Control system does not include relays, you will want to use your X-10 Controller to start and stop your alarms (bell and/or siren and beeper or buzzer). The easiest way to handle this is to connect an X-10 Appliance Module to each of your alarms. However, most alarms work at lower voltages such as 12 Vdc, and therefore, you need an appropriate voltage reducer (sometimes referred to as ac to dc converters, adapters, or transformers) for this purpose. These are easy to find at Radio Shack, Sears, and other stores. Be sure to check that the amperage of the voltage reducer is compatible with your alarm and whether or not you need an ac to dc conversion. The voltage reducer will simply plug into the X-10 Appliance Module and then a two conductor wire will need to be run from the voltage reducer to the alarm(s). Alarms that are not supposed to sound at the same time will need a separate X-10 Module as well as a separate voltage reducer.

Note: Alarms installed as above will not work if there is a power outage.

If your Home Control system has relays on the

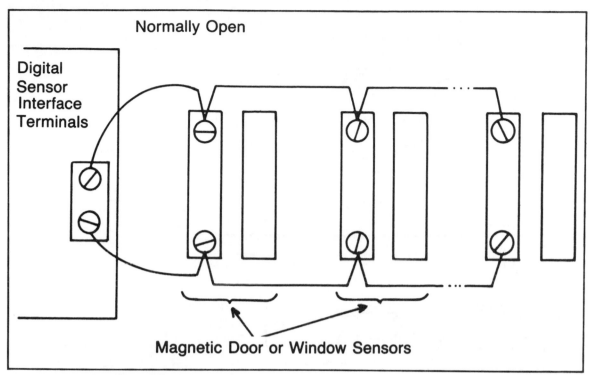

Fig. 10-2. Normally open sensors wired in parallel.

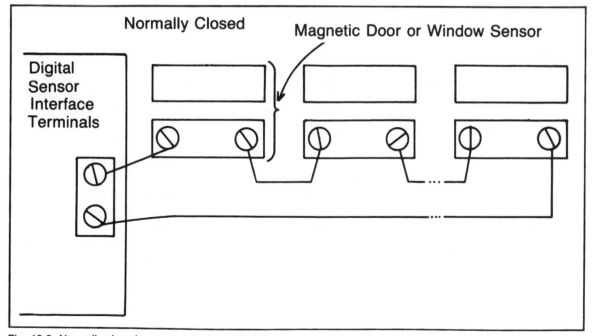

Fig. 10-3. Normally closed sensors wired in series.

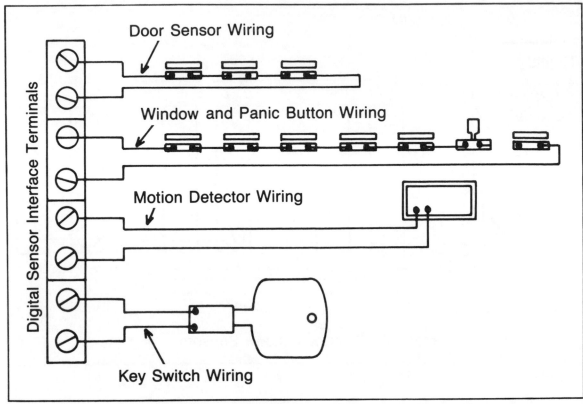

Fig. 10-4. Wiring diagram for burglar alarm system sensors.

controlling side, you can use these to provide power to your alarms. The relays simply turn power on or off as dictated by your Home Control software. Also, if you plan to have a battery backup system for your alarms (see Chapter 17), a relay system can be set up to work even if there is a general power outage in your neighborhood. If your Home Control system includes relays, usually the power source will be a part of the system as well. Your alarms should be wired according to the manufacturer's instructions, and their instructions should also provide the necessary information as to what brands of alarms should work according to their electrical power needs.

Once the wiring is finished, the next step is to adjust your software. The following is a suggested setup:

☐ Have alarm sound immediately when any

window or motion detector senses a break-in.

☐ If a door is opened, the buzzer or beeper should begin to sound within a few seconds, and the alarm should sound after 15 seconds (or whatever time frame fits your needs).

☐ If the key switch (or button switch) is activated within those fifteen seconds (and the door has been properly closed), then the alarm should not sound. Also, after activation of the key switch, have your software programmed to rule out the motion detector while you're at home (so you can walk around the house freely).

☐ If the key switch is activated, 60 seconds should be provided in which to leave the house without the alarm going off.

☐ If the alarm is on and the key switch is activated three times within ten seconds, the alarm should shut off.

☐ If the alarm in on, after five minutes it

should shut off and the system should re-arm.

Your program, of course, can be arranged to react in any way that suits your specific plan. One enjoyable addition to think about adding to your software is to have the hall light go on (only after dark?) and your radio start playing after you have entered the house.

HOW LONG WILL IT TAKE?

The time required for this project will vary depending on how sophisticated your burglar alarm system becomes, and how you plan to do your wiring. A wireless system will obviously require less time than one wired through the walls. As a rule of thumb, each wired sensor (where wires are run neatly around moldings and baseboards), should take between ten to fifteen minutes. The same is true for the alarms, except for the one placed high up on the outside of your house. Wiring is best done for this alarm by drilling a hole through the side of the house and running the necessary wires through this hole. Alternatively, you can run the wire through a second floor or attic window. (Be sure to properly seal the hole for insulation purposes.) This alarm may require anywhere from ten minutes to an hour to install.

Scheduling the software for this project will also take more time than many of the other projects, although an hour should suffice. Also, you will need to test each component of the system, with the time required for this dependent on the number of sensors and alarms installed. Testing should take from 10 minutes to a half hour for most systems.

11. Smoke and Heat Detection

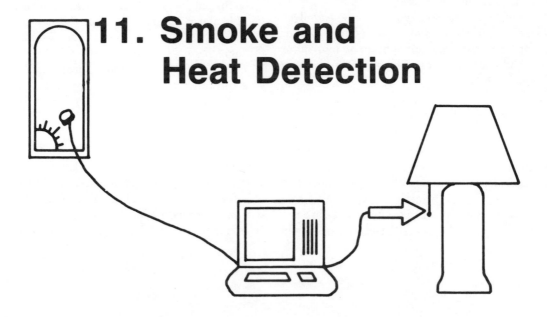

A COMPUTER CONTROLLED FIRE ALARM SYStem is but one of a number of steps you will wish to take in a comprehensive program for fire safety. Your program should include minimizing the chances for a fire to start, as well as maximizing your ability to escape should a fire occur. Consider the following guidelines:

☐ Take the time to understand the causes of fires, and be aware of potential conditions in your home.

☐ Eliminate unnecessary fire hazards. Survey your kitchen, heating system, home appliances, and where combustibles are stored for potential problems which can be eliminated.

☐ Know and practice fire safety rules, and learn how to react to different types of fires.

☐ Develop a fire escape plan and have all family members practice it periodically.

☐ Install an adequate alarm system.

This list is not particularly detailed and you may wish to obtain further advice or materials on this subject from your local fire department, your town library, or from your insurance agent.

If you or your family are involved in a fire, these are the basic rules to follow:

1. Don't panic.
2. Get out of the house following your plan.
3. Feel doors for heat before opening.
4. Keep close to the floor (smoke rises and is less dense closer to the floor).
5. Close doors and windows as you leave.
6. Have the family meet at a pre-determined place.
7. Call the fire department as soon as possible after leaving the house.
8. Never re-enter a burning building.

A smoke and heat detector project is easy to implement as part of your Computer Home Control system, although it usually requires a minimal amount of wiring between the detectors and your sensor interface. This project, however, is an especially valuable addition since it can e set up to thoroughly notify the house occupants of fire. An example of this might be where a fire starts in the basement. The Home Control system can signal those on the second or third floor of the condition, where a conventional smoke alarm installed in the basement might not be heard on all floors of the house.

The fire protection system can also be linked with an outdoor siren or bell to either notify you, if you're outside, or to notify your neighbors. In this chapter, you'll see how to make the connections between smoke and heat detectors, your Computer Home Control system, and the warning alarms around your home. Chapter 12 will be of interest as well, if you want your computer to be able to phone for help.

HOW DOES IT WORK?

Most smoke detectors that you see advertised for home use are good as single station sensor and alarm systems. However, few of the detectors sold at your local hardware or department store are meant to be interconnected or linked to a security or Computer Home Control system. The alarms mentioned in this chapter will have this capability, and although they are usually slightly more expensive, they have expanded possibilities for better protection.

The main difference between this type of smoke or heat detector (sensor) and the kind you may now own is that the latter contains a simple relay which works on either a closed or open circuit. (For further explanation see the discussion of open and closed circuits in Chapter 10.) The relay built into the detector will change from open to closed (or vice-versa) when the detector senses a smoke or a heat condition.

The approach suggested for CHC requires that each detector be wired in parallel or in series (depending on whether the circuit is open or closed) to your sensor interface unit. Your computer, if a fire condition is sensed, will send out a general alarm (and, if you wish, outside) your house.

WHAT MUST I BUY?

Appropriate smoke and heat detectors which include a relay switch can be obtained at stores that specialize in security protection systems. Detectors for a CHC system do not require their own built in alarms. However, you may wish to have some with this feature if you don't have a battery backedup Home Control system. Wiring is easiest if all detectors can be used on a normally open circuit or all on a normally closed circuit.

Heat detectors come in two basic types. The first is a fixed temperature thermostat that upon reaching a precise temperature (such as 135 degrees) will go from open to closed (off to on) or vice versa. The other type is a rate of rise thermostat which will activate by the temperature suddenly rising.

The following list provides specific examples of detectors. These are all manufactured by the Alarm Device Manufacturing Company—ADEMCO.

ADEMCO Model 580DR. Smoke detector (pictured in Fig. 11-1) with relay and alarm horn (power supply—9 volt battery). Can be used on both normally open or normally closed circuits.

ADEMCO Model 590DR. Similar to above but powered by normal (120 volt ac) house current.

ADEMCO Model 502. Fixed temperature thermostat (pictured in Fig. 11-2) that activates at 135 degrees. Model 504 activates at 190 degrees and can be used in attics, hot kitchens, or near a furnace. Both are open circuit devices.

ADEMCO Model 501. Rate of rise thermostat that in addition activates if the temperature reaches 135 degrees. Model 501A is similar but activates at 190 degrees for use in attics, hot kitchens, or near a furnace. Both are open circuit devices.

On the signaling (alarm) side, you can use a bell or a siren as described in Chapter 10. The same alarms may even be used if you add something that will let you know that you have a fire instead of a break-in attempt. If you have decided to take advantage of all three projects for safety and security—the flood, burglar, and fire detection

Fig. 11-1. Combustion (smoke) detector (courtesy of ADEMCO).

systems—you may wish to use the following alarm methods to differentiate the condition:

☐ Flood—flash lights and turn radio on and off repeatedly.

☐ Burglar—flash lights and have siren(s) and/or bell(s) sound.

☐ Fire—turn on lights for escape routes and sound siren(s) and/or bell(s).

WHAT MUST I DO

First, you'll need to decide where to locate your smoke and heat detectors. Fire detectors should be located on each level of your home including the basement and the attic. Each grouping of bedrooms should have at least one smoke detector located in a central hallway, and for those who either sleep with their doors closed, or who smoke in their bedrooms, a smoke alarm should be located within those bedrooms, as well. The garage and the kitchen should have heat detectors rather than smoke detectors because of combustibles present in the air. A smoke detector should also be located between the living room and dining room or in a hallway that adjoins the two. It is also wise to locate a smoke or heat detector in any location that is closed off from the rest of the house by a door.

In terms of mounting detectors, their location should be towards the center of the ceiling, but never in the peak of an "A" frame ceiling or within a half foot from where a ceiling meets a wall. In these areas, the air is relatively stationary and the detectors will be slow to sense a hazardous condition. On side walls, detectors can be located from a half foot (minimum) to a foot from the ceiling.

The National Fire Protection Association's

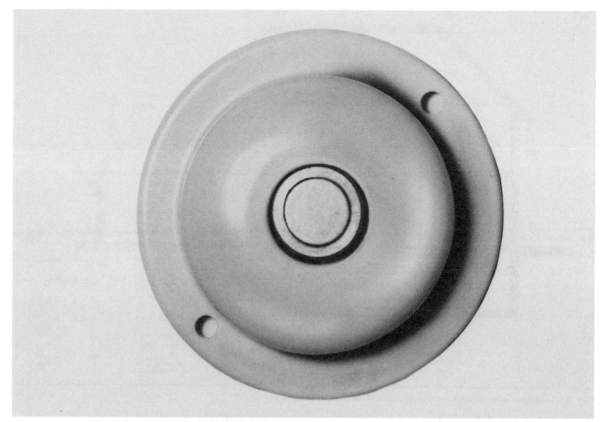

Fig. 11-2. Heat detector (courtesy of ADEMCO).

Standard #74-1978 entitled *Household Fire Warning Equipment* can be consulted for further information by sending $3.00 to them at 470 Atlantic Avenue, Boston, Massachusetts 02210. Again, your own fire department may be a good source for additional information and local requirements.

Once you have figured out where to place your detectors and how many you will need, also carefully decide what type and where your alarms should be located. Once this is done, you can obtain the detectors and alarms and begin installation. The following is the wiring plan of a simple two story house with basement and garage. The wiring shows six smoke and heat detectors wired together to the Computer Sensing Interface unit.

In this instance, the connection is digital and can therefore be connected to either a digital or an analog set of terminals. You may have all detectors connected to a single set of terminals (as in Fig. 11-3); or if you wish to have your computer determine the location of any detector that has become active, you can wire each to a separate set of terminals. Figure 11-4 shows a normally open set of three detectors wired in parallel to one set of terminals.

The signaling portion is handled exactly as found in Chapter 10. Further, you may wish to refer to Chapter 6 in order to light your house to make it easier to get out in an emergency.

Once wiring is complete, be certain you make the appropriate adjustments on your Home Control software. Each detector should be tested to ensure that your computer is able to sense a hazard condition. Your alarm system must be tested to make sure the signaling side works as you expect. Adjust your software so that the alarm can be silenc-

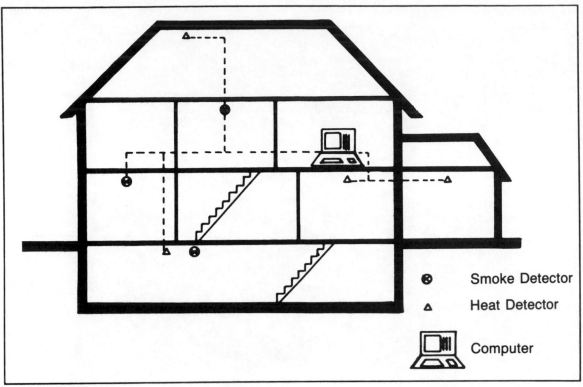

Fig. 11-3. House smoke and heat detector system.

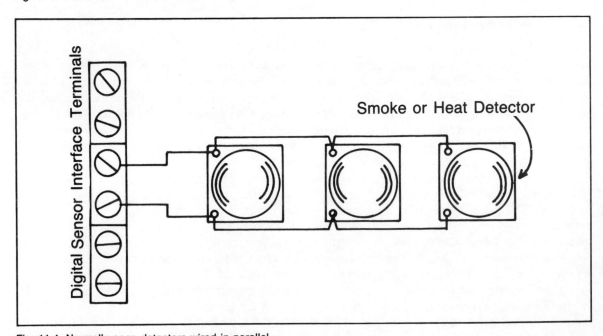

Fig. 11-4. Normally open detectors wired in parallel.

ed temporarily if it sounds by accident and so that it will automatically re-arm after about ten minutes.

HOW LONG WILL IT TAKE?

Actual installation of these devices is quick and painless. To attach the detectors to the ceilings or walls should take less than ten minutes each. Wiring time will vary greatly according to the amount that is necessary and how careful you are to hide the wires. For a four to six detector system including two alarms, you will probably require somewhere between one and a half to three hours including the time necessary to adjust your software and test your equipment. **Be sure not to forget testing.**

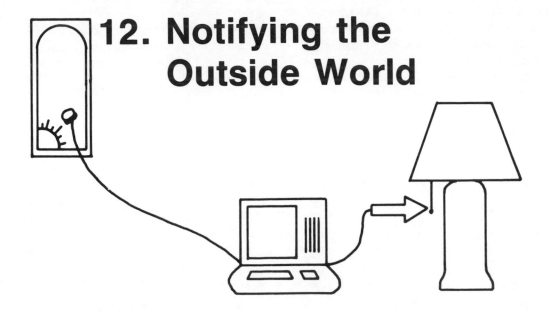

12. Notifying the Outside World

THE LAST THREE CHAPTERS HAVE DISCUSSED safety and security uses for your Home Control system with each describing how to sense a hazardous condition and then signal you of the problem. These three, however, covered only those methods of letting someone on or near the premises of your house know of the condition. For many people, this may be enough security for peace of mind—especially for those who are home most of the time or who can rely on their neighbors to react if a problem arises.

You and members of your family, however, may be away from home during the day, travel for business or vacations, or may not feel terribly good about relying just on neighbors. Or you may have a vacation home or an investment property that would be more secure if monitored in your absence. In these situations, you may feel that a Home Control system which can communicate to the outside world is a must. Even if you are not in these special situations, you still may want to consider hooking up with the outside world. Suppose a break-in happens and suddenly you're aware that a burglar is inside. Just how are you going to react? Wouldn't you feel a little better if you knew that your security system was already contacting the authorities? If a fire starts in the middle of the night, your first concern will be getting outside safely. Wouldn't it be reassuring to know that your Computer Home Control system was in the process of notifying the local fire department?

If you desire this capability, the next consideration is which conditions monitored by your Home Control system should take advantage of this feature. Are you planning to install all of the security measures in Chapters 9 through 11, or just one or two? (Possibly you have other special needs such as a freezer that has hundreds of dollars worth of food stored within. You may want to monitor the temperature (covered in the next chapter) to make sure it doesn't rise to a level where spoilage could occur.) Decide how many elements need to be monitored and how many different messages (corresponding to the various problems) need to be sent. In other words, should your Computer Home Control system simply sound an alert that something is wrong, or should it be more specific—for example: "there is a break-in attempt at a basement window."

Who should be notified? Suppose you install both a burglar and fire security system, and decide to have your Home Control system be able to send two different messages. The burglar message is to summon the police and the fire message is to bring the fire department. One option is to have your system notify each of them directly. However, be aware that many police and fire departments will only react to recorded messages if there are no other emergencies, and others will not react at all. Still others will react, but after the second or third false alarm, they will levy a charge for services rendered!

The reason so many agencies do not positively react is that the proliferation in recent years of burglar and fire alarms with recorded messages has triggered extensive false alarms. (A good way to prevent false alarms on your system is to have your software programmed for a 20 or 30 second delay before calling out after the house alarms go off. This provides you with the necessary time to cancel a false alarm, yet still provides outside help quickly when necessary.) If you decide to have your system call your local police or fire department, be sure to check with them first.

Other possibilities to consider are to call yourself at work, call a neighbor or relative, or call a private company that is set up to receive and react to such messages. Consider, though, just how often you or your friends will be at the location to be called. Calling someone when they are not there is not much assistance. And if you do use a neighbor or relative, be sure to test the system with them so that they have actually heard the message(s), and make sure they know exactly what to do. They should know:

☐ What the message means (i.e., fire, break-in, etc.).
☐ Your address and phone number.
☐ Exactly how to respond. (Should they call the fire department or get the food out of your freezer?) Provide any phone numbers they will

need, and write down any message that they are to give to a third party.

Another possibility is to have your Home Control system contact an answering service or central security station. These can be found by looking in your yellow pages under *telephone answering services* and *burglar or fire alarm systems*. These services will receive the message from your Computer Home Control system and react according to prearranged instructions. Their fees usually run from $15 to $30 dollars per month.

All telephone answering services and central security stations are not equal when it comes to emergencies, so be particular with the service that you choose. Make sure their service operates 24 hours a day, and select one that is familiar with your area and its emergency services. If you are considering hiring a telephone answering service, keep in mind that this is probably just a side line, so double check that they will react appropriately in an emergency.

HOW DOES IT WORK?

There are many different types of equipment that can be used to notify the outside world. Most make use of phone lines, and some cable companies are beginning to offer security services over their TV cables as well. (If you have a cable company that provides these services, you may wish to contact them for further information.) The kind of equipment that you choose will be dependent on your particular requirements, the services offered in your area, and the Home Control system you have established. The following are four basic types of equipment in use today:

☐ Passive busy signal
☐ Noise over line
☐ Voice
☐ Digital

Passive Busy Signal. This is by far the simplest and unfortunately, also the least helpful. This system has applicability in those cases where only a rare check on a condition is necessary. An example might be a vacation home in an area where occasionally the temperature becomes quite cold, and you're concerned that a furnace breakdown could someday result in frozen pipes. In this instance, a Home Control system could monitor the temperature inside the house; and if it dipped below a certain point, the system would make the phone in the house inoperable, providing a constant busy signal. For you to detect the problem, however, you would have to call your vacation home periodically. If you got a constant busy signal, you would know one of two things—your furnace was not working or your phone was not operating correctly! This system works using a relay to complete (short) a circuit between what is usually the red and green incoming wires which are connected to the base of your phone.

Noise Over Line. A few Home Control manufacturers have chosen this as an inexpensive method to provide one type of message over the phone line. Basically, they use the computer with an auto-dial device which can call one or more phone numbers if a hazard condition is sensed. Once a connection is made, a siren sound, produced by the computer (or sometimes by a peripheral device), is sent through the phone lines indicating the condition to the person receiving the phone call.

Voice. Two types of voice systems are available: one uses pre-recorded messages (usually on tape) and the other uses computerized speech synthesis. These products vary widely in terms of capabilities, so be sure to check each product for the features you require. Two examples of those

Fig. 12-1. Talking Home Monitor (courtesy of Tandy Corporation).

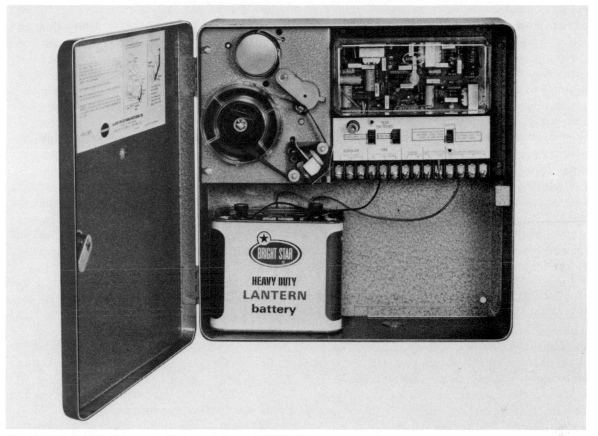

Fig. 12-2. Automatic Telephone Dialer (courtesy of ADEMCO).

that offer a good range of features are the Talking Home Monitor and the Automatic Telephone Dialer.

The Talking Home Monitor (#43-165) from Radio Shack ($199.95) is shown in Fig. 12-1. This unit actually includes some built in sensing capabilities: the ability to detect indoor temperature, loud sounds, and to monitor for a power outage. It can also monitor three other conditions through normally open or closed terminal pairs; and these sets of terminals can be used by your Home Control system (by opening or closing circuits controlled by relays) to activate the Talking Home Monitor. The Talking Monitor, in turn, can use its automatic dialer and voice synthesizer to repeatedly call up to four numbers and notify the receiver of the specific hazard condition. You can also use this equipment to listen to sounds in your

house by calling from any phone outside your house. Further, it can be used as an eight number automatic phone dialer, and comes complete with a battery backup system that operates for up to 15 hours during a power outage.

The Automatic Telephone Dialer (#612) from ADEMCO is shown in Fig. 12-2. This unit is an automatic dialer which uses two prerecorded messages on tape to deliver its warnings. It can be activated either from a normally open circuit closure or from a 5 to 12 dc voltage pulse. The Automatic Telephone Dialer is powered by a six volt battery or by a rechargeable battery pack. It includes an anti-jam feature which stops a burglar from calling your home to prevent the unit from regaining control of the phone line. The unit comes in a lockable steel case.

Digital. Digital communications from your

Home Control system work by sending electronic computer information over the phone lines. It is not understandable unless the receiving party has the computer equipment necessary to decode the messages. There are two basic types of digital systems that can be linked with your Home Control system. The first is similar to the ADEMCO Automatic Telephone Dialer except that rather than voice recordings, digital information is sent over the phone lines. An example is the ADEMCO #679 Two Channel Digital Communicator which has the characteristics of the #612 model except that it sends information digitally. ADEMCO produces a variety of digital communicators, many of which have larger numbers of channels and other features. Most of these communicators are activated through a normally open circuit or a dc voltage pulse.

Your Home Control system can also utilize normal microcomputer communications using an auto-dial modem and an RS-232 port. This requires the necessary terminal or communications software to be part of or integrated into your Home Control software. If you plan to use this method, be sure to contact the manufacturer of your Home Control components to see if they can provide the necessary software. The alternative is some pretty sophisticated machine language programming on your part.

Important: Digital communications between your Home Control system and a central monitoring station is **dependent on the compatibility between the sending and receiving system. Do not attempt to set up your side of the system until you are sure to whom you will be communicating and what their required formats are.**

FEATURES TO CONSIDER

Before leaving this subject, there are some interesting features that you may wish to consider prior to purchasing a particular communications device:

☐ Line seizure: Some auto-dialers have the capability to disconnect anyone using extension phones around the house so that the unit can make its emergency call.

☐ Anti-jam: As noted before, this feature prevents an outside caller from maintaining control of your phone line.

☐ Battery backup in case of power outage.

☐ Ability to call more than one number for the same or for different emergencies.

☐ Ability to take advantage of more than one phone line in your house, should you have more than one.

☐ Ability to make recalls to ensure the information gets to its destination.

☐ Re-arming capability for the next emergency.

☐ Dialing capabilities to 16 (or necessary) digits. Also, can it handle both tone dialing and pulse dialing?

☐ Ability to self test some or all features and notify you if there is a malfunction.

☐ For a digital communicator, does it (in conjunction with the receiving communicator) support a handshaking protocol to assure that the complete message has been sent and received properly?

HOW LONG WILL IT TAKE?

Most of the work involved in notifying the outside world is making sure that the communications method fits both your Home Control system and the requirements of the receiving party. Connecting the communications unit to our system is usually relatively uncomplicated and not particularly time consuming. Be sure to program your software to avoid false alarms, and test your communications equipment periodically to make sure it works.

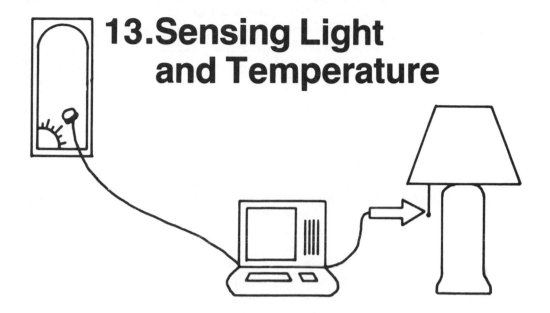

13. Sensing Light and Temperature

YOU'LL RECALL THAT PREVIOUS CHAPTERS have discussed controlling items around the house either by time or by a digital (on or off) condition. The only example of analog sensing so far was the water sensor in Chapter 9. Even in that chapter, however, we really wanted to know if something was on or off. In that case, on meant wet, and off meant dry. It really didn't matter how wet, just that the water sensor was beginning to sense water and therefore a pending flood condition.

Light and Temperature are two other examples of analog sensing that can be monitored by your Home Control system and used, in turn, to control other things. Depending on your application, it may be important to know just how hot or cold, or how bright or dim it is.

In Chapter 6, you learned how to control your front door light. With the method described, you were able to have the light turn on or off at a specific time of day, every day of the week. But some days are bright and sunny, while others are cloudy and dark. Also, as the seasons change, it gets darker earlier in the winter, and stays light later towards the summer months. With a light sensing device, your computer doesn't rely on the time of day to brighten your life. Instead, when it turns to dusk, the computer with a light sensor will take action.

The same is true for temperature sensing. Possibly your home has an attic fan which draws hot air out of the house. You could assume that every day of the summer would be hot and have the fan turn on at a predetermined time each afternoon. But even in summer, every day won't be hot; and in the spring and fall vast temperature swings occur from day to day. By using a temperature sensing device, you can turn on the fan only when necessary. This approach saves money as well as improves comfort.

This is just one temperature sensing idea that you may want to implement. Another example, as mentioned in the last chapter, might be to use a temperature sensor to make sure your freezer was working properly. You could also control a room fan, a window air conditioner, or to be a little more exotic, a greenhouse. A motorized sun shade could be installed that slides up and down inside the greenhouse to keep the temperature at a more constant level.

Note: Do not use the methods presented here to control either your furnace or central air conditioning systems directly. Appropriate methods are described in Chapter 7 and Appendix B which are dedicated to home heating and central air.

HOW DOES IT WORK?

Both the light sensor and the temperature sensor (also known as transducers) described here work on the same principle. Each can be read by the analog sensing capability (described in Chapter 2) on your sensor interface and computer. The amount of voltage allowed to pass through the sensor varies with the amount of light or change in temperature. This variance in voltage is then able to be interpreted by your analog sensor interface. Based on the amount of light or heat which has now been translated into a voltage level, your computer can respond by turning on and off lights, fans, etc., as shown in Fig. 13-1.

WHAT MUST I BUY?

Many different transducers (sensors that vary electrical resistance according to real world conditions such as light or temperature) are available. Cost ranges from a few dollars to $30 or more depending on the products' sensitivity, ease of use, prior calibration, and design features (i.e., packaged with easy mounting or connection features). The first place to look is the manufacturer of your other Home Control equipment. Sensors sold with these units are usually precalibrated and often the manufacturer's software is preset for their use. This makes setup much easier.

An inexpensive example of a light sensor is a *cadium-sulfide cell* (photocell) from Radio Shack which sells for $1.29 (catalog #276-116). Temperature sensors (known as thermistors) are

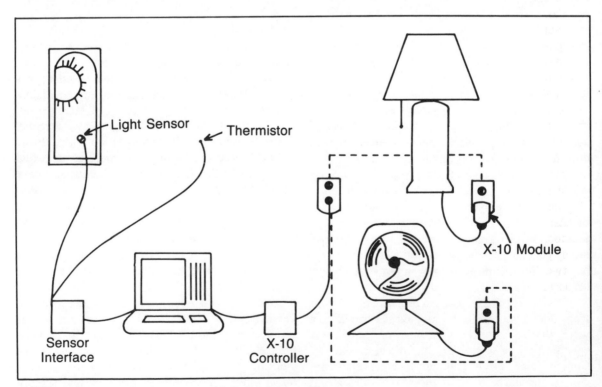

Fig. 13-1. Light and temperature sensors linked to lamp and fan.

available in a wide variety; simple, uncalibrated ones run well under $10. These are easily found at TV and appliance repair shops. (One major supplier with many distributors is Fenwal Electronics, 63 Fountain Street, Framingham, MA 01701). Thermistors are rated by their resistance in ohms at a nominal temperature of usually 25° Celsius (77° F). For experimental purposes, a regular glass bead (or probe model if measuring temperatures in liquids) of about 50 K to 100 K ohms of resistance should be suitable. Some thermistors are linear to temperature (resistance varies proportionately when temperature varies), and these are usually a bit higher priced. In most cases, however, linear thermistors are not necessary for Home Control sensing, since your system will be able to interpret appropriate temperatures.

Figure 13-2 shows what each of these sensors looks like. Both sensors are shown at roughly their actual size. As you can see, the entire temperature sensor can be much smaller than a match head.

Take a look at the home survey you completed in Chapter 4 to rethink which items might be best controlled using these methods. Of course, you can use one sensor (either light or temperature) to control more than one application. As an example, one light sensor could be used to turn on more and more lamps (or to brighten lamps) as the sun goes down. Or, one temperature sensor could sense progressively warmer temperatures and respond by first turning on fans and later, room air conditioners. Therefore, be sure not to over buy when purchasing these sensing device. There are applications, however, for which you may need more than one. An example might be if you wanted to build an indoor and an outdoor thermometer that can e read by your computer. For this purpose, you would need two thermistors, one located indoors and one outdoors.

WHAT MUST I DO?

After purchase, you'll have to select the best location for your sensors. Often these can be placed near the computer, and require very little additional wiring in your house. As an example, you may wish

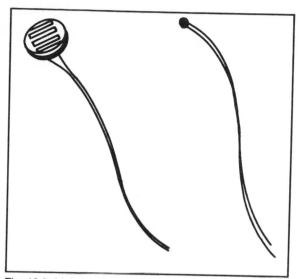

Fig. 13-2. Light sensor (left) and thermistor (right).

to have your light sensor tell how dark it's getting outside, but your computer may be located on the northern or eastern side of the house. Of course the sun sets in the west. This, however, doesn't mean you have to string wire to a western window. Your sensing equipment will work just as well by sensing the light available on the inside of a window located near your computer. When it gets dark enough outside, your computer will be able to sense it from whichever window your sensor is located.

Thermistors should be located as you would any thermometer—not in direct sunlight—so that accurate readings are made. Also, be sure you avoid areas subject to rain or excessive moisture if you intend to locate a sensor outside. While this would not damage your sensor interface, it may shorten the useful life of the individual sensors.

Figure 13-3 shows how to connect your transducers to your computer sensor interface. As you can see, the installation merely consists of running a double stranded wire between the sensors and a pair of the analog terminals on your sensor interface. Once the wiring is finished, all that remains is to connect the appropriate X-10 Modules to whatever is to be controlled. Then turn on your computer and use your software to find the analog readings of your sensors. Uncalibrated transducers

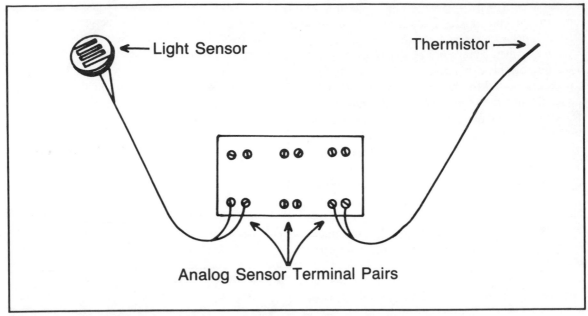

Fig. 13-3. Analog terminal wiring of light and temperature sensors.

can be adjusted (under software control) satisfactorily for your use with the following procedures:

Light sensors work by varying the amount of voltage that is sent to your analog terminals according to how much light they are sensing. A higher analog reading on your computer means that more light is being sensed, and a lower reading means that less light is being sensed.

This discussion is a little technical, but if your sensor interface has a 6-bit analog system (see your manufacturer's description) your computer will likely display a number between 0 and 255. A ten bit system will present numbers between 0 and 1023. The greater the number of bits your system uses, the finer the increments, or variations in voltage, that can be detected by your sensor interface. As sensors vary their resistance, the amount of voltage allowed to pass through them will vary (usually ranging from 0 to 5 volts on most systems). A 6-bit system breaks the 5 volts into 64 possible analog readings, the 8-bit system is able to break the same voltage range into 256 distinct analog readings, and the 10-bit system can break the voltages read into 1024 possible readings. When you purchase a Home Control Sensor Interface, this

is one thing to consider if you wish extremely fine sensing capabilities. However, for most home needs, a 6-bit system will be satisfactory. An exception to this would be if you wish to accurately monitor outdoor temperatures and you live in an area that can get as cold as -30° F in the winter and 100° F in the summer. Since a 6-bit analog system can only distinguish between 64 different readings it would be impossible to show each separate degree of real world temperature variation.

By varying the amount of light that reaches your light sensor, decide how much light it should receive before turning on each item (i.e., lamp, front door light). Record these analog readings and adjust your scheduling software to reflect these readings. For example, suppose you have a 6-bit system and you notice that sunset is close when your computer shows an analog reading of 20. If you wish your front door light to turn on at or below this reading, this should be reflected in your software. When the sun goes down a bit further, you may wish to have a living room lamp come on and possibly your radio should start playing. Don't forget that later in the evening you may wish to have your Home Control system turn off your lights and radio according to the time.

To calibrate your thermistors (if they are not precalibrated) you will need a good thermometer, a couple of plastic sandwich bags, and a pan filled with water (see Fig. 13-4) After hooking up your temperature sensor, turn on your equipment and take an analog reading of the voltage running through the thermistor. Note the temperature on the thermometer and record it in Table 13-1. (Before proceeding, it is assumed that your analog terminals are low voltage—usually 5 volts. **Do not perform the following procedure if you have high voltage equipment**. Also, be careful to keep the pan of water away from your computer or any electrical devices other than the thermistor as described below.) Now place the thermistor in one plastic bag and the thermometer in the other. (The sensor is placed in the plastic bag to protect it from the water, and the thermometer is placed in a bag to make sure we are consistent in the readings received by both.) Use hot and cold tap water (and possibly some ice) to slowly vary the temperature in the pan of water. As you are doing so, record the current analog readings along with the thermometer readings, as you go, in order to calibrate the full scale of the thermistor.

Once you have completed calibrating, simply adjust your schedule software so it reacts according to the temperatures being sensed and in turn controls whatever you wish to have controlled. For example, you may equate an analog reading of 50 (6-bit hypothetical reading, but go by your chart because this will vary according to several factors)

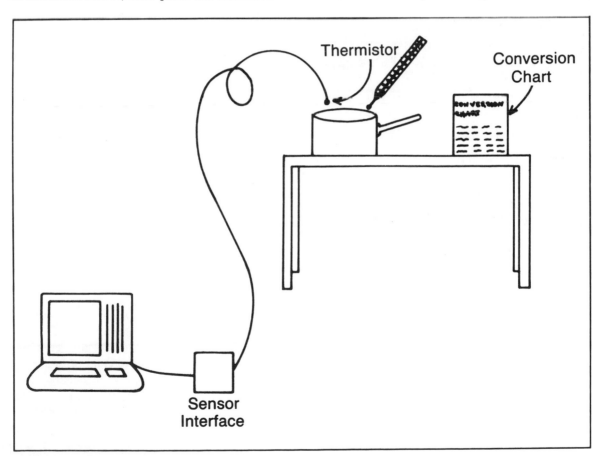

Fig. 13-4. Calibrating a thermistor.

Table 13-1. Temperature to Analog Reading Chart

Benchmark Degree	Actual Degree	Analog Reading	Benchmark Degree	Actual Degree	Analog Reading
-10	———	———	60	———	———
	———	———		———	———
	———	———		———	———
0	———	———	70	———	———
	———	———		———	———
	———	———		———	———
10	———	———	80	———	———
	———	———		———	———
	———	———		———	———
20	———	———	90	———	———
	———	———		———	———
	———	———		———	———
30	———	———	100	———	———
	———	———		———	———
	———	———		———	———
40	———	———	110	———	———
	———	———		———	———
	———	———		———	———
50	———	———	120	———	———
	———	———		———	———
	———	———		———	———

to be 80 °F. You may wish to adjust your software so that your attic fan turns on after this analog reading is reached. If the temperature drops to 73 degrees, possibly the fan should be shut off, and so on.

HOW LONG WILL IT TAKE?

Once you have your temperature sensor and light sensor, physical installation should take about 10 minutes for each. However, it may require up to an additional hour if you need to do your own calibration. As usual, a short amount of time will be needed to update your software scheduling. You will need to monitor the actual functioning of your setup to be sure it is working as you planned.

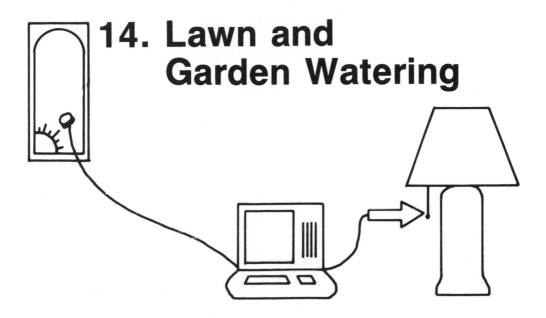

14. Lawn and Garden Watering

LAWN AND GARDEN WATERING CAN BE AS simple as a time controlled Appliance Module that turns on and off your sprinkler, or as complex as a complete underground watering system that (based upon soil moisture content) waters your lawn and gardens to the precise amount needed for the greenest, healthiest foliage in the neighborhood. (Be careful though, for Home Control doesn't include mowing!) To your Home Control system, neither are particularly complex. You can install your system to give you as much flexibility as you wish. Lawns can receive frequent watering while less thirsty plants can get only once a week sprinkling. If you have a sloped area on the property where runoff creates a problem, you can provide this area with short but frequent dosages so that water is retained instead of carrying the soil away.

HOW DOES IT WORK?

The simplest method for watering your lawn or garden is to water it for specified periods during the day or week. This can be handled simply with an X-10 Appliance Module connected to turn water on and off using the procedures related in Chapter 6. However, most of the commercially available electric water valves operate at 24 volts dc, so a voltage reducer (transformer) is required. The voltage reducer is connected to the X-10 Appliance Module and is also connected to an electric water valve (see Fig. 14-1). In this way, your X-10 Controller can operate the water as it would a lamp or a radio. The water is fed from the house plumbing system, through the electric water valve, to a hose hooked to your lawn sprinkler. Software control of the system is based on a schedule which you can develop like any appliance you are controlling.

A second method doesn't use time as the exclusive controlling factor. Instead, it also uses the moisture content of the soil. In this way, your lawn won't be watered just after a two inch downpour! This method uses the same signal (control) as described earlier; however, the sensing is based on an analog reading of the soil moisture content.

Basically, the moisture content is measured by

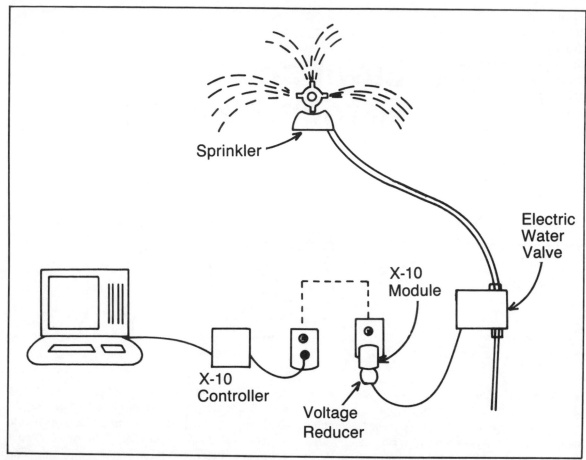

Fig. 14-1. Simple computer control of a lawn sprinkler.

the "relative conductivity" of the soil. The relative conductivity means the varying amounts of electricity that can pass through a medium—in this case soil. If the relative conductivity is high, this means the soil is moist. If the relative conductivity is low, the soil is dry, and the lawn or garden needs watering. Your Home Control Sensor Interface will use an "analog" reading of this relative conductivity to determine the moisture content of your soil; and based on this reading (as well as time), your X-10 Controller will send a message(s) to the X-10 Module which controls your electric water valve.

You will need to decide whether you wish to water your lawn or garden according to time alone, or in combination with sensing the soil moisture content. In either case, another decision is required:

would you like a permanent underground system, or would a simple garden hose linked to a lawn sprinkler suffice? If you made a property sketch in Chapter 4, use this to note the location of your outdoor faucets and decide where and how your sprinklers should be placed. Figure 14-2 may give you some thoughts on how to design your system. Also, for additional ideas, visit your local hardware or lawn and garden supply store to check the various types of stand-alone sprinklers. Many sell do-it-yourself components for underground systems, as well.

WHAT MUST I BUY?

After you have chosen and designed a system, for

each lawn or garden sprinkler (or lines of sprinklers if your water pressure is strong) you will need an Appliance Module, an appropriate voltage reducer, and an electric water valve. Since your front and back lawn probably receive the same amount of rain, you can more than likely use only one well placed sensor for moisture detection. The same water (moisture) sensor described in Chapter 9 on basement flood sensing can be used for soil moisture sensing.

Beyond this you will need whatever hosing (underground or regular) and sprinkling devices necessary to complete your system. Also, you may need garden tools (shovels, etc.) if you plan to dig trenches for a permanent system. The following manufacturers of lawn watering equipment may be of interest to you:

☐ The American Grandby Company, Liverpool, NY 13088, make the Lawn Genie line of equipment, including the Model R-204LG 1"NCN Solenoid Valve, a 24 volt electric water valve for about $20.

☐ The RainBird Sprinkler Mfg. Corp., Glen-

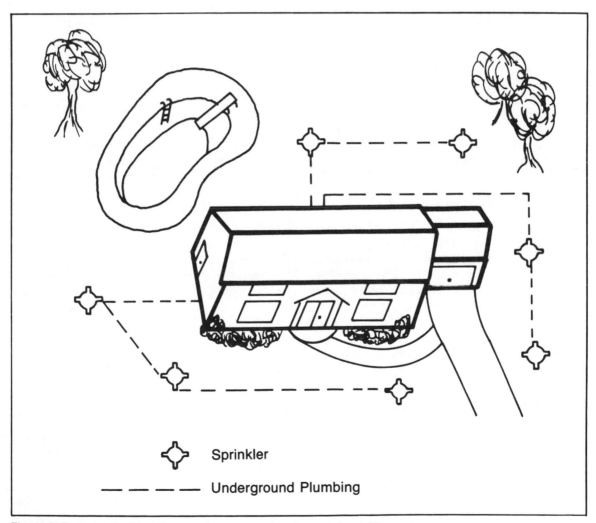

Sprinkler

Underground Plumbing

Fig. 14-2. Property plumbing diagram of a permanent underground sprinkling system.

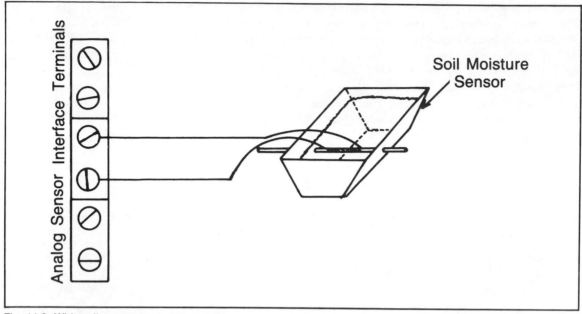

Fig. 14-3. Wiring diagram of a moisture sensor.

dora, CA 91740, makers of pop-up and regular underground water sprinklers.

WHAT MUST I DO?

If you plan to incorporate moisture sensing in your lawn and garden watering system, a set of analog input terminals in the back of your sensor interface should be connected to the two strands of wire from your moisture sensor as shown in Fig. 14-3. This figure also shows the simple sensing device at the other end of the wire. This should be buried in the soil so that the exposed wires (wrapped around the dowel) are about one inch below the surface of the soil.

Test your sensor by using your Home Control system to evaluate the relative conductivity of the dry soil. It should be very low or zero. Now moisten the soil as if there had been enough rain to penetrate the depth of the soil to the wires buried underneath. Once the soil is moist, re-evaluate the relative conductivity. Note the change in the value of the analog circuit.

Moisture sensing only needs to be done periodically—maybe once or twice a day. This is certainly different from the type of sensing necessary for the flood control system, so be sure to adjust your software schedule accordingly. You may wish to use your software to have the sprinklers turn on only if two conditions are met. The first condition would be a specific time of day, and the second would be if the analog reading of the moisture sensor shows that the soil is dry.

The electric water valve and the plumbing for your system should be installed according to the manufacturer's recommendations. Underground plumbing will likely need to be drained in winter months if the weather in your area dips below freezing. If the need for draining is planned during installation, this should be a fairly easy process. Usually, removable plugs at the low points of your plumbing will be necessary. If your electric water valve will be located outdoors, make sure that you are using appropriate wiring (likely 18 gauge approved for burial).

You should have your sprinkler(s) turn on and off each day only for the period of time necessary to moisten your lawn or garden to the correct amount. This will likely be 1/4 to 1/2 inch of water per watering, and can easily be calculated. As

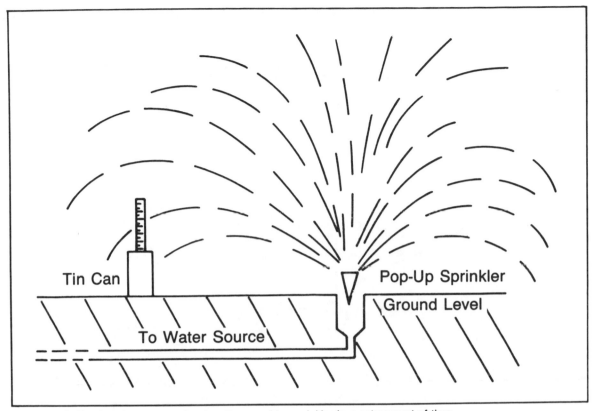

Fig. 14-4. Calibrating the amount of water dispensed by sprinkler in a set amount of time.

shown in Fig. 14-4, place a tin can (fully open on top) in an average coverage area on your lawn or garden. Turn the sprinkling system on and determine how long it needs to run to get the desired amount of water in the tin can. This is how long your Home Control system should allow the sprinkler to be left on in order to give your lawn the correct amount of water coverage.

You may wish to consider the following items in determining when it's best to water:

☐ Moisture content of lawn.
☐ Appropriate time of day for lawn and garden to be watered (possibly evening or morning).
☐ Potential changes in water pressure (low

pressure at certain times of day in some areas may cause poor operation of sprinkler system).
☐ Pedestrian traffic or family use of lawn and garden areas during certain parts of the day.

HOW LONG WILL IT TAKE?

This project can vary substantially in setup time. If the only thing you are doing is setting up a single sprinkler connected to an electric water valve that operates by time alone, the process should take about 20 minutes, plus a little time for measuring water coverage (the tin can procedure). However, if you are designing a full blown underground watering system with multiple water lines, you may need the weekend to complete this project!

15. Controlling Your Swimming Pool

IF YOU HAVE (OR ARE HOPING TO HAVE) A BACK-
yard swimming pool, spa or hot tub, your Home
Control system can be set up to make maintenance
easier and to leave you with more time for fun in
the sun! Although there may be other pool-related
features controllable with your system (such as the
lights around your pool), this chapter focuses on
three: a filter timer, a water level sensor, and a
robot cleaning system.

**Important: Always use fully grounded
methods for control of your swimming
pool. Pool pump filters should always be
carefully grounded by use of their three
prong plug and/or other methods described by the manufacturer of the equipment.
Do not defeat these grounding precautions.
Further, make sure that even low voltage
sensors keep water and electricity
separated. Also, X-10 Modules are not
suitable for outdoor (unprotected) conditions. Protect these modules from damp-
ness and extreme temperatures.**

SWIMMING POOL FILTER TIMER

It may be that the easiest pool-related item to control with your Home Control system is your pool
filter. One basic method of control is an X-10
System using a three prong (universal plug) Appliance Module. However, this Appliance Module
has a resistive load of 15 amps and a motor load
of one-third horse power (HP), and will only be
satisfactory for small pool filters. Many filter
motors have higher ratings and should not be handled using this method. If your filter motor has
higher ratings and your Home Control system has
relays, check the ratings of the relay system to
determine whether they can handle this type of
load. The relays on Home Control systems,
however, are unlikely to be set up for such high
ratings.

If your filter motor requires higher ratings and
you either have no relay system incorporated in
your Home Control system or the ratings are not
high enough, the best solution is to have an Appliance Module control a relay purchased for this
specific purpose. Because proper grounding is so

important, it is suggested that you use a qualified electrician to install the relay to your pool filter wiring. The electrician can install a relay so that the relay's switch mechanism leads to a plug which can be inserted into an Appliance Module to allow control through your X-10 System.

WATER LEVEL SENSOR

A pool filter motor must have water flowing through the pump in order to operate properly. Without the resistance of the water in the pump, the motor will run too fast, overheat, and eventually burn out. If this happens, you need a new motor. The most common cause of the filter pump not obtaining sufficient water is when, either through evaporation or a leak, the pool water level drops below the skimmer or pump intake hosing. Your Home Control system can monitor for a drop in the water level in several different ways, and should a drop occur, it can shut the pool filter off and notify you of the problem condition.

One way to sense a low water condition is to use a water-flow switch which opens or closes depending on whether or not water is flowing through a pipe. ADEMCO (Alarm Device Manufacturing Company) makes a normally open (off) water-flow switch #452 which is pictured in Fig. 15-1. (This equipment was actually designed to sense water-flow conditions in a fire alarm sprinkling system.) The water-flow switch can be connected to a two-inch diameter pipe. When the pump is working properly, the open contact will be closed (on); and when the pump is off or not receiving water from the pool, the switch will be open. You will need to replumb the filter intake line by adding a short piece of two inch pipe to which the waterflow switch can be fastened. A hole on the side of the pipe is also necessary for the mechanical switch to fit through. The water-flow switch should be wired to a digital pair of terminals on your sensor interface.

Your software will need to be adjusted so that when, and only when, the filter is turned on, the water-flow switch will be monitored. If the contact switch opens (and stays open for thirty seconds or more) when the filter is on, your Home Control system should turn the filter off. The 30 second delay should prevent occasional opening of the switch from a temporary water surge.

Other methods to determine a drop in your pool water level are outlined if you care to experiment. The first would be by use of a thermistor (temperature sensing device) as described in Chapter 13. Some thermistors are designed as probes—the glass housing is elongated—and can be used to sense temperature changes in liquids. The elongated thermistor can be securely glued through a small hole in the intake pipe from the pool so that the glass protrudes into the flowing water. When enough current is passed through them, thermistors will begin to heat up. (Use different thermistors to experiment, but don't use voltage levels beyond 5

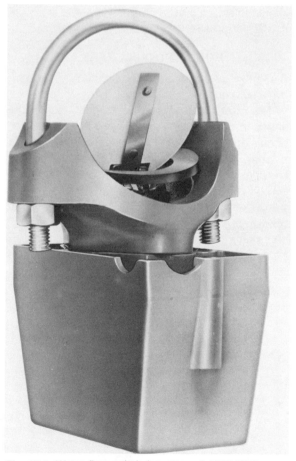

Fig. 15-1. Water flow switch (courtesy of ADEMCO).

volts since you're working close to water.) The flow of water, due to convection, will keep the thermistor cooler than if the water is not flowing. Using an analog pair of terminals on your sensor interface, you should be able to tell the difference between when water is flowing and not flowing.

Another experimental method would be to rig some sort of mechanical flotation device (possibly using a cork) at the side of your pool. This flotation device could open or close a switch (digital circuit) connected to your sensor interface depending on the water level in the pool. (Don't forget, your software will need to be able to account for the ups and downs of waves created by diving and swimming.)

For any of the methods used, once your Home Control system senses a drop in the water level it should first turn off the filter; and second, it should signal you in some way (flash lights, etc.).

ROBOT POOL CLEANER

A number of automatic pool cleaners (swimming robots) are available which either stir up the water so the filter has a better chance of catching any debris or dirt, or that vacuum the bottom and sides of the pool. Some of these work using the main filter's intake or return water flow as a (nonelectric) power supply, while others require either a secondary booster or a separate pump for their water power supply. If your model is powered from the water of the main filter, the earlier section on controlling your filter will automatically control this type of pool robot. If you have a model that makes use of an entirely separate pump, you can use the same procedure as described earlier to control your filter pump.

Other pool cleaning robots make use of a booster pump system that takes some of the filtered water directly upon leaving the main filter and before it returns to the pool. (A good example of this type of pool cleaning robot is the Polaris VacSweep, made by Polaris, P.O. Box 1149, San Marcos, CA 92069). A "T" pipe in the plumbing allows water from the main return line to be pulled into a secondary line where a pump boosts the water flow strength before the water returns to the pool through the robot.

Such secondary pumps require the main filter to be on in order to obtain enough water to prevent overheating. Home Control of your secondary pump motor can be handled by using a physical setup similar to control of the main filter. However, your software control will be different.

The software schedule should only turn the secondary pump (robot's pump) on after the main filter pump is on, and it should always turn the secondary pump off prior to the main pump. With old fashioned electric/mechanical timers, this meant giving at least a half hour leeway between the two pumps turning on and off. With your Home Control system, both use the same clock, and therefore only a minute's difference between the on or off sequence is necessary. Do not have both turn on at the same time, however, because it takes a few seconds for the main filter pump to get the water circulating correctly.

16. Audio/Video Control

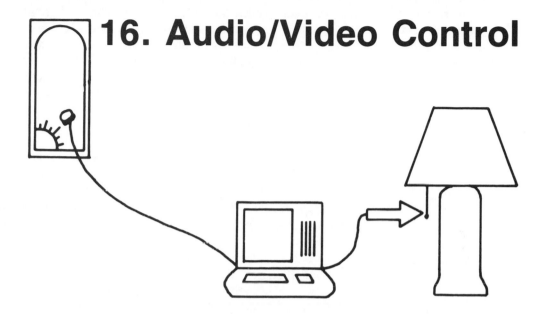

A RECENT PHENOMENON IN AMERICAN HOMES is the *media room*. With the rush of new technologies, no one wants to admit to being in the dark ages of the family TV room. Ten to fifteen years ago, a TV (likely black and white) and a record player were standard in most homes. But today's complete media room (see Fig. 16-1) boasts a modular assortment of the basics: a monitor, video tuner, video cable, video cassette recorder, video disc player, video camera, video game player, computer with modem for information, banking, and shopping, a component—yet integrated—stereo which includes an AM/FM tuner and amplifier (or receiver), linear tracking turntable, graphic equalizer, cassette deck, compact disc player, headphones, and a set of 3-way speakers. Did we forget the satellite dish on the roof?

Of course, at least three or four of these components come with a remote control unit. And after finding each of these (they seem to wander if you have children), control really becomes simple. Of course, since the other half of your system is not remote controlled, you still have to remember which remote control works which gadget, and then walk to the nonremote items to make additional adjustments.

Take a moment and think about how many buttons and switches (and dials for older models—dials seem to be passe these days!) you have on your equipment. With such a system, have you ever had to explain to your babysitter how to turn on your TV? Did you provide her with an electronics certificate? Did you find her reading a book when you got home?

Home Control will not immediately solve these problems. But thankfully there are a few things available that give the media room owner a chance! First, some companies do complete home media designs and installations and make available customized remote capabilities via wall or table control panels which can be located throughout a home. Two examples are Boulten Music Systems, located at 979 Third Avenue in New York City, 10022 (212-697-4900) and Audio Command Systems whose main office is at 46 Merrick Road, Rockville Centre, NY, 11570, (516-766-5055). Figure 16-2 shows Audio Command System's remote controller. Both of these companies have many major installations for the rich and famous to their credit—often costing tens of thousands of dollars and, of course, using only the best equipment. Often these firms work with designers and architects to create specialized cabinetry, custom furniture, and include custom colors and finishes for the end products.

For those of us with more modest requirements (or means), some of the manufacturers of audio and video components are beginning to offer components which are more integrated than has been available in the past. One such system by Jensen, the AVS-1500 Receiver (shown in Fig. 16-3), integrates a TV tuner which is cable ready for 133 channels, an AM/FM Stereo Receiver (50 watts/channel), an Audio Signal Processor (does such things as creating simulated stereo from mono sources), a Switcher which integrates all input sources (even includes Simulcast switch for combining TV broadcast with audio from FM stereo), and all can be controlled from a wireless remote control unit. The system may be purchased with matched monitor and speakers.

In October of 1984, RCA began delivering a system called Dimensia. This system, at first glance, appears like any other audio/video integrated system and includes components (which can be purchased separately) such as a 26″ monitor/receiver, VHS Hi-Fi VCR, CD player, analog audio turntable, audio cassette recorder, tuner, amplifier, and speakers. What makes this system vastly different from regular systems is the

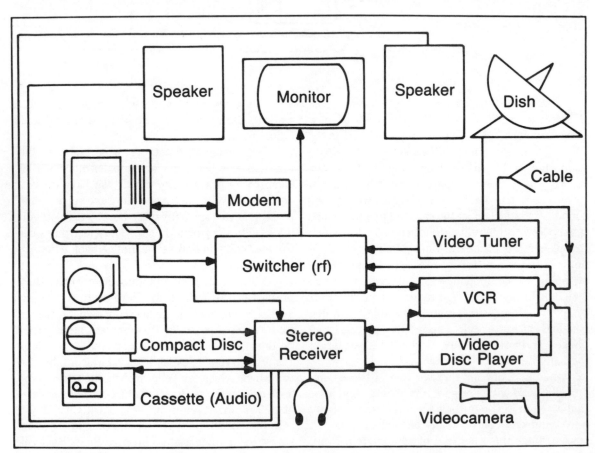

Fig. 16-1. Components of the media room.

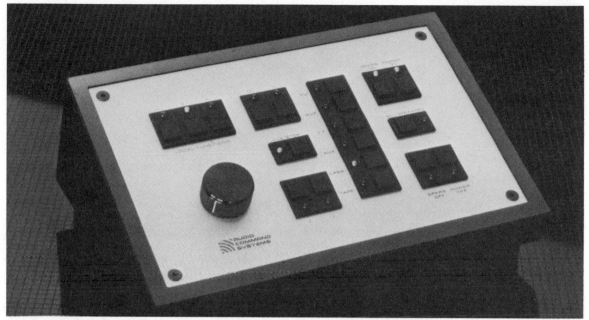

Fig. 16-2. Audio Command Systems' remote controller (courtesy Audio Command Systems).

remote control feature as shown in Fig. 16-4. Where most remote controllers can handle only one specific component, this controller manages the entire setup, and does so with simple and logical commands. Although each component has its own computer circuitry, all react to this central controller in an interactive, well designed and coordinated way. The chore of operating the media room has been conquered.

Wiring of Dimensia has also been simplified. Usually, the various components of such an integrated system requires criss-crossing wires from each component to every other to enable all pieces of the system to work with each other. RCA instead

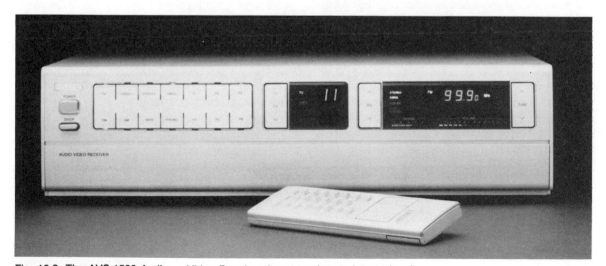

Fig. 16-3. The AVS-1500 Audio + Video Receiver (courtesy Jensen International).

Fig. 16-4. The Dimensia system (courtesy RCA Consumer Electronics Div., Indianapolis, Indiana).

has chosen a method of piggybacking connections in a more logical approach for an integrated system.

Another major feature will be evident if you have operated a VCR for timed program recording. Even though many VCR units have prompting features, trying to push the correct buttons in the appropriate sequence can be a frustrating experience. RCA has at least partially alleviated this annoyance by superimposing prompts on the monitor picture. For many fumble fingered individuals, this feature will be of great help.

COMPUTER LINK UP

But this book is about Computer Home Control—so why all this talk about integrated audio/video systems? Well, the problem with computer control of audio/video devices is not for a lack of customer demand, or so claim the manufacturers of Home

Control equipment. Rather, the problem is that for a computer to control an integrated A/V system, the A/V equipment must be capable of linkage. Extremely few component audio and/or video manufacturers have produced computer compatible items for the home market. (Exceptions mostly relate to the video disc market—a discussion of which will be provided later.)

It's true that manufacturers have produced component monitors, switchers, receivers, etc., to which computers can send their audio/video output. Indeed, many manufacturers provide components with inputs for all the popular items which may feed their systems, and these components have one or more inputs for computers labeled "Computer RGB Input," "Computer Composite Input," "Computer Audio Input," etc. What manufacturers haven't offered, however, is for the computer to actually control the components. The reason for this is that most consumers are not particularly interested in computer control of one or two individual components of a system.

To have real value, the computer must control the *whole* system. This in the past has been a monumental task because it means that the computer must be linked with each separate component. Home Control manufacturers would have to be able to understand and then hardwire to each component in the system through relays, or the like. Of course, each manufacturer's system is slightly different—again compounding the problem. In a sense, the actual innards of the components have to be reworked, which as you can imagine is not a very cost effective proposition. However, now that the linking has been simplified by such companies as Jensen and RCA, the computer linkage is also simplified many fold. All that is necessary is for the computer to emulate the master remote controller of such an integrated system.

Although sophisticated computer control of audio/video systems is not widely available, it's likely to be more so in the not too distant future. These computer-audio/video links may come from the audio/video or computer manufacturers themselves. It is more likely, however, that Home Control manufacturers will develop them first.

All is not rosy, however, for there is still a very large standardization problem. Let's take Dimensia, for example. Dimensia is fine for those that will buy only Dimensia components, but non-Dimensia components will need to be controlled manually or with their own remotes. Even if many of the manufacturers begin to offer Dimensia-like products (fully integrated), it's unlikely—although one can hope—that the communications between the remote controller and the components will be standard from one manufacturer to the next. Therefore, if you wish to buy a component that is not part of the same line as your other equipment, you will likely have this incompatibility problem for the foreseeable future.

FEATURES TO CONTROL

The simplest kind of Home Control of Audio/Video

is by using an X-10 Module to turn on a radio, TV, receiver, etc. However, more interesting features can be incorporated into your system by extending the audio/video system to other parts of your house through relay control of speakers. Also, functional control of components (for example: computer control of the radio station setting on a receiver) can be part of your Home Control system—with a little extra effort. Further, a lot of activity has occurred in the area of computer linked video discs. Since this is one type of device that audio/video manufacturers have provided the capability for direct computer linkage, these will also be covered in a more extensive overview format.

Relay Control of Remote Speakers

Many receivers (or amplifiers) offer the capability to operate more than one set of speakers, either by turning a dial or by pressing a button. Usually, either the A set can be on, or the B set can be on, or both can be on at once. Home Control can add to this by offering timed control by turning on and off both the receiver, and the various speaker sets, as appropriate.

An example of this might be linking the receiver in a den with three different speaker sets—one set located in the den, itself, another in the dining room, and a third set in the master bedroom. Each morning that you wish to be awakened, the Home Control system would switch the bedroom speakers to the on position via a relay. Once this is accomplished, your Home Control system could then (using the X-10 System) switch on the receiver. Now, instead of an irritating alarm buzzer or a tinny sounding clock radio, you can wake to your favorite FM stereo station's music or the early morning news. A short time later, as you head towards the kitchen, the speakers in the adjacent den might be timed to come on.

On those days when everyone is at work or school, the receiver and speakers might be turned on periodically in different locations for security purposes to make your house sound as if someone was there. Further, you could have the den speakers turn on for your arrival home, and the dining room speakers could switch on to signal the advent of dinner. All this, of course, would happen automatically according to your preset instructions.

As shown in Fig. 16-5, the receiver is controlled simply by an X-10 Module while the individual speaker sets are controlled by relays. These relays may either be internal to your Home Control equipment, or may be attached to and controlled by separate X-10 Modules. If two sets of speakers are unlikely to be used at the same time, one relay can control both by having one set of speakers on when the relay is switched one way (power applied) and the other set of speakers on when the relay is switched the other way (no power applied). (If an X-10 Module is used—depending on the power requirements of your relay—a voltage reducer may be necessary between the X-10 Module and the relay.)

Relay Control of an Audio/Video Component

This project is slightly more advanced than most in this book, and may require soldering electrical parts as well as opening either an audio or video component. In some cases this may void your warranty for the equipment that is involved.

There may be a particular audio or video component that you wish to have managed by your Home Control system. Examples might be the control of a video cassette recorder or your receiver. Suppose that you own a VCR with limited recording programability, such as one of the models with the capability to program one time length within a 24 hour period. You might wish to expand this capability with your Home Control system by timed control of relays that would operate the push button controls of your VCR. (Only push button controls—as opposed to dial or slide switch operated devices—can be operated using this method.)

Figure 16-6 shows how such a system should be wired to control the record and stop functions of the VCR. The relays could be internal to your Home Control system or controlled by X-10 Modules. The VCR buttons will likely be *momentary* contact switches, in which case the relay should

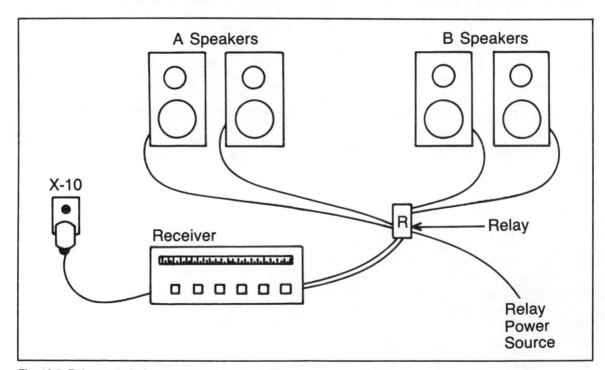

Fig. 16-5. Relay control of a component stereo system.

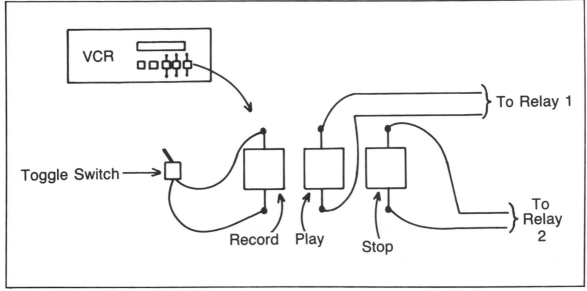

Fig. 16-6. Relay control of VCR. Toggle switch must be in closed position (on) for Home Control recording.

only be on for a moment and then returned to the normal (off) state. Some VCR's also allow for channel selection via momentary contact switches, and these two may be controlled by your Home Control system. If this is part of your plan, your software will have to track which channel is the starting point, as well as any moves therefrom.

If your VCR (or other audio or video component) has a remote control unit, wiring may be simplified and less problematic if you wire to the remote unit rather than directly to the component, itself. (This approach could be illegal, however, depending on the F.C.C. regulations governing the remote control transmitter.)

Computer Control of a Video Disc Player

Computer control of a video disc player is really a subject for a complete book, and therefore this will be a very brief overview. The major aspect of computer control of a video disc player is that the video disc player itself is used as a sophisticated memory device—somewhat similar to a disk drive. The video disc player can be linked to a computer and a monitor so that advanced control of data (usually in the form of a high quality video movie) can be randomly (but specifically) accessed by the com-

puter. This process is similar to random access of a standard disk drive, but usually for input only. More advanced video disc players (costing usually beyond $15,000) have recording capability.

As opposed to a disk drive, information contained on the video disc itself is not normally sent to the computer, but is instead sent to a monitor for viewing. Therefore, the information on the video disc is not used for input to the computer as is computer data, programs, files, etc. The only information fed from the video disc to the computer is a signal for control purposes—for example, to let the computer know that a certain segment of viewing has been completed. Often, however, even this type of information is controlled by the computer by being programmed to know the time length necessary for a certain video disc segment to play.

The memory of the actual shiny gold or silver video discs (they produce a kind of rainbow effect) can be extremely large—up to about four billion bytes of information or over 50,000 still pictures. One disk can store about two hours worth of video—enough for most full length movies.

Various applications for this technology include education and training systems (where the user can actually interact with the computer/video disc player combination) advanced computer games, business presentations, advanced interactive retail store catalogs (where high quality visuals are important), or where other advanced cataloging and high interactivity are necessary or preferable—such as a very advanced form of encyclopedia. As an example, imagine learning about prehistoric dinosaurs. Depending upon your question, your computer controlled video disc system could not only help you find the answer, but could also show you a Hollywood portrayal of what "Dino" looked like! Or you could learn to fly a twin engine airplane where based on your operation of the controls (keyboard, joystick, etc.) the picture on the monitor in front of you would begin to take-off, dive, spin, or land just as if you were actually in the plane.

Futurists predict that this is a technology just waiting for a few good pieces of software to make it fly. Two companies that are betting on this technology and have (or are planning) relatively inexpensive links (hardware and software) to the Apple, IBM PC, and the Commodore computers are Digital Research Inc. and Vutrack Systems.

As always with start-up technologies, a few problems exist. With video disc control the major problem is of standardization. This includes a number of differing formats (similar to the noncompatibility of VHS and Beta in VCR formats), as well as differing methods in the computer control (hardware and software) of the video disc players. However, once a consumer market really begins to develop, these should resolve into two or three generally accepted formats and linkage combinations. Figure 16-7 shows a sampling of the current

Video Disc Players			
Brand	**Model**	**Approx. Price**	**Port Type**
Hitachi	8500	$1200	Serial
	9500	$1600	Serial
Pioneer	LD 700	$800	Serial
	LD V4000	$900	Serial
	LD V6000	$1600	Serial
	LD V1000	$1200	Parallel
Sony	Laser max	$800	Serial
Panasonic	TQ 2024	$2985	Serial

Fig. 16-7. Currently available video disc players which include computer linkage port.

video disc players available in the U.S. market.

TIPS FOR THE MEDIA ROOM

Since a good number of you who are interested in Home Control are also interested in the media room concept (based on information expressed to Home Control manufacturers), the following few paragraphs are for you. However, this short section is not intended to suggest that a home computer should necessarily be located in the media room. The computer location should make sense according to how you use your computer, and whether or not you will be constantly sharing the media room with other members of the family. If others will be making extensive use of the media room while you're trying to develop a complicated computer program or completing a lengthy document on your word processing software, it's suggested that you locate your computer away from the distractions of this particular room. However, if your computer is used for lighter efforts or if one of your major interests in Home Control is to develop a highly sophisticated computer linked A/V system, the media room may be just the place.

The term "media room", as opposed to the family TV room, has been used recently to describe a room in the home where the chief functionality of the space has been designed to integrate audio/video and other electronic media into a center for entertainment and education. Often designs for these rooms are such that they are tremendous electronic entertainment centers, but are not at all set up for general social entertainment. That's okay, of course, as long as that's the understood purpose of the area prior to implementation of the plan, and often there may be other areas in the home for more casual recreation. Many media rooms, however, are not so strict in design and have been developed with some compromises to suit many family functions. If you decide to develop a media room, your particular design should first consider the various needs for the particular room that will be used.

Once the foregoing concerns have been covered, probably the next most important decision to make is where to place the monitor and speakers, and where the audience will be located. These relative locations will make a critical difference to bringing out the most from your equipment, and may play a significant factor in your choice of added equipment. Generally, the audience should be centered from roughly 2/3 to 1 1/2 the distance between the speakers along a perpendicular line that begins at the center point between the speakers (see Fig. 16-8). These rough distances may also be a help in determining the size of the monitor that might be used. It would normally be located midway between the speakers.

The remainder of your equipment should be placed with two factors in mind:

☐ First and foremost, convenience in the use of your equipment once all is installed.

☐ Second, but yet a factor, ease in terms of wiring and maintenance.

With the mass of equipment in the market today, it's unlikely that much real advice can be provided here on the selection of particular components. However, a good recommendation is to have a plan as to what your overall intentions are for the media room. Then judge any new component purchases against this plan. Some examples of this might be as follows:

☐ Do you intend to use your monitor exclusively for video movies and broadcast shows, or will it be used with your computer as well? Does it have the appropriate ports for your present (or future) computer (or other needs)? If you are planning to work with spreadsheet or word processing programs, is the resolution good enough to support text?

☐ Does the particular receiver, switcher, etc. have enough ports to conveniently operate all the equipment you plan to have?

☐ If you considering one of the "rack" audio (or audio/video) systems, what happens when you buy your next component? Will it look a little funny sitting on the floor? Might it make better sense to use a large cabinet (or closet) that offers plenty of space for additions or replacements?

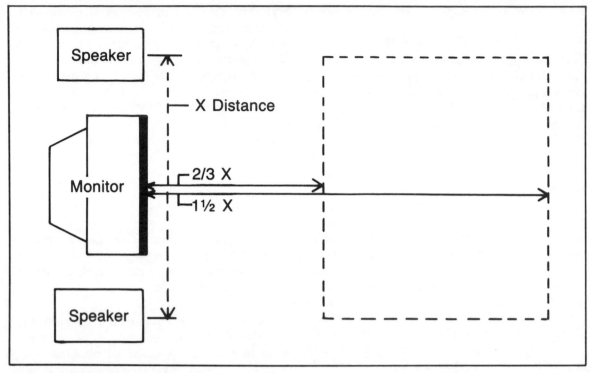

Fig. 16-8. Dimensions of the media room.

☐ Does it make sense to buy a particular remote controlled item if other components will be operated manually?

☐ Will the new equipment integrate well with your existing equipment, or will it be of little advantage to the overall system? For example, does it make sense to upgrade to a $500 amplifier if your speakers only cost $200?

Assuming your hardware is in order, be sure to plan in some convenient storage space for your software and manuals—the records, audio tapes, video tapes, computer disks, etc. And don't overlook the furnishings in the room. Heavy draperies that cover your picture window across

from your large screen TV may be appropriate if you wish to do some viewing during daytime hours. If you plan to be watching or listening for extended periods of time, make sure the room has comfortable furniture—the kind where you can put your feet up and relax. Of course, if possible, locate your controls where they can be operated from this relaxed position!

For those of you who wish some detailed advice in designing such a room *The Media Room*, a book by Howard J. Blumenthal (published by Penguin Books: Baltimore, 1983) is a good place to start. Also, be sure to check with your local audio/video specialty stores to get some further ideas and live demonstrations.

17. Getting It All Together

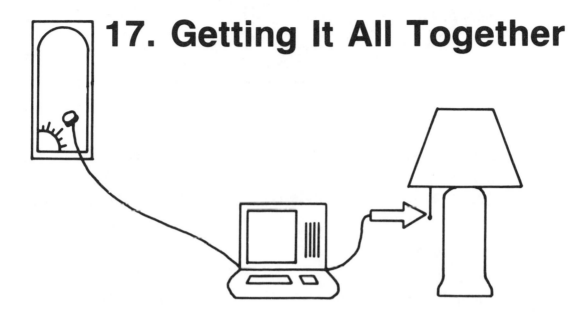

ONE OF THE MAJOR BENEFITS OF COMPUTER Home Control is that it allows what would normally be a number of independent systems to be combined into one super intelligent system. If you incorporated all the ideas in Chapters 6 through 16 (and likely some of your own) as separate independent systems, imagine all the mini-sensor/controllers that would be scattered within your house, each with its own set of buttons, timers, and procedures to understand, memorize, and adjust. Of course, much of the wiring and peripherals would be redundant as well, so your costs would be higher and your flexibility would be much, much lower.

A Computer Home Control system is an integrated approach (as shown in Fig. 17-1) offering high flexibility, simplicity in installation and control, ease of future expandability—and all this at a more reasonable cost than separate systems. This chapter covers a few notes and procedures that are important to make sure you enjoy your Home Control system for many years to come.

SETUP NOTES

If you're having difficulty selecting among specific components for your Home Control system, don't hesitate to contact the manufacturer or distributor with any and all questions you may have. Buying and installing a Home Control system is much like a component stereo system in that all the pieces must work in harmony. Unfortunately, detailed product information is not likely to be available at the nearest shopping center. You won't find two or three Home Control stores with knowledgeable sales help to answer your questions. Five or ten years in the future, maybe! Keep in mind that today this is a fledgling industry; the manufacturers and distributors are very willing to discuss your specific questions since many of their customers are in the same position and need some help.

Another basic rule that can save you trouble later is to unpack your Home Control equipment carefully and read all instructions completely prior to installation. Check the packing list to make sure

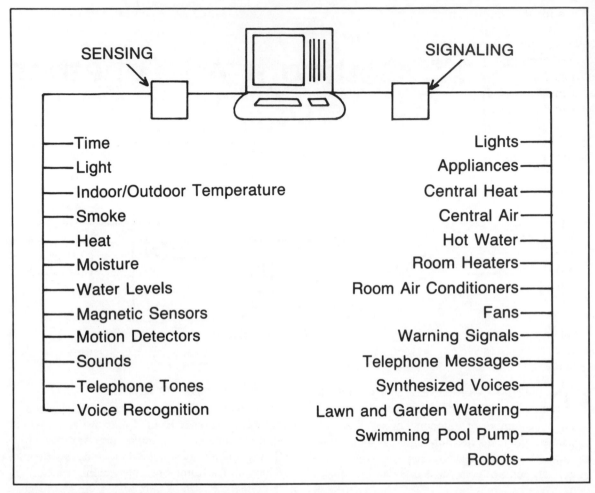

SENSING

SIGNALING

- Time
- Light
- Indoor/Outdoor Temperature
- Smoke
- Heat
- Moisture
- Water Levels
- Magnetic Sensors
- Motion Detectors
- Sounds
- Telephone Tones
- Voice Recognition

- Lights
- Appliances
- Central Heat
- Central Air
- Hot Water
- Room Heaters
- Room Air Conditioners
- Fans
- Warning Signals
- Telephone Messages
- Synthesized Voices
- Lawn and Garden Watering
- Swimming Pool Pump
- Robots

Fig. 17-1. Integrated approach to Home Control.

that all the equipment has been included. Many of the Home Control sensor interfaces and controllers (or single unit combinations) include simple tests to be performed during installation to make sure all functions and capabilities are operative. Take the few extra minutes to do these tests to ensure that the equipment is in order.

Many, though not all, Home Control systems require that your computer remain in one stationary location. Consider carefully where this should be; for once your installation is complete, a later relocation would be cumbersome and time consuming. Obviously, a place that is damp, exposed to extreme temperatures, or in the middle of your main traffic

flow where knocks or spills are likely, is less than desirable. Wiring ease for your system to the sensors should be a consideration, as well.

When installing equipment and making connections, use care to make sure that none of the components become damaged. As an example, a thermistor used to sense temperature can be about the size of a pin-head with two hair-sized wires for connections. Not only can these be easily damaged, but they are even easier to misplace. Imagine trying to find a thermistor in a hay stack! Home Control components, like any peripherals, need careful handling. Once your equipment is installed, keep it reasonably dust free and follow any maintenance tips for the components.

After your overall wiring plans for the house are complete, you may find that many of the wires head from your sensor interface in the same direction. Most sensor interface systems will use less than 12 volts (usually 5 volts) and 22 to 26 gauge wire (the higher the gauge, the smaller the wire). This wire may be purchased in color coded multiconductor cables where six to ten separate wires are housed in one cable less than a quarter inch in diameter. One or two of these cables from your sensor interface (if a number of wires need to travel together) may take care of most, if not all of your sensor wiring requirements. When wiring 24 volt applications—such as between the voltage reducer (transformer) and the electric water valves—use 16 to 18 gauge wire. If any wire will be buried underground, be sure the specifications confirm that it is approved for burial.

If you will be installing your Home Control system over a period of time, be sure to consider future wiring at the beginning. Including extra conductor strands during the original wiring can often save doing virtually the same work all over again at a later time.

If long lengths of wire are used between your sensors and your sensor interface, you may occasionally get misreadings (false alarms, etc.). This is more likely to be a problem if you are in an *electrically noisy* area where heavy duty motors or other high powered electrical appliances are being used. Such false readings can be easily controlled with the use of a few electronics parts—a capacitor (and possibly a resistor)—linked to your wiring. These are inexpensive pieces that can be purchased locally at any electronics store. However, for proper sizing and hook-up instructions, contact the manufacturer of your sensor interface equipment.

DATA BACKUP

Whether you purchase software or program your own, **make sure you have backup copies**. The first thing to do when you receive your software on a diskette or cassette is make at least two backup copies. Since most of the manufacturers do not copy protect software (because it is only usable with their

Home Control Equipment), the process of making a backup copy is usually straight forward. Follow the computer instruction manual for cassette (tape) copies, or your Disk Operating System (DOS) manual for diskette copies. After making these, write protect the original and one copy (so that you can't accidently SAVE a program or data on the same cassette or diskette), and store it in a safe place. Disks are write protected by placing a piece of tape over the notch(s) located on the side of the disk, and tapes are write protected by breaking off the small tabs located at the back of the cassette.

Each time you develop or update a schedule for your Home Control system, it should be backed up as well. Though the schedule itself does not require much time to actually re-enter, it can be very time consuming to recall just how every component interacts with the system. For example, you'd have to remember what sensor is linked to which item(s) it controls, as well as all the time related data (i.e., the time your coffee pot, alarm clock, water sprinkler, etc. should go on and off each day of the week). Therefore, it's shorter in the long run to make copies of your schedules each time you make any changes.

BATTERY BACKUP

A battery backup may not be a requirement for your system. However, if you do want this capability, the easiest (and likely the cheapest) way is to purchase a Home Control system which includes one built-in. Keep in mind the following considerations to be sure the battery backup you purchase meets your needs:

☐ X-10 Controllers and Modules will not work if the house power goes out. Therefore, anything that must work during a power outage should not be controlled by your X-10 system (unless your whole house is backed up by an alternate electrical supply—an expensive method to choose).

☐ If your Home Control system does not have a separate microprocessor to control your house independently of your computer, then your computer must have a power backup as well.

☐ All peripheral equipment such as sirens or

telephone dialers expected to perform during a power failure must have a power backup.

☐ When manufacturers claim that their product has a battery backup system, be sure to find out just whey they mean. Do they mean that only the clock time and software will be retained in your computer's memory during a power outage, or will the sensors, relays, and appropriate voltages to power burglar and fire alarm functions remain operative? There is a big difference between the two, so make sure you investigate the manufacturer's definition. Also, how long does the backup remain operative? Five minutes? Ten hours? This is another important feature to consider.

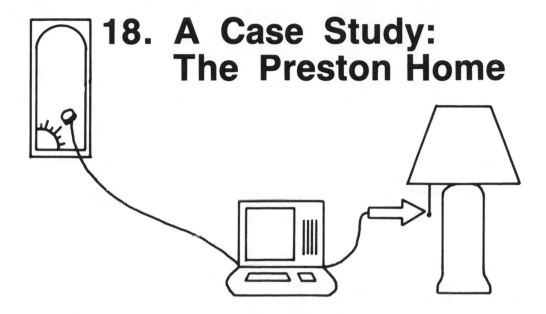

18. A Case Study: The Preston Home

A T THIS POINT, YOU KNOW ALL THE PIECES. This chapter will help you pull all your theory and knowledge together as you follow the Prestons in an actual case history. You'll share firsthand how they installed their Home Control system and how it operates. Even if you choose a completely different system, much of the information here should shed some light on just what is involved, or how different alternatives should be evaluated to find the one most practical to you.

Fred and Lisa Preston live in a suburb of New York City. Lisa works in Manhattan as an analyst for a Wall Street firm and Fred, whose job is located in New Jersey, is a sales manager for a nationwide commercial real estate broker. The Prestons have a son, Christopher, who is almost two and who stays with a neighbor while both Fred and Lisa are at work.

The Prestons have a computer that both Fred and Lisa use for work extensively. Lisa tracks the companies she is responsible for analyzing on database and spreadsheet programs, while Fred uses the computer to develop proposals and agree-

ment letters for clients. Fred also uses the computer to compile a monthly sales report which summarizes the work of his six salespersons when these are not completed on a compatible computer at work. The computer also serves to keep track of the family's financial and tax records, and is periodically tied into an online information service, through a modem, that the Prestons use for home banking and computer shopping.

The Prestons own a two story colonial home in New Jersey (Fig. 18-1) where they have lived for about three years. During that time they had discussed installing a burglar/fire alarm system, and their interest became more acute when some friends in the next town were recently the victims of a burglary. Lisa decided to call a few security companies to get estimates after asking some neighbors for references who had security systems of their own. Two written estimates were obtained which were both between $2500 and $3000.

The following Sunday, Fred was paging through the "Home" section of the newspaper and came across an article which gave an overview to

Fig. 18-1. The Preston's computer controlled home.

Home Control. The article discussed three products that could be linked to a computer to control lights and appliances. One of the products covered was the HomeBrain by HyperTek, Inc., and Fred noted that this product appeared to have an extensive security system. Fred also found that this product used the X-10 System as a Controller. Lisa had recently purchased an X-10 Timer and three Modules which were currently used to control their front door light, a lamp in their living room, and the coffee pot in their kitchen. Fred decided to give HyperTek a call on Monday and request further details.

At work on Monday, Fred called HyperTek and described what he was looking for in terms of security. He found that the HomeBrain could satisfy his needs in this area, and it was also determined that the HomeBrain was compatible with the Preston's computer. Fred requested a brochure and price list, and decided to order the HomeBrain's Reference Manual. By the end of the week, all materials had arrived in the mail.

After both Fred and Lisa had read the brochures, they were confident that the HomeBrain suited their needs. They were particularly pleased that the HomeBrain would not monopolize their computer, since both of them used their system extensively for other purposes, as described earlier. They also liked the idea of having extensive battery backup capabilities included with the

114

HomeBrain, since there were occasional power failures in their area. Lisa, who usually took care of the family finances, particularly liked the idea of the potential energy savings with the HomeBrain. They decided to devote Sunday afternoon to designing their Home Control system so that they would have a systematic and complete plan to take advantage of the HomeBrain's benefits.

THE PRESTON HOME CONTROL DESIGN

By the time Fred and Lisa began to actually develop their Home Control plan, they had a lot of information on file from the security companies and from the HomeBrain brochures. Sunday afternoon they toured their property (both inside and outside

their house) and within a few hours had developed the drawings which appear in Figs. 18-2 through 18-6 on the next several pages.

The Outside

As they walked outside their home, Lisa and Fred noticed that their front lawn and gardens always seemed a little brown in the summers, while the backyard—possibly because of their pool—stayed green throughout the season. Therefore, they decided to develop a simple sprinkler system (using a moisture sensor) for the front lawn only (see Fig. 18-2). They agreed that the pool had stayed much cleaner since they had purchased a robot pool cleaner last year, but they felt its performance—as

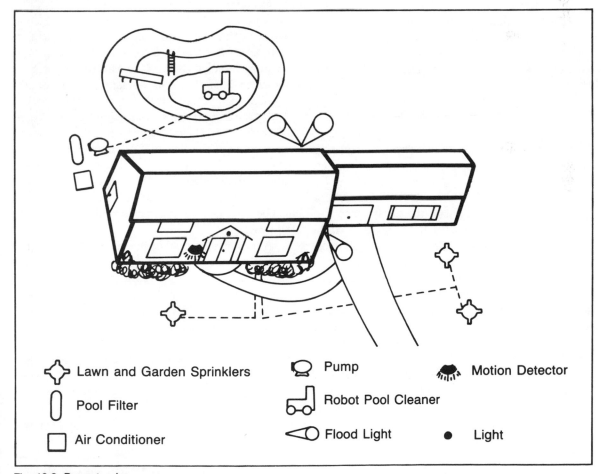

Lawn and Garden Sprinklers   Pump   Motion Detector

Pool Filter   Robot Pool Cleaner

Air Conditioner   Flood Light   ● Light

Fig. 18-2. Property plan.

well as the pool's filter—could be optimized if both were under computer control. A water level sensor would also be used to monitor the level of the pool.

Fred noted that often when they were in the backyard, no one could hear the front door bell. He decided to install a buzzer in the back of the house tied to when the front door bell switch was pushed (see Figs. 18-3 and 18-5). And since they wanted to have the front and back doorbell offer a better welcoming system, they decided to have both linked to their Home Control system. They agreed to have a motion detector placed near the front door to further add to their entrance welcoming system (more details provided later in this chapter).

For security reasons and for convenience, it was decided that all outdoor lights would be controlled by the Home Control system. Also, in order to know the temperature outdoors—particularly to control their attic fan—a thermistor would be located in a shaded area on the north side (front) of the house.

The Security System

Lisa and Fred wanted both a burglar and fire security system. The fire detection system would include three heat detectors located in the kitchen, garage, and attic; and four smoke detectors placed in the basement, front hall, upstairs hall, and recreation room located to the right of the garage (see Fig. 18-3). As shown in Figs. 18-4, 18-5, and 18-6, the burglar detection system would monitor all doors and windows, and include two motion detectors on the first floor, as well as the motion detector next to the front door. An indoor buzzer and siren, and an outdoor siren would be utilized. A panic button would be located in the master bedroom, and a keypad switch would be located between the front and back door.

Because the house once leaked in a corner of the basement, a water detector would be placed there. Another would be located near the washing machine (see Figs. 18-3 and 18-4).

Since weekdays no one was usually at home, Lisa and Fred decided that the HomeBrain must be able to use the telephone lines to notify someone

of an emergency if one arose. To accomplish this link the Prestons would use a Talking Home Monitor wired to the HomeBrain.

The Inside

Both heating and cooling would be controlled by the HomeBrain using the X-10 System (more information on their heating and cooling systems can be found later in this chapter), and many lights throughout the house would be managed by the HomeBrain for both security and convenience. Three TVs are located in the house, and these would be controlled by X-10 Appliance Modules. The computer, which is located on the second floor of the house, could also be turned on and off via an Appliance Module. The stereo in the den had previously been wired to speakers in the master bedroom, the recreation room, as well as the den itself. Control of the stereo receiver for this system would be handled by an X-10 Module, while control of each of the room speakers would be accomplished by relays in the HomeBrain.

Because the Prestons wanted to distribute control throughout their house (since their computer was located on the second floor in the guest room), stand-alone X-10 Controllers were to be located in the den, the kitchen, the recreation room, and the master bedroom. The keypad in the front hall could also be used as an extension for manual control of the system.

A thermistor would be installed in the front hall which could be used to record internal temperature variations for better heat/air conditioning control. A light sensor was to be located at a basement window to tell how dark or light it was outdoors. The reason a basement window was chosen was merely wiring ease to the HomeBrain; it really didn't matter what window in the house was used.

THE FINANCES

Lisa developed some figures on what the Prestons might be able to save by better controlling energy consumption. The Preston home has a gas hot air heating system, a central electric air conditioner,

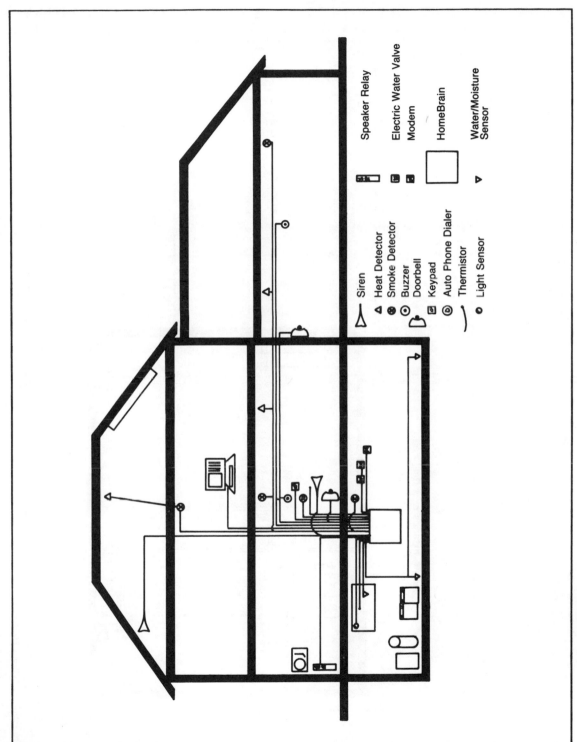

Fig. 18-3. Cross section of the Preston home.

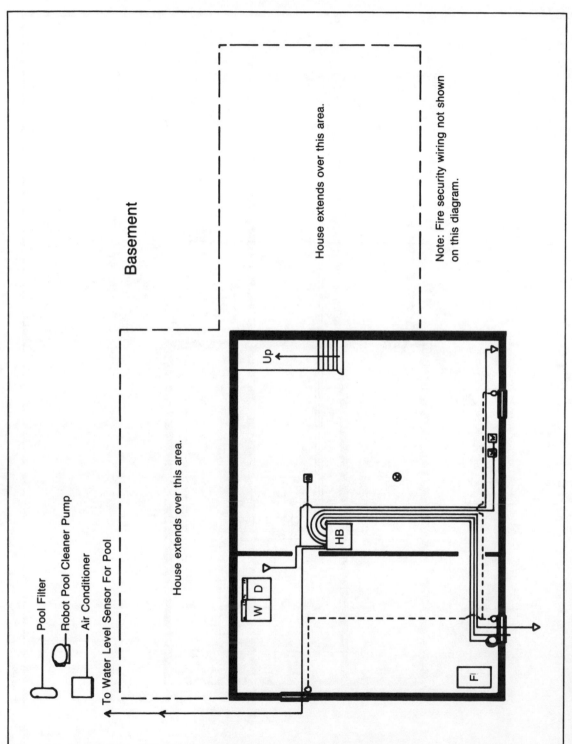

Fig. 18-4. Basement floor plan.

First Floor

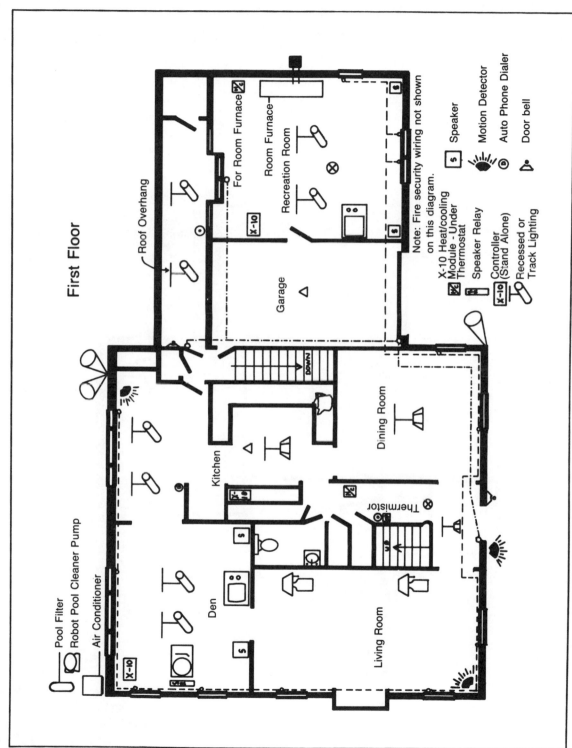

Fig. 18-5. First floor plan.

119

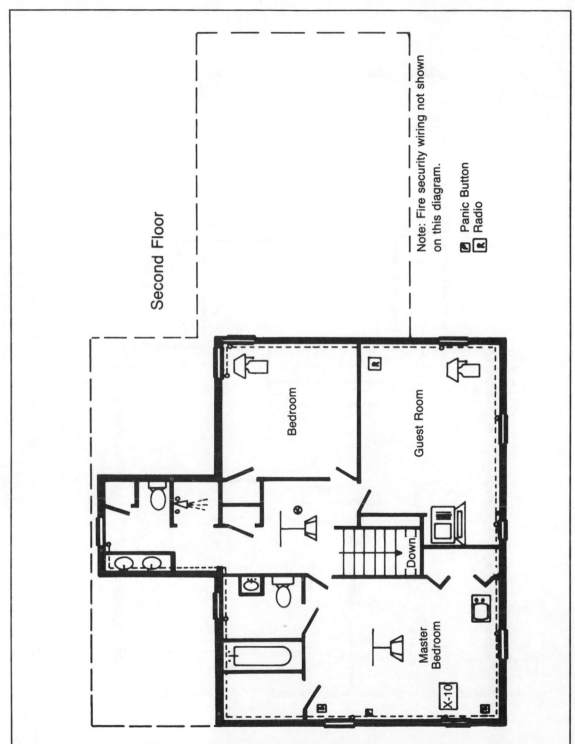

Second Floor

Note: Fire security wiring not shown on this diagram.

P Panic Button
R Radio

Bedroom

Guest Room

Master Bedroom

Down

X-10

Fig. 18-6. Second floor plan.

and a gas hot water system. Also, a small additional gas furnace is located in the recreation room (see Fig. 18-5). She noted that savings would be achieved by controlling both heating systems as well as their air conditioning unit. It was decided that the gas hot water system was not easily controllable by the HomeBrain, and therefore was not linked to the system.

At the town library, Lisa found a few books on home energy conservation which gave some tips on how to estimate energy savings prior to implementing home energy projects. Armed with this information and the previous year's utility bills, she was able to complete her figures and estimate their savings.

Lisa found that her family's potential savings from having computerized control of their heating and air conditioning needs was particularly high. This was based on the fact that she and her husband worked during the day and that both they and their son were out of the house for an average of over nine hours a day. Also Lisa recalled all the times that she and Fred had discussed adjusting the heat or air conditioner before going to bed, but somehow this rarely seemed to be accomplished.

Small mishaps in the control of heat in the recreation room had also been a concern to Fred and Lisa. Although the house's central cooling system did not extend here, this room was used frequently in the summer, especially in the evenings, since it was located near the pool. However, in the winter the room was rarely used except on Sundays and this often caused one of two problems. Since the thermostat was located inside the recreation room, someone had to run out ahead of time to turn up the thermostat. Even worse, many times the heat was never turned down when everyone went back to the main part of the house—which meant that the heat would stay on until the following Sunday when the room was once again used. Although Lisa did not complete a full study of this room, she did estimate that they had spent roughly $270 heating it last year, and that they should be able to save one third of that cost or $90.

The main heating and air conditioning systems in the Preston's house were set up in two zones.

However, at some time prior to their taking occupancy of the house, the thermostat wiring had been adjusted to react as a one zone system. Lisa noted that additional savings would be easy if they reconverted the thermostat wiring, but decided to calculate their main energy savings as if they would be maintaining the one zone system. Lisa's calculations (reworked using the methodology found in Chapter 3) can be found in Fig. 18-7. Her savings estimate, using a 10 degree adjustment for both heating and air conditioning, totaled $568 per year. If the $90 savings from the other furnace is included, that's a total of $658.

Although not part of her calculations, Lisa realized that additional savings could be achieved by making better use of their attic fan via the HomeBrain. This would be accomplished by using the fan as a substitute for their air conditioning system to take advantage of the times when the outside air was cool.

The following day Lisa called their insurance agent and found that their plans to incorporate a burglar/fire alarm system into their house would save $85 on their homeowners policy each year. The agent mentioned the things needed to be a part of their system, all but one of which had already been incorporated. The only further requirement was that two home fire extinguishers be maintained in the home.

With this added advantage, Lisa had determined their total savings per year to be $743. Both Fred and Lisa agreed that these savings represented a tremendous advantage over a standard burglar alarm system. But beyond this, there were four other advantages. First, the Home Control system's energy savings will pay for all aspects of the system in just a few years. Second, the money spent related to energy conservation would be partially offset by tax advantages (see Chapter 3). Third, if they ever decided to sell their house, the fact that the house has built-in Home Control features should certainly enhance its value. (This would be true even if they decided to move the HomeBrain along with them, since any wiring or peripherals that were left could be used by others who desired a Computer Home Control system.) And fourth, and

	Preston Figures
Heating System (main)	
1. Heat factor (Fig. 3-2) (for reference only)	H
2. Last Year's Heat Cost	1950
3. Thermostat set-back in Degrees	10
4. Interpolate Savings percentage (from Table 3-1)	12%
5. Weekly Schedule: Winter Heating (hours lowered):	
Monday	17
Tuesday	17
Wednesday	17
Thursday	17
Friday	18
Saturday	15
Sunday	11
Total	112
Divide by 7 = Average hours set back:	16

6. (Avg Hrs set back)/(8 Hrs) × (Saving %) × (Heat Cost) = Savings

$$16/8 \times .12 \times \$1950 = \quad \$468$$

	Preston Figures
Cooling System	
7. Cool factor (Fig. 3-3) (for reference only)	MM
8. Last Year's Cooling Cost	410
9. Thermostat set-ahead in Degrees	10
10. Interpolate Savings percentage (from Table 3-2)	13%
11. Weekly Schedule: Summer Cooling (hours raised):	
Monday	17
Tuesday	17
Wednesday	20
Thursday	17
Friday	17
Saturday	9
Sunday	8
Total	105
Divide by 7 = Average hours set raised:	15

12. (Avg Hrs set raised)/(8 Hrs) × (Saving %) × (Cool Cost) = Savings

$$15/8 \times .13 \times \$410 = \quad \$100$$

Total Heating and Cooling Savings = $568

Fig. 18-7. Preston heating and cooling savings worksheet.

most important, by installing a computerized system, Lisa and Fred would have a truly flexible Home Control system offering its many advantages for years to come.

Based on these facts, the Prestons decided to go ahead with the HomeBrain option. After Fred and Lisa developed a list of materials required for their installation (see Fig. 18-8), Fred placed the order with HyperTek the following day. During the conversation, Fred agreed to send copies of his drawings to HyperTek so that they could see exactly what he wished to accomplish.

INSTALLATION

Within three weeks, all equipment and software had arrived. During this time Lisa and Fred had already completed much of the wiring necessary for the burglar, fire, and flood detection systems. While performing the wiring, they had been careful to label each wire that terminated where the HomeBrain was to be located so that appropriate connections could be made. As with most houses, some unique features were taken advantage of to complete the wiring. In the Preston's case, they made extensive use of the crawl space under the rear section of their house, as well as a laundry shoot which eased wiring to the first and second floor.

The only thing left to do was to make the actual connections to the peripheral equipment, and to install the X-10 equipment. Fred had called a local electrician who had agreed to wire an X-10 controlled relay system for the pool filter and robot pool cleaner.

On Saturday, the remaining installation work began. Fred mounted the HomeBrain on a basement wall, and made the necessary connections to the RS-232 port of his computer. Following the instructions received from HyperTek, Fred connected the battery and tested the computer to HomeBrain link. He then connected the HomeBrain end of each of the labeled wires to be used in conjunction with the sensors or relay controlled equipment. Figure 18-9 details the necessary connections that were made. During this time Lisa had been connecting the various sensors at their appropriate locations.

After these tasks were complete, the day was still bright and Fred turned off all power in the house so that they could quickly install the X-10 Wall Switch and Receptacle Modules. Figure 18-10 shows the location of each module, the module type used, the X-10 HOUSE/UNIT CODE, and the item controlled.

During the late afternoon the indoor siren and both the indoor and outdoor buzzers were installed, as well as the stereo speaker relays and motion detectors. Lisa and Fred decided they had done enough for one day, and that they would complete their installation the next morning.

Sunday morning, Lisa installed the keypad in the front hall and the telephone dialer in the kitchen while Fred connected the outside siren which was to be actually located inside the attic next to the attic vents.

The only things remaining were the work to be completed by the electrician for the pool and the sprinkler system. Fred decided to tackle the sprinkler system during the following weekend.

Figures 18-11 through 18-25 show some of the completed aspects of the installation.

SETTING UP THE SOFTWARE

The final step in completing their system was for Fred and Lisa to adjust the HomeBrain software to specifically reflect their particular needs and circumstances. As they installed the wiring, they had been careful to follow the connections specified in the HomeBrain Standard Package documentation. This meant connecting specific wires to specific terminal pairs. Although the HomeBrain could be wired in many different ways, by following this Standard Lisa and Fred would automatically take advantage of HyperTek's *logic* suggestions. Logic here means relating what is sensed to any particular reaction or sequence of reactions, and the associated timing involved. Since HyperTek has had many installations to their credit, Lisa and Fred decided it would be best (and easiest) to make use of their knowledge, and then adjust as necessary

Description of Item — grouped as **X-10 EQUIPMENT** (Three Prong Appliance … Stand Alone Controller) and **OTHER EQUIPMENT** (Door Sensor … Modem)

Location of Item	Three Prong Appliance	Two Prong Appliance	Wall Receptacle	Lamp Module	Wall Switch	Three-Way Wall Switch	Thermostat Controller	Stand Alone Controller	Door Sensor	Window Sensor	Bell or Siren	Buzzer	Keypad	Panic Button	Motion Detector	Door bell Switch	Smoke Detector	Heat Detector	Water or Moisture Sensor	Thermistors	Light Sensor	Water Control Valve	Sprinklers	Dialer	Remote Speaker Relay***	Pool Pump Relay***	Modem
OUTSIDE OF HOUSE											1	1			1	2			2	1			3				
BASEMENT										3							1		2		1	2				2	1
FIRST FLOOR																											
Front Hall			1		1	1	1*		1		1	1	1				1										
Living Room				2		2	1*			3			1							1					3		
Den		2			2			1		3					1												
Kitchen		1			1			1		1					1			1						1			
Dining Room					1					2																	
Back Hall					2				1																		
Garage									1									1									
Recreation Room		1			1		1**	1	1	3							1										
SECOND FLOOR																											
Hallway and Bath										1																	
Master Bdrm and Bath		1			1			1		4				1				1									
Child's Room				1						2							1										
Guest Room	1			1						3																	
ATTIC	1	1																									
TOTALS	2	6	1	4	9	3	2	4	4	25	2	2	2	1	3	2	4	3	4	2	1	2	3	1	3	2	1

*Uses wall receptacle module noted for front hall.

**Includes appliance module.

***Includes X-10/Relay Combination.

Fig. 18-8. Required materials for the Preston's Home Control plan.

Item(s) Wired	# Of Items	Type	Connection #(s)**
Computer	1	RS-232	RS-232 Port
Front Door Sensor	1	D	21
Other Door Sensors	3	D	22
Window Sensors	25	D	23
Sirens	2	R	65
Buzzers	2	R	69
Keypad LEDS	2	R	66,67
Keypad	1	D	16
Panic Button	1	D	23*
Front Door Motion Detector	1	D	26
Security Motion Detectors	2	D	24
Front Door Bell Switch	1	D	27
Back Door Bell Switch	2	D	28
Smoke & Heat Detectors	7	D	25
Lawn & Garden Moisture Sensor	1	A	5
Pool Water Level Sensor	1	D or A	6
Basement Flood Detectors	2	D or A	7
Outdoor Thermistor	1	A	2
Indoor Thermistor	1	A	3
Light Sensor	1	A	1
Water Control Valves	2	R	70
Dialer	1	R	64,68,R*
Modem	1	RS-232	RS-232 Port
Speaker Relay	1	R	71

Type Codes:

Input: D = digital, A = analog
Output: R = relay, R* = relay and X-10 combination
RS-232: via RS-232 port

* On same line as window sensors.
** Numbers refer to Standard Package locations on HomeBrain's panel: analog locations from 0 - 15; digital locations from 16 - 31; and relay locations from 64 - 71.

Fig. 18-9. Wiring connections for Preston Home Control plan.

Location	Module Type	CODE	Controlled Item
FIRST FLOOR			
Front Hall	Wall Recept	A1	Thermostat
	Wall Switch	B1	Front door light
	3 Way Switch	B2	Front hall light
	3 Way Switch	B3	Upstairs hall light
Living Room	Lamp	B4	Lamp
	Lamp	B5	Lamp
Den	Wall Switch	B6	Ceiling track lights
	Wall Switch	B7	Ceiling track lights
	2 Prong Appli	B8	Stereo
	2 Prong Appli	B9	TV
Kitchen	2 Prong Appli	B10	Coffeepot
	Wall Switch	B11	Tiffany lamp
	3 Way Switch	B12	Overhead light
Dining Room	Wall Switch	B13	Chandelier
Back Hall	Wall Switch	B14	2 outdoor spots
	Wall Switch	B15	2 outdoor ceiling lts
Recreation Room	2 Prong Appliance	D1	TV
	Wall Switch	D2	2 overhead lights
	Appliance	A2	Thermostat
SECOND FLOOR			
Hallway	2nd Switch - 3 Way	B2	Front hall light
	2nd Switch - 3 Way	B3	Upstairs hall light
Master Bedroom	Wall Switch	C1	Overhead light
	2 Prong Appliance	C2	TV
Child's Room	Lamp	C3	Night Light
Guest Room	Lamp	C4	Lamp
	3 Prong Appliance	C5	Computer
	2 Prong Appliance	C6	Radio
ATTIC	3 Prong Appliance	A3	Attic fan
BASEMENT	3 Prong Appliance	E1	Pool filter*
	3 Prong Appliance	E2	Robot pool cleaner*

* In combination with relay.

Fig. 18-10. X-10 Module types and locations for Preston Home Control plan.

Fig. 18-11. Motion detector on outside of house takes note of visitors approaching front door.

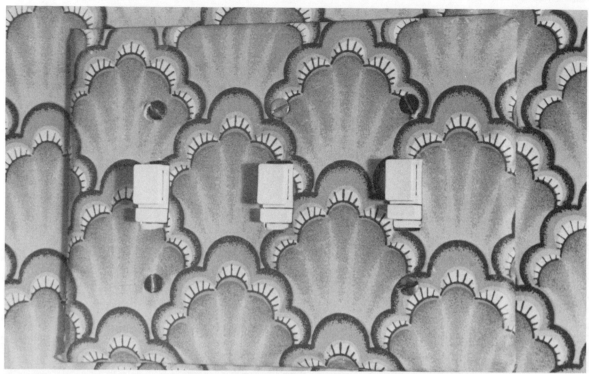

Fig. 18-12. First floor hall X-10 Wall Switch Modules for front door, lower and upper hall lighting.

Fig. 18-13. Keypad and buzzer located in first floor hall.

Fig. 18-14. The Talking Home Monitor is in position to call for help in the event of an emergency.

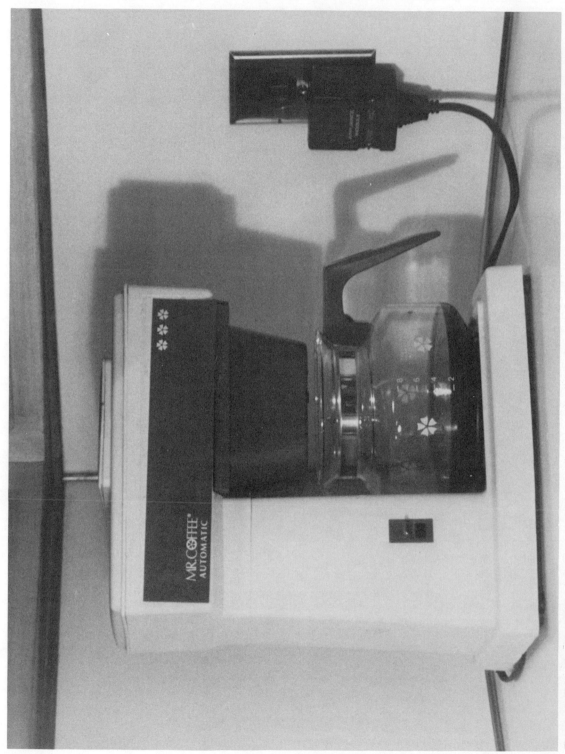

Fig. 18-15. The coffee is turned on from the master bedroom's X-10 Controller. The Home Control system checks to make sure it's turned off at the appropriate time.

Fig. 18-16. Heating and cooling control using X-10 Thermostat Controller.

Fig. 18-17. The Preston den has remote and computer control of audio, video, and even the lighting.

Fig. 18-18. A vibration window sensor monitors for unexpected guests in the den.

Fig. 18-19. A smoke detector located in the second floor hall constantly monitors for traces of fire.

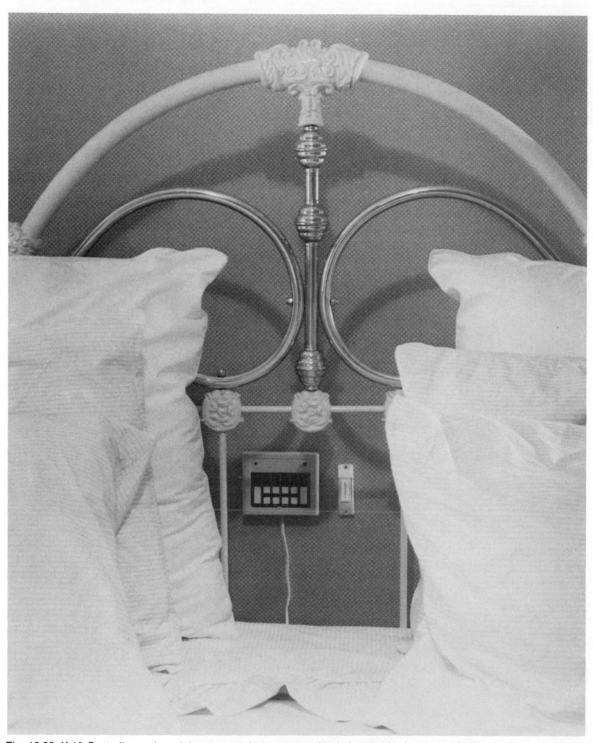

Fig. 18-20. X-10 Controller and panic/emergency button conveniently located in the master bedroom.

Fig. 18-21. Electric water valve located in basement turns the sprinklers located in front lawn on and off.

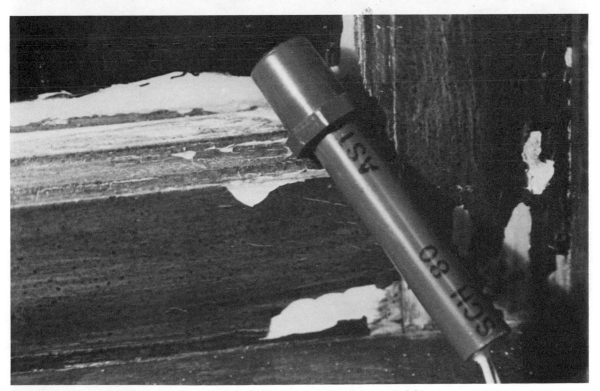

Fig. 18-22. From a basement window, the light sensor keeps track of day and night.

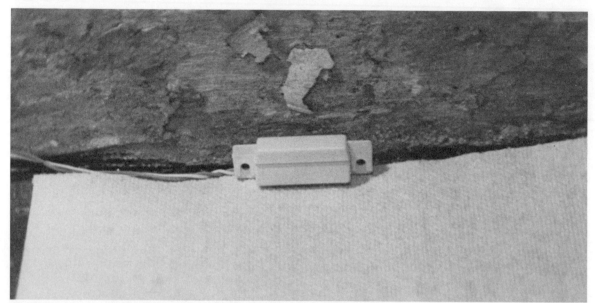

Fig. 18-23. If the basement floor becomes flooded, this moisture sensor will detect the condition. Note the paper towel used to absorb water and speed detection.

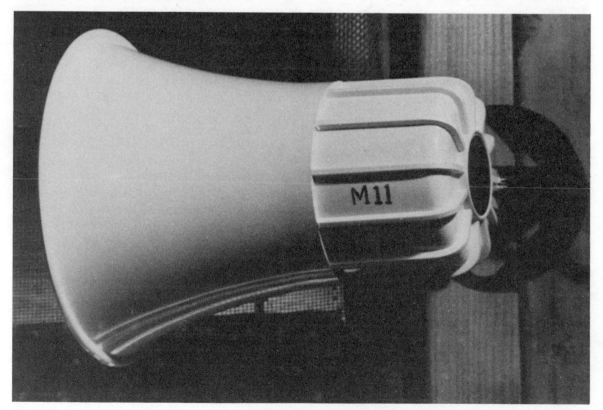

Fig. 18-24. Located at the attic vents is a siren to signal the neighborhood of an emergency.

Fig. 18-25. The HomeBrain in the process of being wired.

any specifics to enhance their particular system.

They found that by following this procedure, most of the adjustments necessary were simply in the schedules of the X-10 Modules located throughout the house. Three HomeBrain Software packages were used by the Prestons to complete their installation: the Toolkit, Create, and Display programs.

The Toolkit

The following is an overview of what was necessary once all wiring was completed and the Preston's computer was turned on. Figure 18-26 shows the main menu screen that appears when the Toolkit program is loaded. The first item on the menu is Communications Setup. Note the bottom of the screen gives an explanation of the current menu item. Here the description reads: "Communications is the term used to describe the sending or receiving of information. This module will allow you to customize the communication driver within this

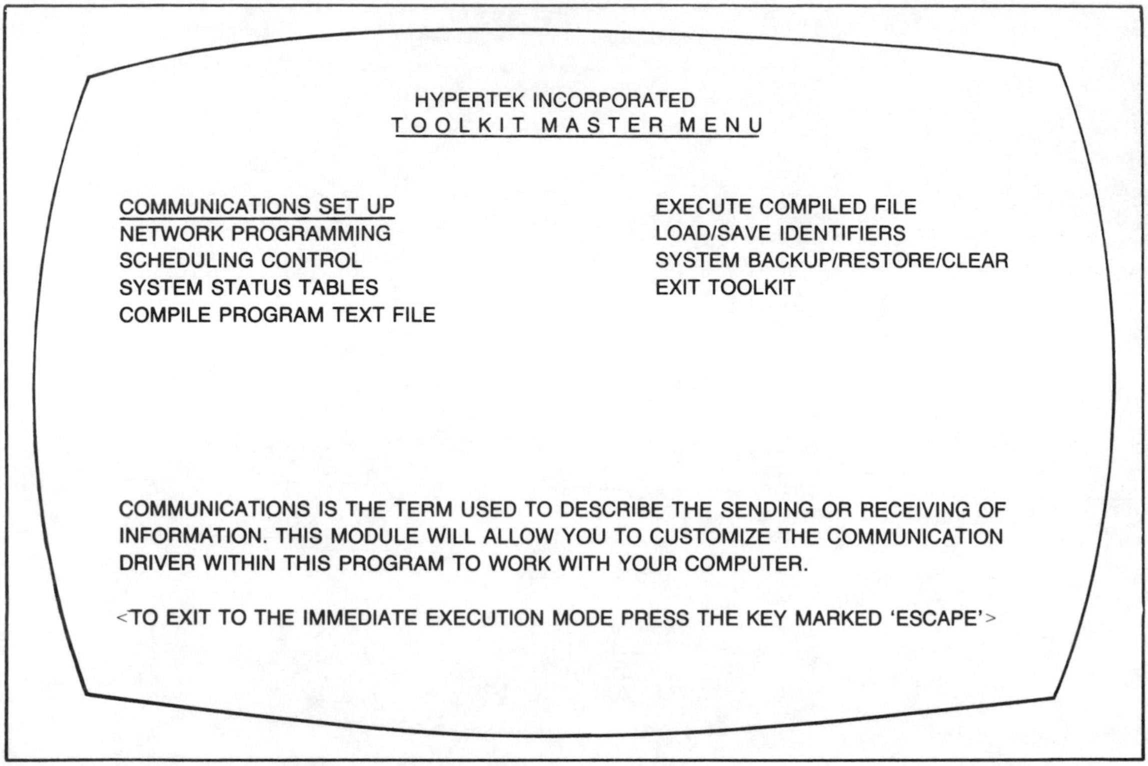

```
        HYPERTEK INCORPORATED
        T O O L K I T   M A S T E R   M E N U


  COMMUNICATIONS SET UP              EXECUTE COMPILED FILE
  NETWORK PROGRAMMING                LOAD/SAVE IDENTIFIERS
  SCHEDULING CONTROL                 SYSTEM BACKUP/RESTORE/CLEAR
  SYSTEM STATUS TABLES               EXIT TOOLKIT
  COMPILE PROGRAM TEXT FILE




  COMMUNICATIONS IS THE TERM USED TO DESCRIBE THE SENDING OR RECEIVING OF
  INFORMATION. THIS MODULE WILL ALLOW YOU TO CUSTOMIZE THE COMMUNICATION
  DRIVER WITHIN THIS PROGRAM TO WORK WITH YOUR COMPUTER.

  <TO EXIT TO THE IMMEDIATE EXECUTION MODE PRESS THE KEY MARKED 'ESCAPE'>
```

Fig. 18-26. The HomeBrain Toolkit program's main menu.

program to work with your computer." In other words, this menu item checks that your computer and your HomeBrain can talk to each other, including a check on your RS-232 wiring, and such things as data transmission speeds, etc. If anything is out of sync, the software will try to correct the problem or at least suggest a probable cause.

The bottom line of the menu notes an *Immediate Mode* which can be entered at any time to use the computer to immediately instruct the HomeBrain to do most any of its functions—turn on a light, show the position of a relay switch, read the time or date, etc. Once the communications was checked, the first thing for the Prestons to do was to inform the HomeBrain of the correct password. This was achieved by going to the Immediate Mode and typing in the factory set password. The actual entry is "ENAPAS 0,0,0,0" Enter . Of course, the password has been since changed by the Prestons for security purposes. After the password was pro-

vided, the current time and date were also entered.

For a little practice Fred and Lisa remained in the Immediate Mode and tested their HomeBrain's X-10 System by turning on and off a few lights and the stereo. Everything was in order, so they returned to the main menu.

The next step was to check out the analog and digital wiring that they had already completed, and to see if the relays would control items as expected. To begin this process Fred went to the menu item "System Status Tables" which, among other things, allowed him to check the digital and analog readings that the HomeBrain was receiving from the various sensors located around the house. It turned out that two adjustments were necessary to the wiring in order to obtain the expected readings, but once identified by the Status Tables, the actual corrections were small tasks to complete. The two items needing adjustment were a loose wire to a motion detector, and a smoke detector which had originally been connected incorrectly.

The relays were checked by returning to the Immediate Mode and giving the commands to switch them on and off. Each item here worked as expected. When the Talking Home Monitor reacted to the fire or burglar condition relay being switched to on, it spoke its warning: "Alert condition one exists" or "Alert condition two exists". However, it had not yet been given the appropriate phone numbers to call. Consequently, it would beep for a few seconds and then say "No number!" Actually, this was by design to enable Fred and Lisa to first check out their system without giving false alarms to those designated for the security calls.

After the wiring adjustments were made to the motion and smoke sensors, all appeared to be in order. Since the Prestons were using the Standard Package, they now needed to adjust the Standard Package software file to reflect their specific needs. This could be accomplished in more than one way:

1. Using the Network Programming and Scheduling Control modules.

2. Revising a standard word processing file (which uses standard ASCII codes and therefore would work with most word processing programs).

A HomeBrain program is actually made up of many short subprograms called *networks*. Using the *Network Programming* module, any of these subprograms can be created, adjusted, or deleted according to the particular needs of the user. The Scheduling Control modules allow the timing of schedules (i.e., what time or day an X-10 Module will be turned on or off) to be adjusted, as long as each schedule has been defined within a network. Since most of the necessary adjustments to the Preston's system were due to schedules of X-10 Modules, they decided to update the Standard Package using these methods.

However, an alternate way to handle this would be to use a word processing file of the entire Standard Package software; and by using most word processors, adjustments could be made to reflect the Preston's needs. The adjusted word processing file would then need to be compiled (a process by which the computer—using the Compile Program Text File module—predigests the material to make it understandable to the HomeBrain) before being executed by the system. One of the main advantages of using this word processing method is that it makes adjusting (editing) very easy to accomplish if you are familiar with a particular word processor's software. Execution (or implementation by the HomeBrain) of the file is then accomplished by the Execute Compiled File module.

The following few paragraphs are a brief discussion of the remainder of the menu items shown in Fig. 18-26.

The first remaining menu item is the Load/Save Identifiers module. *Identifiers* are words that can be substituted by the user of the system to make reference to specific items easier. In other words, your smoke detector may be connected to input #25. However, instead of remembering this in the future or having to constantly look up such items in a reference table, it is easier to assign an identifier to it (i.e., smoke = 25). Identifiers can be defined while using a word processor (when programming or adjusting your software), or in the Immediate Mode of the HomeBrain software.

The menu item System Backup/Restore/Clear allows the user to backup (save) a complete image (file) of what has been programmed into the HomeBrain on the computer's disk system, to Restore (load) an image from the disk system to the HomeBrain, or to Clear the image (all information) currently in the HomeBrain.

The last menu item, Exit Toolkit, allows you to leave the Toolkit program.

The Create and Display Programs

The Preston's HomeBrain was now fully operational with all functions operating according to Lisa and Fred's specific wishes. One last set of steps, however, would provide the finishing touches to their system to give them full monitoring and ease of control over their Home Control system. To accomplish this the HomeBrain Create and Display packages were used.

Figure 18-27 shows the Create main menu

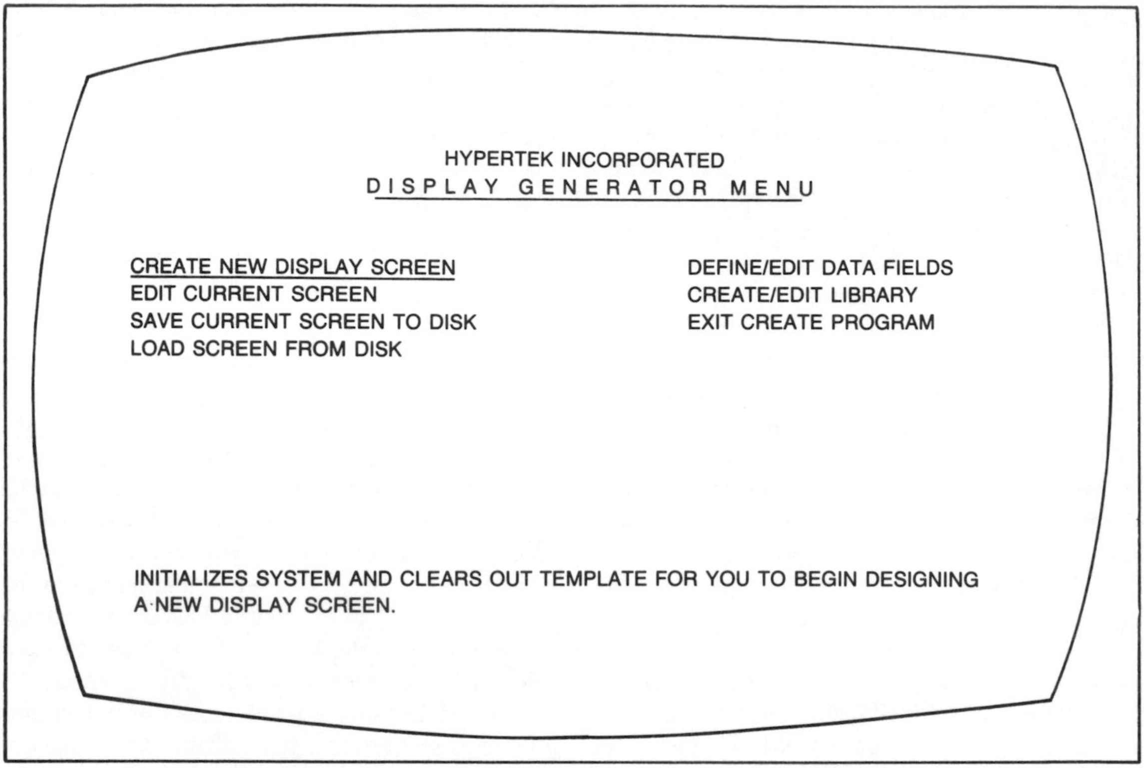

```
                    HYPERTEK INCORPORATED
              D I S P L A Y   G E N E R A T O R   M E N U


    CREATE NEW DISPLAY SCREEN          DEFINE/EDIT DATA FIELDS
    EDIT CURRENT SCREEN                CREATE/EDIT LIBRARY
    SAVE CURRENT SCREEN TO DISK        EXIT CREATE PROGRAM
    LOAD SCREEN FROM DISK




    INITIALIZES SYSTEM AND CLEARS OUT TEMPLATE FOR YOU TO BEGIN DESIGNING
    A·NEW DISPLAY SCREEN.
```

Fig. 18-27. The HomeBrain Create program's main menu.

screen (shown as the "Display Generator Menu"). A short summary of each of the menu items follows:

Create New Display Screen. This module will delete any display in the computer's memory and allows the user to create a completely new display screen. Display screens can be text descriptions of functions in the house, or diagrams (floor plans, cross sections, etc.) which will later (through the use of the Display Program) allow for the constant monitoring of the entire system.

Edit Current Screen. Allows user to alter or adjust any screen already in memory.

Save Current Screen to Disk. Developed screens must be saved to disk for later use.

Load Screen from Disk. Restore a previously saved screen to the computer memory for editing, etc.

Define/Edit Data Fields. This menu item links real world conditions being sensed by the HomeBrain to representative wording or displays on a particular screen. For example, on various displays created by the Prestons, a fire condition is shown by the word "SMOKE". The "Define/Edit Data Fields" module allows for this definition.

Create/Edit Library. Associates individual screens into a complete library for viewing on the Display program.

Exit Create Program. Terminates program.

The Display main menu screen is shown in Fig. 18-28. After loading the Display program, the program itself automatically looks for a library of screen files. If found, the library of screens is displayed in the left hand column under Active Screens. A library can contain five screens, and any number of libraries can be maintained for a particular set-up. The Preston's screens include floorplans of the basement, ground (first) floor (shown in Fig. 18-29), second floor, and attic, as well as a property layout. Other screens (contained in a second library) include functional descriptions regarding fire, security, energy management, lighting, and even a vacation mode screen.

Options contained on the Display menu include the following:

Load New Screen Library. For users with more than one library of screens, this feature allows access to other libraries.

Print One of the Active Screens. Allows a hardcopy printout of any particular screen.

Dial-Up a Remote Intelligence Unit. Allows user (with the aid of a modem) to contact a HomeBrain unit over the phone lines.

Exit Display Program. Terminate program.

Lisa did most of the design work using the Create program to develop the Preston Home Control libraries. Some of their other library screens

are displayed later in this chapter.

THE PRESTON SOFTWARE LOGIC

Although details of how software works would vary from Home Control system to Home Control system, the logic used in the Preston's system (by and large the logic of the HomeBrain Standard Package) will be helpful to anyone developing their own design. Therefore, the descriptions that follow discuss the software in terms of logic rather than programming specifics.

Fire Safety

If a fire condition was sensed by any of the seven heat or smoke detectors located around the Preston home, the HomeBrain will respond for a fifteen minute period by performing the following procedures or until the condition is no longer sensed. The Fire Control Status screen is shown in Fig. 18-30.

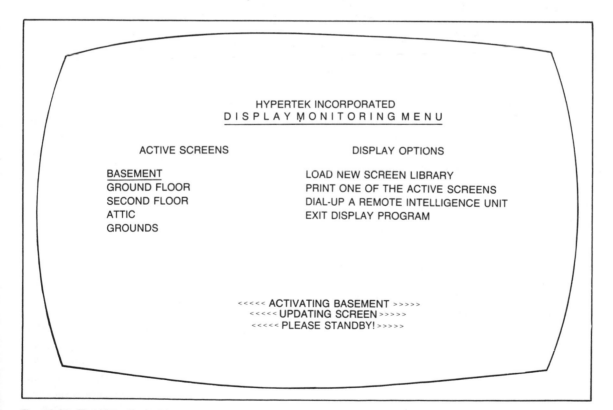

HYPERTEK INCORPORATED
D I S P L A Y   M O N I T O R I N G   M E N U

ACTIVE SCREENS   DISPLAY OPTIONS

BASEMENT   LOAD NEW SCREEN LIBRARY
GROUND FLOOR   PRINT ONE OF THE ACTIVE SCREENS
SECOND FLOOR   DIAL-UP A REMOTE INTELLIGENCE UNIT
ATTIC   EXIT DISPLAY PROGRAM
GROUNDS

<<<<< ACTIVATING BASEMENT >>>>>
<<<<< UPDATING SCREEN >>>>>
<<<<< PLEASE STANDBY! >>>>>

Fig. 18-28. The HomeBrain Display program's main menu.

```
FEB 1, 198X                                                    12:55:03
              ***********************************************
                        HYPERTEK HOMEBRAIN
                     RESIDENTIAL CONTROL SYSTEM
              ***********************************************
                            FIRST FLOOR
              ***********************************************
    BACK
    :::::::::.S....  : ::::::::::::.....S.. : :::::::
    ::              DEN                              ::
    S:   B6 LITE     ON     : B11-LITE OFF           ::
    .:   B7 LITE     ON     : B12-LITE OFF .......::
    ::   STEREO      ON     : COFFEE OFF :           ::
    S:   TV         OFF                           S
    .:   SPEAKERS ON
    ::......                                     :  S
    ::                     : : KITCHEN      :  ..  NOTES:
    S:                     : :...           :      ::   SECURITY-ARMED
    .:   LIVING RM         : :::            :      ::   S = SECURE
    ::                     :...:            :      ::   N = NOT SECURE
    ::   B4 LAMP OFF       H:               :      ::   F = SMOKE ALARM
    ::.  B5 LAMP OFF       :_:  :DINING ROOM::          < QUIET >
    ::                     :_: F :            ::   H = HEAT SETTING <HIGH>
    S:                     :__:   B13 LITE OFF :S
    .:                                         :
    ::                  . B2 OFF .             ::
    :::::::..S. . : : : : : : :    :::::::.S..::::::
                       B1 LITE OFF       FRONT
```

Fig. 18-29. Computer display of the Preston's first floor.

☐ Turn on specific inside lights (upper and lower hall, etc.) to guide occupants out of the house.

☐ Flash outside lights to assist fire company in locating house.

☐ Sound interior and exterior sirens.

☐ Adjust X-10 Thermostat Controller to turn off heat or air conditioning in order to stop smoke from being sent through the ventilation ducts. (The Prestons use the HomeBrain to control heating via the X-10 method, but the HomeBrain can be used to control the furnace or air conditioner more directly and thereby have a more positive shutdown of the ventilation system. In actuality, the Preston method only uses the HomeBrain's X-10 Controller to place the heating or cooling system in a mode where it is less likely to be on.)

☐ After a thirty second delay, the HomeBrain triggers the dialer to call for help. (The Talking Home Monitor is used by the Prestons and is set-up to dial four telephone numbers repeatedly until a positive communication is made. This positive communication means that the Talking Home Monitor will keep on trying until a receiving party actually calls back the Preston home and acknowledges to the Talking Home Monitor that the message has been received. The dialer is capable of distinguishing the type of emergency to the receiving party.) Fred and Lisa have chosen the numbers of four friends and relatives who have been thoroughly briefed on how to respond to such a call. Care was also taken to choose phone numbers where it would be likely that someone would be available to receive the message.

Security

The HomeBrain is setup and responds like a standard security system and continuously monitors all window and door sensors located throughout the house. The Security Control Screen is shown in Fig. 18-31. There are four zones as follows:

□ Front door
□ All other doors
□ All windows
□ Two internal motion detectors

The doors have exit and entrance delays associated with them. The system is controlled from the security digital keypad which has two LEDs (light emitting diodes or small lights—one green and one red) to indicate whether the system is secure and armed. The system is not able to be armed if it is not secure. The same five digit code is used when leaving or returning to the house. The specific keypad the Prestons use has a potential for 95,000 different five digit codes. Only one of them will work. Therefore, such keypad security is extremely high.

Should a break in security occur, the HomeBrain will sound the sirens, turn on specific interior lights, flash specific outside lights, and if the system is not disarmed within thirty seconds, the dialer (Talking Home Monitor) is activated. After fifteen minutes or when the system has been disarmed, all sirens, buzzers, and the dialer are turned off. Lights are returned to normal (their prior state).

When an entry door is opened, the procedure is similar except that a delay of thirty seconds occurs during which time the occupant has a chance to signal his or her arrival by punching the correct code into the keypad. If the correct code is not punched within the first fifteen seconds, the buzzers are activated as a reminder. If the correct digits are still not pressed, the HomeBrain considers this a security break and reacts as described earlier.

When an occupant arms the system, the HomeBrain starts a thirty second count for an exit delay. During this time the occupant may leave the house through any of the doors. However, should a window security break occur during this time, the

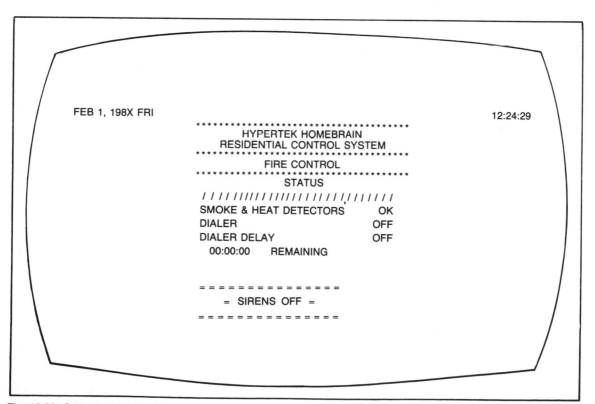

Fig. 18-30. Computer display of fire safety system.

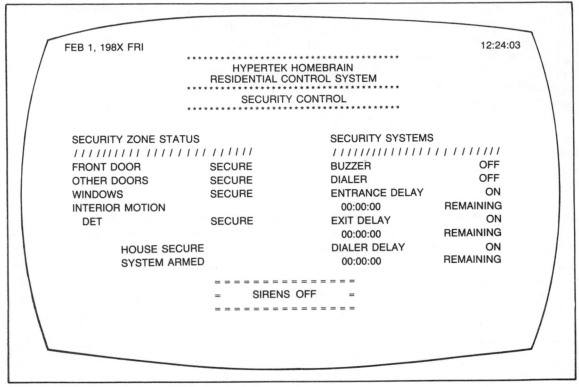

Fig. 18-31. Computer display of security system.

HomeBrain will respond immediately.

The interior motion detectors can be armed or disarmed independently of the other components of the system. This provides additional protection when the Prestons are not at home, yet allows them to freely wander the house when they are.

Of course, any of the delay times used by the Prestons are software adjustable.

Energy Management

Although there are many ways to control the heating and cooling systems using the HomeBrain, the Preston's use timed control of their Thermostat Controller Modules to regulate all systems. As discussed earlier, their method uses a ten degree differential for heating and cooling during those periods when the house is unoccupied, or when they are sleeping. The recreation room furnace—also under similar control—has been placed under a fif-

teen degree differential. The Energy Management screen is shown in Fig. 18-32.

Two thermistors are also used. The interior thermistor is used as a check on the system and allows for a display of the interior temperature on the computer monitor (via the HomeBrain). The second thermistor is located outdoors and is used to measure outdoor temperatures particularly in the spring or summer to activate the attic fan as an alternative to the air conditioning system. The temperature of the outside air can also be viewed on the monitor, which both Fred and Lisa have found useful to help determine how they and their son should dress in the mornings.

Lighting Control

The Prestons have extensive lighting control with the X-10 Modules throughout the house. The type of logic they have used groups the control of lights into the functions that they serve. As an example, take a look at Fig. 18-33 which displays a screen of the lighting near the front door. Each of these lights has its own particular schedule according to a time and day schedule, yet each of these has a reaction related to what is being sensed at the front door. This includes the following:

☐ If motion is sensed near the front door, the HomeBrain sounds the buzzers (located in the front hall and outside the backdoor) for one second.

☐ If motion is sensed while it is relatively dark outside, the buzzers will sound and the HomeBrain will send a signal to turn on the front door light for a duration of five minutes—after which it returns to its prior state (according to the particular schedule for this light).

☐ If the door is opened (possibly the Prestons returning home) and it is dusk or dark out, the front hall and kitchen lights turn on. (Although each schedule is not actually shown, note that, in Fig. 18-33, the same kitchen light operates under two different schedules depending on which day it is.) The front hall returns to its prior state after five minutes.

☐ If the time is after eight o'clock in the evening then the upstairs hall light turns on as well.

The stereo could have also been linked to welcome the Prestons home, but they found that timed control of their receiver coupled with the relay control of which speakers were playing made the system suit their life style better.

Vacation Mode

Much of the Preston's Home Control system operates similarly whether operating in a normal or a vacation mode. As examples, the fire and burglar systems react in the same manner whether

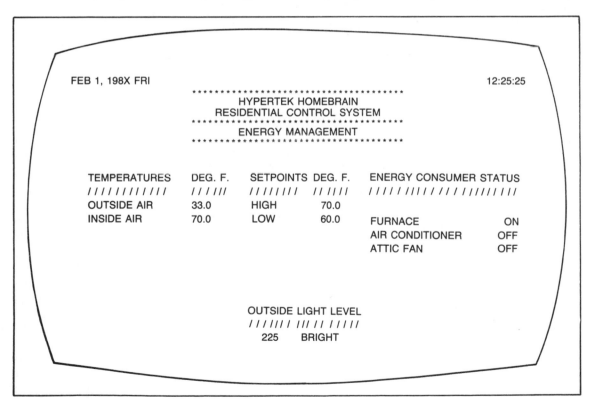

Fig. 18-32. Computer display of energy management system.

they are away from the house for a few hours or for an extended vacation. But other subsystems change to be more efficient while in vacation mode. If the Prestons decide to leave their home for more than a day, they can place the house in vacation mode by noting both the departure and return date to the HomeBrain (Fig. 18-34). During operation of the vacation mode (between these preset dates) the system will:

☐ Maintain heating or cooling to maximize cost savings (set-back or set-ahead mode).
☐ Control some lights according to their normal schedule, yet have others operate according to a randomized schedule. Stereos and TVs are also operated in this randomized fashion.

The HomeBrain normally flashes the green LED on the keypad to show that it is working. During the vacation mode, this LED remains on. At the return date specified, the system automatically brings the house back to normal control.

Other Functional Notes

Many other logic links have been incorporated into the Preston's Home Control system, most of which work as described in previous chapters. Some of these include such items as the pool pumps shutting off if the water drops, and the lawn moisture sensor is looked at by the system once a day (at appropriate times of the year) to see if the lawn needs watering. If water is needed, the electric water valves are turned on for an appropriate duration. The water sensors in the basement are constantly monitored. If water is sensed, the lights in both the first floor and second floor hall will flash and the buzzers will sound every fifteen seconds. If no action is taken by an occupant within twenty minutes, an X-10 Module/relay combination will

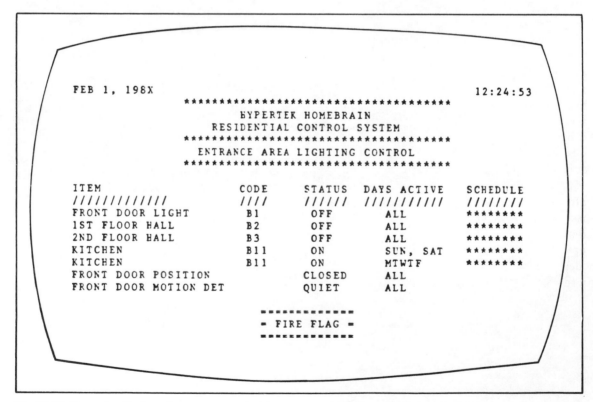

Fig. 18-33. Computer display of entrance area lighting.

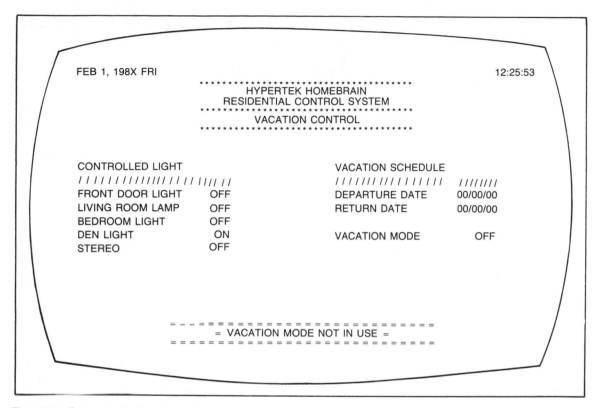

```
FEB 1, 198X FRI                                                   12:25:53
                    ************ HYPERTEK HOMEBRAIN ************
                         RESIDENTIAL CONTROL SYSTEM
                    ***************************************
                              VACATION CONTROL
                    ***************************************


     CONTROLLED LIGHT                      VACATION SCHEDULE
     / / / / / / / / / / / / / / / / / / //// //   / / / / / / / / / / / / / /   ////////
     FRONT DOOR LIGHT      OFF            DEPARTURE DATE      00/00/00
     LIVING ROOM LAMP      OFF            RETURN DATE         00/00/00
     BEDROOM LIGHT         OFF
     DEN LIGHT             ON             VACATION MODE          OFF
     STEREO                OFF




                    = = = = = = = = = = = = = = = = = = = = = = = =
                         = VACATION MODE NOT IN USE =
                    = = = = = = = = = = = = = = = = = = = = = = = =
```

Fig. 18-34. Computer display of vacation control system.

signal the dialer. (The X-10 Module/relay combination was installed because all the HomeBrain relays had been dedicated to other functions.)

Since Fred uses a personal computer at work that is compatible with the one at home, he decided that he would like to have full monitoring and control capabilities of his home while he was at work by connecting a modem to the HomeBrain and using a copy of the Display software which he keeps at work. By running his computer and modem at the office, he can now monitor and control the HomeBrain and his home from this more distant location just as if he were working from the computer at home.

The Prestons have had their Home Control system for slightly over a year, and they have become extremely comfortable with all of its benefits. They also claim to have had a lot of fun demonstrating it to friends and relatives. Some of them have begun to install their own Home Control systems. Although other systems may be smaller or larger, the Preston's basic experiences, as recorded here, are typical to many families who have taken advantage of Computer Home Control.

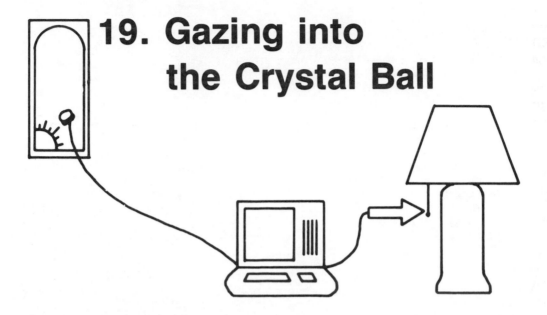

19. Gazing into the Crystal Ball

THIS BOOK HAS COVERED READILY AVAILABLE, practical applications for Computer Home Control. But Home Control can go much further if you have an interest in more exotic applications. These can be developed from what has been discussed in this book, though some may require additional hardware and/or software. For example, you could have draperies open and close according to the position of the sun, or have your Home Control system operate a highly complicated active solar heating plant for heating and hot water needs. You could add a video camera to your burglar alarm system in order to see who is at your front door. With proper identification, you could have your front door open automatically. If you wished, you could even use your Home Control system to replace your house keys and provide access to your home using a digital key-pad.

Another possibility is managing the activities at a party via Home Control. Guests could be directed to appropriate parts of the house when you wished. For example, lights and music could start on the patio for cocktails, and when dinner's ready, a path of lights might lead to the dining room. The patio music stops, and background dinner music begins to play inside the house. After dinner, the lights in the living room go on to half their brightness, the music becomes a little louder, and coffee is served. And when the party is over, the music stops and the lights slowly brighten to their full extent—no subtle hints to leave here!

But some of you may still want more.

CONVERSING WITH YOUR HOUSE

One of my early concerns about a computerized Home Control system was that while my computer was taking care of the house, it might be distracted by someone playing with its keys. Therefore, the first program I wrote included a voice synthesizer, and when any key was pressed (except for a shifted left arrow which gave access to the main program), the computer would respond by saying, "PLEASE, DON'T TOUCH THOSE KEYS!"

Seriously, voice synthesis can be very handy for updating your schedules by acting as a prompting mechanism. Further, it can provide status reports on your system: "THE LAWN DID NOT NEED WATERING TODAY . . .", warn of emergency conditions: "FIRE CONDITION SENSED!", or greet someone at the front door: "HELLO, SOMEONE WILL BE WITH YOUR SHORTLY" or "SORRY, NO ONE IS AVAILABLE TO COME TO THE DOOR AT THIS TIME". A wide variety of computer voice synthesis products are available today, and most are operable by those with only a minimal knowledge of BASIC programming.

The flip side of conversing with your home is having your computer understand your spoken commands. Though products to accomplish this are few in number, the pace of their availability is increasing rapidly. One interesting product like this is Waldo which is produced by Artra, a company in Arlington, Virginia. This product presently is only available for the Apple II (pictured in Fig. 19-1) and Heath/Zenith H/Z-89 computers. Waldo can understand verbal commands: "WALDO, TURN UP THE HEAT . . .", and it can accomplish the task by using an X-10 Controller (included). Waldo can even respond through one of two optional voice synthesizers: "THE HEAT HAS BEEN RAISED. ANYTHING ELSE YOU DESIRE?" One particularly nice feature about Waldo is that you don't need to be actually holding a microphone when giving Waldo his instructions. As long as you're in the same room as Waldo's microphone, he will be able to understand and respond.

MAN'S BEST MECHANICAL FRIEND

The discussion of Waldo leads into another fascinating possibility—a pet robot. Robots are now reaching the home market similar to the home computer around 1977. Industry watchers predict that these devices in the home market will grow proportionately to the massive increase in units sold of microcomputers.

Essentially, a robot is a computer with mobility and/or limbs. Hero 1, shown in Fig. 19-2, can be

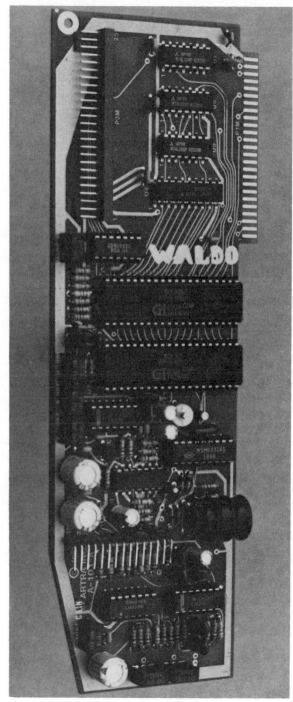

Fig. 19-1. Waldo, the Home Control system that talks and listens (courtesy Artra, Inc.). The pictured card plugs into the Apple II line of computers.

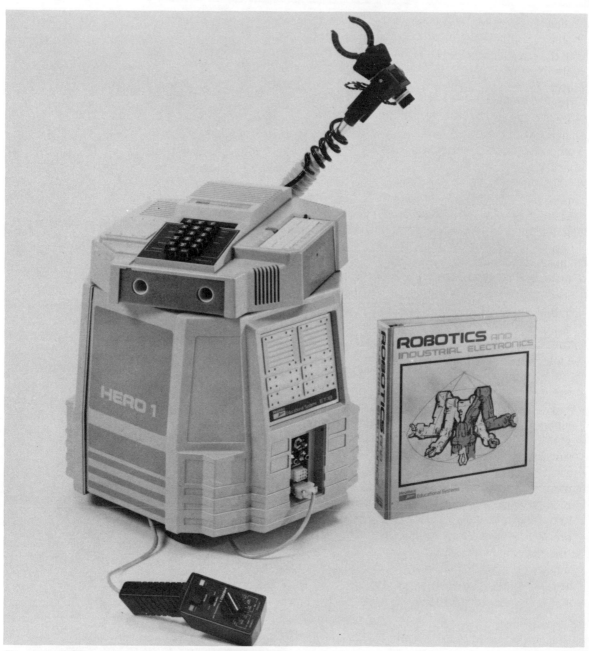

Fig. 19-2. HERO I robot (courtesy of the Heath Company).

programmed to use its mechanical arm. Some have voice synthesizers and a few are capable of voice recognition. One robot listed in Appendix A even has a complete music and video game entertainment center built-in. But alas, most of these little fellows, although marvels of technology, are still a bit clumsy and are currently limited in their practical applications. This should change very rapidly as better software becomes available and a few simple attachments are added. The development of robots is similar to when the first personal computers became available—the hardware was fine, but the software was extremely limited. Therefore, only those who understood how to program computers could really make any use of them. With the advent of strong application programs—spreadsheet and word processing for example—things really got moving. Suddenly, the personal computer began making sense to a much wider market.

Figure 19-3 shows TOPO, the robot pet from Androbot. Robots currently can be used to greet guests, to serve drinks, wake you up in the morning, and their best use might be as a tool to actually learn the subject of robotics, itself. Some are able to handle regular home computer functions such as word processing, etc., as well. Most can be operated on a stand-alone basis, while some robots can be programmed through a separate computer. For a computer controlled house, a robot capable of being programmed by a home computer would be a logical addition, for such a robot will be able to work more harmoniously with your overall system.

The practical success of the home robot is doubtless tied to their ability to perform housekeeping. Some robot manufacturers have promised vacuum attachments for their droid by early 1985. But washing windows, emptying the dishwasher, mowing the lawn, or doing the laundry still seem remote. More likely achievements in the near future will be along the lines of opening doors, carrying more substantial objects, or monitoring the inside of the home for hazard conditions such as smoke or unexpected motion. One never knows, however. The robot by 1990 may be a widely accepted super home appliance and man's best mechanical friend.

THE HOME OF THE FUTURE

Although a great deal of speculation centers around the house of the future, this book will only touch a few areas of this very interesting subject. A few futurists have incorporated many elements of Computer Home Control into two existing designs. These are the *House of the Future* located in the Arizona desert and *Xanadu* located near Disney World in Orlando, Florida. The House of the Future is a 3100 square foot building composed of many triangular shapes. Computer controlled solar collectors line the south facing wall and provide three quarters of the home's heating needs as well as most of its hot water needs. Ceilings vault to heights of 32 feet, and fountains surround the central gathering place called the *conversation pit*.

Xanadu is strikingly different in contrast in that the shape of the structure more nearly resembles a mushrooming of globes. Actually, the house was constructed by spraying a type of plastic foam (which acts as a strong insulator) over huge balloons. Once the foam hardened, the balloons were deflated and removed for potential re-use. The globes interconnect to form a 6000 square foot, two story living space.

Both futuristic homes make extensive use of their respective computer systems to control such things as security, energy management, and lights and appliances. And further both computer systems are used for the management of information and entertainment. Each house has extensive audio and video equipment linked to their computers, and this combination provides a futuristic home office, a computerized dietitian, an automated education laboratory, and outside links to computerized information, shopping, and banking systems, to name just a few.

Of course, many of these types of functions are becoming well within the reach of home computer users today. The important thing found in both the House of the Future and in Xanadu are that all these functions and applications have been integrated together and can be experienced in combination with one another.

YOUR HOME OF THE FUTURE

This book offers Home Control ideas and suggestions to incorporate into your present home. But some of you may be considering building a new home either now or in the future. Therefore, it's wise to keep in mind that many of these simple

Fig. 19-3. TOPO with his Androwagon (courtesy Androbot, Inc.).

ideas can be incorporated even more efficiently into new homes and, with a little preplanning, at an extremely low additional cost.

If you are considering building your own home of the future, the following are suggestions for your design. It should be noted that these are not being advocated only for the super modern home. They are suitable for any new home whether the particular design is a colonial, a cape, a tudor, a ranch, or whatever.

Make Room for the Computer

The computer will soon be as much a part of the home as the television, washer/dryer, or the dishwasher is today. And just as these items are planned into your homes, so should the computer be planned into tomorrow's homes. A new plan should include a *computer area* so that the computer and peripheral attachments (i.e., printer, disk drives, TV or monitor, storage for books, manuals, and software packages) can be housed conveniently.

One possibility would be to include a large closet in the home to be used for this purpose. The closet approach allows what often may be a working area to be closed up and out of the way when not in use (aesthetically pleasing and child proof). The location might be in a family room, den, or bedroom. The kitchen isn't ideal because of spillage problems. The closet should be roughly the size of a double door clothes closet (although possibly a few inches deeper), and contain overhead shelving for storage, as well as a collapsible (but sturdy) shelf for the computer, printer, TV or monitor, disk drives, etc. At least two three-prong electrical outlets should be included, preferably buffered from voltage spikes (these spikes can destroy a computer's circuitry.) Also, a phone jack should be provided (two jacks if multilines are a potential in the house—one to be used for a computer modem and the other as a regular telephone outlet). Adequate lighting should also be available inside the closet.

Of course, other possibilities—if you can spare the room—include a separate home office with lots of space for your computer and other materials, or a workshop/hobby area in an extra bedroom, the attic, or the basement.

Make Adjustments for Computer Home Control

When planning your house, keep in mind that it's easiest to incorporate signaling and sensing ideas from the beginning. Although this book has made extensive use of the X-10 System, any items which you would prefer to control by a hardwired relay system are easier to install during the original construction. And rather than replacing regular wall switches and wall outlets, shouldn't X-10 switches and outlets be part of the original scheme? Actually, if you have your Home Control plans well designed before construction begins, the builders can install most or all of the peripheral Home Control equipment for you.

Be sure to include any potential sensor wiring details in your discussions with your builder or architect. The base wiring should terminate in a box located at the computer's intended location and can be used for the following:

- ☐ Burglar alarm system.
- ☐ Smoke alarm system.
- ☐ Light sensor(s).
- ☐ Lawn (moisture) sensor.
- ☐ Flood sensor(s).
- ☐ Temperature sensor(s).
- ☐ Water level sensor.

A FINAL NOTE

No one can predict exactly in what shape the future will arrive. Technology in the computer field itself is wide open and changing so rapidly that even the experts can't keep up. Home Control is still in its infancy and subject to enormous advances. Innovative as some of the concepts in this book may seem, new and exciting developments are always on the horizon. However, the basic cost savings, safety, and convenience applications described in this book can be yours today and for years to come. Hopefully, this book will inspire you to take advantage of a truly exciting way to improve your life today with tomorrow's technology.

For those of you who wish additional information, check the Optional Reading appendix.

Appendix A: Home Control Product Directory

SENSOR INTERFACE AND SIGNALING DEVICES (combined)

Waldo

Artra
P.O. Box 653
Arlington, VA 22216
703-527-0455

Base Price = 599.00

For Apple II computers, a voice recognition (controlled) X-10 Home Control system which also contains stereo sound generators and an amplifier. Waldo starts with software and manuals for $599. Two types of synthesized voices are available—each at $199; and the X-10 capability can be expanded to control 256 X-10 Modules (basic unit controls 16 Modules). Waldo is also available for the Heath/Zenith H/Z-89 computer.

HC-1

At Home With Computers
Suite 203
823 East 53½ St.
Austin, TX 78751
512-451-2713

Base Price = 2000

X-10 compatible controller for the IBM PC with sensing capability. Plugs into internal PC slot and includes clock, and parallel and serial ports. Connections for sensors are located on outside of PC. Board includes its own cpu and memory which allow it to operate independently of the PC. System provides for calendar function and an optional weather package is available for about $1000.

Autocrat

Bi-Comm Systems
2963 Yorkton Boulevard
St. Paul, MN 55117
612-481-0775

System attaches to most any computer via an RS-232 port and provides X-10 Control as well as sensing capabilities. After being programmed by computer, this system can operate on its own. Can be linked to modem for over phone line operation. Instructions and software included. Bi-Comm also makes the PC-1 ($355) that is a board for the Apple II. This system has similar characteristics to the Autocrat system, but needs constant link to the Apple for control.

TomorrowHouse

Compu-Home Systems, Inc.
1660 S. Albion #806
Denver, CO 80222
303-758-7043

Base Price = 895.00

Works with Apple II+ or *IIe* and includes both sensing and signaling capabilities, as well as a calendar (reminder) capability. 16 separate X-10 Modules can be controlled, by sending audio tones to the BSR Ultrasonic Control box. 16 analog and 16 digital sensor terminals are included. Compatible with Thunderware Thunderclock ($199), BSR Ultrasonic Wireless Controller, and voice synthesizer. System includes battery back-up, 48 channel I/O circuit card, cable, Compustat central heat/air interface, 4 temperature sensors, and wall mounted junction box. Software includes graphic display of floor plan and temperature changes. Complete manual provided. System can handle wide variety of Home Control functions including security, spa/hot tub control, and record-keeping of some of its functions. A new product, TomorrowHouse *II*, can talk and with an optional Applecat *II* modem will be able to speak over the phone and understand and react to touch tone signals received from the caller. The new product can control up to eight heat/cooling zones and will have more complete security system capabilities. TomorrowHouse *II* availability for the Apple *II*c—late 1984, and for the IBM PC—first quarter 1985. Refer to Fig. A-1.

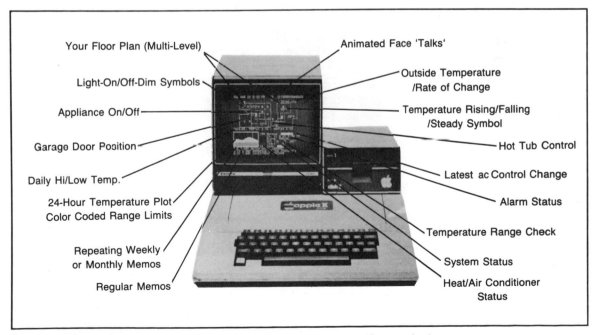

Fig. A-1. TomorrowHouse Home Control system (courtesy Compu-Home System, Inc.).

Fig. A-2. SmartHome Control System using "mouse" (courtesy of CyberLynx Computer Products, Inc.).

SmartHome I

CyberLynx Computer Products
4828 Sterling Drive
Boulder, CO 80301
303-444-7733

Starter System = 495.00

SmartHome I is compatible with the IBM PC or Apple II computers and includes its own microprocessor and power supply. The computer is used to program the equipment, but does not have to be on for the system to work. The system can be used in conjunction with an rf (wireless) burglar, fire, and medical alert alarm system. SmartHome I does timed controls of lights and appliances, or immediate control can also be accomplished with a hand-held 12 key transmitter. An infrared motion detector is available. Smart-Home I's software uses interactive graphics and can be programmed by using a joystick or mouse! Refer to Fig. A-2.

Home Control System

Harris Labs
1106 Westwood Drive
Marshalltown, IA 50158
515-763-8529

Extensive home control system usually custom built into house during construction. Home Control of all electrical appliances. Starting prices of about $6000 and up.

156

HomeBrain

HyperTek Inc.
P.O. Box 137, Route 22 East
Salem Industrial Park
Whitehouse, NJ 08888
201-534-9700

Base Price = 1499.00

HomeBrain is one of the most sophisticated Home Control systems and includes 16 digital and 16 analog sensor ports, 8 relays and a 256 item X-10 Control capability. System includes an extensive battery backup able to work a burglar and fire alarm system for up to three hours during a power outage. Retains memory without power for one month. Has its own separate microprocessor and can work by itself after it has received programming. Extensive documentation and software for many computers. The standard software package features energy management, security, and fire safety capabilities, as well as season and vacation modes.

Home Security System

Jance Associates
P.O. Box 234
East Texas, PA 18046
215-398-0434

Base Price = 195.00

Using a Commodore 64 or VIC 20 in conjunction with the Home Security System, can provide a complete burglar alarm system (including a Vic 20 computer) for about $300. The system is also set up to interface with the X-10 Burglar Controller. The Home Security System includes software (disk or cassette), input/output (sensor/control) interface cartridge, an alarm, wire, magnetic switches, warning beepers, independent power supply (for alarms), panic button, and a de-activate button. IBM PC model available soon for $399.

The Eye

Lehigh Valley Computer Corp.
523 S. Clewell Street
Bethlehem, PA 18015
215-868-1303

Base Price = 249.95

The Eye is an Apple II card (similar Commodore product available) which includes a clock, a battery back-up, a small alarm, three digital input terminals, the ability to control X-10 Modules, software on disk, 4 magnetic switches and a 30 page manual. Also available are extra magnetic switches ($3.50), X-10 Modules ($18.95), window bug ($10.75), Temp/Fire detector ($12.95), Siren including X-10 switch ($69.45), Switch Mat ($39.95), Ultrasonic Motion Detector ($162.50), and an electronic Dialer ($199).

ADC-1

Remote Measurement Systems
POB 15544
Seattle, WA 98115
206-525-3369

Base Price = 369.00

RS-232 port compatible Home Control unit with 4 digital and 16 analog sensor ports for sensing light, temperature, humidity, etc. X-10 Control as well as 6 hardwired circuits provided. User manual provides descriptions of BASIC programs necessary to operate ADC-1. Software for many computers is available. Sensors include:

Temperature	$ 7
Light	$ 6
Wind Speed, Direction	$45, $80
Soil Moisture	$56
Relative Humidity	$60
Elec. Energy Consump	$75

S-100 Bus Products

Sci-Tronics Inc.
523 S. Clewell St.
P.O. Box 5344
Bethlehem, PA 18015
215-868-7220

Sci-Tronics offers three S-100 Bus, IEEE-696 compatible boards each including manuals and software is available (extra) for integrated applications between the boards. The Real Time Clock board can track hours, minutes, seconds, day of week, month, and day of year ($199). The Energy Watcher board measures electrical power usage ($259). Similar more sophisticated EW boards available. An X-10 and Leviton (commercial grade X-10 type system) Remote Controller board is available for $259.

Computerized Alarm System

Transition Technology
1458 West Birchwood
Chicago, IL 60626

Base Price = 34.95

Plans and software for a computerized alarm system for Radio Shack's Color Computer. The Company is willing to perform custom programming to add functions such as:

☐ Real time clock.
☐ Battery backup.
☐ Check alarm status over phone.
☐ And others.

SIGNALING DEVICES

Automatic Telephone Dialer

Alarm Device Manufacturing Co. (ADEMCO)
165 Eileen Way
Syosset, NY 11791
800-645-7492

The Auto Telephone Dialer #612 is specifically made for burglar and fire alarm system communications. It has two channels (burglary & fire) and operates from a six volt battery. Add-ons available for line seizure, trigger delay, and recharger.

This company makes many items for burglar and fire alarm systems that can be adapted to Computer Home Control. To find their nearest distribution center dial 800 ADEMCO1.

HC-1 Home Commander

Automatic Micro, Inc.
2542 Billingsley Road
Worthington, OH 43085
614-766-0670

Base Price = 295.00

X-10 Controller that has its own microprocessor built in. Once programmed, will carry out commands separately without tie to programming computer. Plugs into serial (RS-232) port and can controls 256 X-10 Modules separately.

CSI-1200

Circuit Science
4 Townsend West
Suite 3
Nashua, NH 03063
603-880-4066

Base Price = 169.00

RS-232 (serial) compatible for home computers to independently control 256 X-10 Modules. Comes with a 20 page manual that explains how to operate by programming the computer using BASIC commands.

RS-232 to X-10 Interface
Heath Company
Benton Harbor, MI 49022
616-982-3285

Base Price = 129.95

X-10 Controller capable of working with any computer that has a serial (RS-232) port. Can control up to 256 X-10 Modules separately. Heathkit's controller (Cat.#GD1530) can be programmed using BASIC and examples of such programs are provided.

The Control Center
Intelectron
1275 A Street
Hayward, CA 94541
415-581-4490

Base Price = 149.95

Similar to X-10 Control system. Uses house wiring to send messages from Control Center to Modules. Two Modules are included. The Control Center (although a stand-alone item) recalls which lights or appliances it has switched on.

CIM-112
Savergy Inc.
1404 Webster Avenue
Ft. Collins, CO 80524
303-221-4200

Base Price = 479.00

Hardwired controller to be interfaced with either Commodore 64 or VIC 20 computers. Eight hardwire relay circuits. System can be connected to house wiring at utility or basement electrical box. Low voltage relay capability is available through the "Powerport", another product offering for $99. Software for the Powerport is $49.

Talking Home Monitor
Tandy Corporation
(Radio Shack)
1 Tandy Center
Fort Worth, TX 76102

Base Price = 199.95

This unit can be used to provide emergency messages over the phone lines and includes its own sensing capabilities. Has automatic dialing capabilities as well as a built-in voice synthesizer. Includes battery back-up that lasts up to 15 hours.

PC Mate Device Master
Tecmar, Inc.
6225 Cochran Road
Cleveland, OH 44139
216-349-0600

Base Price = 245.00

IBM accessory slot compatible. Includes capability to control 16 X-10 Modules by linking to X-10 Ultrasonic Controller (not included), and has a clock, a calendar, and includes a backup battery. Menu driven software available at $35.

Thunderclock Plus
Thunderware, Inc.
P.O. Box 13322
Oakland, CA 94661
415-254-6581

Base Price = 150.00

Thunderclock is a card for the Apple II that includes a clock, and an X-10 interfacing capability. The clock/calendar is compatible with Pro-DOS based software. With an optional X-10 adapter ($49) this card can be linked with a X-10 Ultrasonic Controller to control up to 16 X-10 Modules independently.

SENSOR INTERFACE AND SENSOR DEVICES

Motion Detectors
Alarm Device Manufacturing Co.
(ADEMCO)
165 Eileen Way
Syosset, NY 11791
800-645-7492

Various types of motion detectors are available from this company including ultrasonic, microwave, and passive infrared.

This company makes many items for burglar and fire alarm systems that can be adapted to Computer Home Control. To find their nearest distribution center dial 800 ADEMCO1.

Smoke and Heat Detectors
Alarm Device Manufacturing Co.
(ADEMCO)
165 Eileen Way
Syosset, NY 11791
800-645-7492

A wide variety of smoke and heat detectors are available from ADEMCO. Some detectors are specifically made to be used with "smart" systems and include the ability to (through a relay) send a signal to a remote device.

This company makes many items for burglar and fire alarm systems that can be adapted to Computer Home Control. To find their nearest distribution center dial 800 ADEMCO1.

COCO-Port
Green Mountain Micro
Roxbury, VT 05669
802-485-6112

Base Price = 49.95

The CoCo-Port attaches to Radio Shacks's Color Computer (cartridge slot) and is a general purpose 8-bit input/output port which can be used to receive signals, or (in conjunction with relays) to control electrical appliances. Documentation is complete, but this product is for those that are not afraid of soldering and POKE-ing and PEEKing through their computer. The designer Dennis Kitsz wrote two articles on this device which appeared in Color Computer Magazine in the April and May 1983 issues.

Dascon-1
MetraByte
254 Tosca Drive
Stoughton, MA 02072
617-344-1990
    Base Price = 485.00

Dascon-1 is a complete, high precision, low speed data acquisition and control system designed to plug directly into the IBM PC. Can be used for scientific and/or laboratory quality functions, or it could be integrated into a sophisticated set-up for Home Control. Has twelve bit analog I/O capabilities. Board is provided with software and documentation. This manufacturer offers a wide variety of I/O boards, other equipment, and software for the IBM PC.

CCAD Analog Interface
Technical Hardware, Inc.
P.O. Box 3609
Fullerton, CA 92634
714-870-1882

Base Price = 169.50

Software and hardware included for this unit which can be used to sense real world conditions. Includes 16 input channels, a clock, a 12 bit analog to digital converter and 3 output lines. This product is specifically designed to link with Radio Shack's Color Computer.

BSR (USA) LTD. X-10 PRODUCT LINE

BSR System X-10 Controller and Modules

BSR (USA) Ltd.
Route 303
Blauvelt, NY 10913
914-358-6060

BSR is a producer of a wide assortment of stand-alone command controllers. Refer to Fig. A-3.

Telephone Responder/Controller Set. Can control X-10 Modules from any phone ($149.99).

Timer Console. Automatically controls X-10 Modules with a twenty-four hour clock and features a battery backup ($89.99).

Ultrasonic Command Module. For instant control of 16 X-10 Modules ($49.99).

Ultrasonic Cordless Controller. Used in conjunction with Ultrasonic Command Module for wireless control of X-10 Modules ($24.99).

Mini Controller. For instant control of 4 X-10 Modules ($29.99).

Burglar Alarm Interface/Controller. Connects to security system to turn on or flash lights if security system senses intruder. Can also activate one Appliance Module ($49.99).

Thermostat Controller Sets. Use X-10 System for control of heating and/or cooling system ($79.99 with Appliance Module, or $59.99 without module).

X-10 Modules. BSR modules are available at AT&T Phone Centers, Sears, Radio Shack, and many other stores nationwide. Many of their products are also sold in sets.

Lamp	$22.50
3 Prong Appliance	22.50
2 Prong Appliance	22.50
Wall Switch Module (push button control)	22.50
Wall Switch Module	16.99
3 Way Wall Switch Set	29.99
Wall Outlet Module	29.99
Heavy Duty 220 Volt Modules	
15 Amp	44.99
20 Amp	49.99

New Product. BSR now has a computer interface for Radio Shack and (in the near future) other computers. The Radio Shack Color Computer version can control 256 X-10 Modules, contains its own separate microprocessor and clock (and once programmed can be detached from computer). It uses color graphics and a joystick to aid programming, has a 100 hour battery backup, and has push-buttons for manual control of X-10 Modules when the controller is not connected to your computer.

Fig. A-3. BSR X-10 System (courtesy BSR (USA) Ltd.).

VOICE PRODUCTS

Sybil

Centigram Corporation
1362 Borregas Avenue
Sunnyvale, CA 94089
408-734-3222

Base Price = 495.00

Speech synthesis board which plugs into the IBM PC. Includes a speaker jack for an 8-ohm speaker.

Speak Up!

Classical Computing, Inc.
P.O. Box 3318
Chapel Hill, NC 27515

Base Price = 29.95

A machine language voice synthesizer program for Radio Shack's Color Computer. No hardware is required beyond what is needed for the computer itself, except a cassette recorder for loading the software.

Software Automatic Mouth

Don't Ask Computer Software
2265 Westwood Blvd.
Los Angeles, CA 90064
213-477-4514

Atari and Commodore models sell for $59.95. Apple II and III models sell for $124.95. Supplied with a 10,000 word dictionary of English to phonetic spellings. Software Automatic Mouth (SAM) can talk from either English or phonetic spellings.

PC Parrot

Dragon Data Systems
1068 Homer Street, #110
Vancouver, BC, Canada V6B4W9
604-255-0584

Base Price = 39.95

The PC Parrot for the IBM PC is a software synthesizer that can digitize sound and can be used in conjunction with a BASIC program.

Intex-Talker

Intex Micro Systems
725 S. Adams Rd.
Birmingham, MI 48011
313-540-7601

Base Price = 295.00

Stand-alone device that plugs into serial port or a 34-pin Centronics type plug. Uses a set of English phonetic rules. Works with most computer brands.

Mimic Speech Processor

Mimic, Inc.
P.O. Box 921
Acton, MA 01720
617-263-2101

The Mimic Speech Processor can be linked to any computer with a parallel port. The product works by digitizing speech which can later be played back according to software control. Complete systems for many computers sell at less than $200.

Supertalker

Mountain Computer
300 El Pueblo Road
Scotts Valley, CA 95066
408-438-6650

Supertalker II for the IBM PC sells for $565. Supertalker SD200 for the Apple sells for $199. Digitizing method which can store 120 seconds of speech.

The Parrot

Research in Speech Tech, Inc.
P.O. Box 499
Fort Hamilton Station
Brooklyn, NY 11209
212-259-4934

Base Price = 69.95

Phoneme based speech that plugs into the Sinclair ZX 80/81 or Timex Sinclair TS1000.

Apple Talker

Softtape
5547 Satsuma Avenue
N. Hollywood, CA 91601
213-985-5763

Base Price = 29.95

The Apple Talker (for Apple II Computers) is a software voice synthesizer.

The Voice

Speech Systems
38 W. 255 Deerpath Road
Batavia, IL 60510
312-879-6880

Base Price = 79.00

Hardware speech synthesizer which uses Votrax SC-01. This product works with Radio Shack's Color Computer, and attaches to the cartridge port (disk system can still be used with Y-cable - $29.95). Can be heard through TV or through external speaker. Includes demonstration programs and documentation. Many related programs which make use of the speech capability are available from company, or user can write his or her own using BASIC. Company working on an X-10 and voice recognition system.

Echo II and GP

Street Electronics
1140 Mark Avenue
Carpinteria, CA 93013
805-684-4593

The Echo II voice synthesizer for the Apple II sells for $149.95. The Echo GP for computers with a serial (RS-232) Port sells for $299.95. The Echo II comes as a plug-in card and includes software and documentation. Echo GP also comes with documentation, and remains outside the computer as a stand-alone peripheral.

PC-Mate Speech Master

Tecmar, Inc.
6225 Cochran Street
Solon, OH 44139
216-349-0600

Base Price = 395.00

IBM PC compatible product that operates with Speech Master Software Support package (optional) which sells for $95. This product offers both a 143 word stored vocabulary (for high quality speech) and a text to speech capability (unlimited vocabulary with slightly reduced speech quality). System uses DIGITIZER and VOTRAX methods. A Voice Recognition board with a capability of interpreting up to 200 spoken words is available from Tecmar starting at $995.

Solid-State Speech Synth.

Texas Instruments
Attn: Consumer Service
P.O. Box 53
Lubbock, TX 79048
800-858-4565

Base Price = 99.95

Works with TI 99/4A computer. Comes with a vocabulary of about 300 words.

Voice Box

The Alien Group
27 West 23rd Street
New York, NY 10010
212-741-1770

Works with Atari 400 and 800 computers, $169; with Apple II computers, $215; and with Commodore VIC 20, $95. Uses the serial (RS-232) port.

Personal Speech System

Votrax
500 Stephenson Highway
Troy, MI 48084
800-521-1350

Base Price = 395.00

Uses synthesis-by-rule and can be linked to any personal computer with either a serial port or a Centronics-type parallel port.

Type-N-Talk

Votrax
500 Stephenson Highway
Troy, MI 48084
800-521-1350

Base Price = 249.00

Works with most computers that have an RS-232 port. Unit can voice any text typed into the memory of the computer.

V100 Interactive Voice Synth

Vynet Corporation
2607 South Winchester Blvd.
Campbell, CA 95008
408-370-0555

Available for the Apple II or IBM Personal Computer. This product is an interface device to the telephone line, does touch-tone dialing and decoding, and can talk through the telephone by using voice synthesis. With this device, a caller is able to command the computer by using a touch tone phone (from anywhere) and the computer can take appropriate action(s) and respond (by voice) to the caller. Apple version - $395. IBM PC version - $450.

ROBOTS

TOPO, FRED, and BOB

Androbot, Inc.
101 E. Daggett Drive
San Jose, CA 95134
408-262-8676

TOPO is a robot that has a radio link for communicating to its host computer. Currently, interfaces and software are available for linkage to an Apple, Commodore, or IBM PC. Includes voice synthesis and motorized base among its many features. TOPO's base price is $1595. Little brother FRED (Friendly Robotic Education

Device) will be able to walk, talk, and be controlled by a hand-held remote device. BOB, on the other hand, will sell for about $4500 and will include an 8088 microprocessor.

Hero 1
Heath Company
Dept. 529-138
Benton Harbor, MI 49022
616-982-3285

Base Price = 1500.00

Hero 1 costs $1500 in kit form ($2500 assembled). Uses an on-board 6808 microprocessor that interfaces with all sensors, experimental circuit board, drive motors, and real-time clock. Hero 1 is 20" tall and weights 39 lbs. Robot can detect sound, light, objects and motion, and has synthesized phoneme-based speech. Comes with useable arm and gripper. A scaled down version of Hero 1 called Hero Jr. is available for $500 (kit) and $1000 (assembled). Education courses available.

Smart Rabbit
Hobby Robot Co., Inc.
P.O. Box 887
Hazlehurst, GA 31539
912-375-7821

Twenty two inch tall robot with motorized movement. Can be controlled with Timex 1000/ ZX81 and Commodore Computers, as well as others. Upgrades available include moving head and arms (with grippers), and an electronic expansion bus. Base price starts around $400.

Hubot
Hubotics Inc.
6352-D Corte Del Abeto
Carlsbad, CA 92008
619-438-9028

Base Price = 3495.00

A walking, talking robot that includes a sonar collar to help Hubot avoid obstacles. Has a tray to serve drinks, and a working 12" TV screen that seconds as a monitor. Includes a 64 key computer with 128K and CPM 2.2. Interface included for expandability, and disk drive built in. Can play Atari 2600 games and has an AM/FM stereo cassette tape deck with graphic equalizer. Hubot is 44" high and weights 100 lbs. Works on 12 volt, 50 amp rechargeable battery. Attachments promised soon.

RB5X
RB Robot Corp.
18301 West 10th Street
Suite 310
Golden, CO 80401
303-279-5525

The RB5X Robot includes the ability to locate its charger when its batteries become low. Base price starts about the $2000 range, and many add-ons are available. RB5X walks, talks, is capable of playing games, and should have a vacuum attachment soon.

Scorpion
Rhino Robots
P.O. Box 4010
2505 S. Neil St.
St. Champaign, IL 61820
217-352-8485

Robot that includes a microprocessor, an RS-232 interface (so that most any computer can link with Scorpion), a motorized base, sound generator, electronic eye and bumper sensors. Other more sophisticated robots are available in either kit or assembled units from this company. The base price of Scorpion - about $700.

MISCELLANEOUS PRODUCTS

ADT-Safewatch
ADT Security Systems
One World Trade Center
New York, NY 10048
212-558-1100

Base Price = 995.00

Various central station home security systems which can be linked to an ADT central monitoring station. Systems can include smoke detection and medical emergency capabilities. Modular design which can be tailored to customer's needs.

Protect Center - Mod #9000
Anova Electronics
Three Waters Park Drive
San Mateo, CA 94403
415-572-9686

Base Price = 299.95

Wireless sensor system (RF detection transmitters) which provide protection against burglar, fire, flood, medical emergencies, and utility failure. Includes battery backup. Also available are Door/Window Intrusion Transmitters ($39.95), Personal Emergency Transmitter ($49.95), Alarm Module with three distinct alarms ($49.95), Wired Auxiliary Siren ($39.95), and a Telephone Dialer Interface for use with the Telephone Center Mod #7000 ($39.95).

Control Center - Mod #8000
Anova Electronics
Three Waters Park Drive
San Mateo, CA 94403
415-572-9686

Base Price = 199.95

Timed control of up to 16 lights and appliances. Includes a battery backup which maintains its schedule in the event of a power failure. Also available are Lamp, Appliance, and Wall Switch Modules at $29.95 each. System may be used in conjunction with the Protection Center Mod #9000, noted prior.

Telephone Center - Mod #7000
Anova Electronics
Three Waters Park Drive
San Mateo, CA 94403
415-572-9686

Base Price = 399.95

Advanced automatic telephone answering system, dialer, and speaker phone. A Remote Control Beeper is available for $29.95 for message playback from any telephone. System may be used in conjunction with the Protection center Mod #9000, above.

Remote Controlled A/V Systems
Audio Command Systems
46 Merrick Road
Rockville Cntr., NY 11570
516-766-2627

Firm sells high quality, high tech complete home audio/video systems which can be controlled using remote control panels located anywhere in the house. Audio Command Systems handles everything from design to installation.

ECM-1500
Ellsworth Chow & Murphy
1748 Hamilton Avenue
Palo Alto, CA 94303
415-326-8575

Base Price = 1850

A powerful X-10 Controller system that allows individual control of up to 256 X-10 Modules. Offers seven-day programability and recalls item status. Optional extended battery available. Refer to Fig. A-4.

Fig. A-4. ECM-1500 (courtesy Ellsworth Chow R. Murphy).

RF-2200 Surveillance System

GBC Closed Circuit TV Corp.
315 Hudson Street
New York, NY 10013
800-221-2240

Base Price = 299.50

Package includes video camera, mounting bracket, power module, RF switch, and a 50 foot cord to plug into regular TV. Add-ons available including different lenses and a housing for protection outdoors.

HomeMinder

General Electric
Video Products Division
Portsmouth, VA 23705

HomeMinder is an X-10 controller for the operation of lights, appliances, heating and cooling. A hand-held remote control unit, similar to an ordinary TV remote controller, is used to operate the system. Graphic displays generated on the TV screen lead the homeowner through step-by-step operating instructions.

HomeMinder is available in two versions: a free-standing unit that connects to the back of any TV set, and as a feature built into a 25-in. GE component television.

The HomeMinder system works through existing house wiring and GE offers a number of the X-10 Modules, as shown in Fig. A-5, re-titled as the "LampMinder", "ApplianceMinder", etc.

GE system provides extremely simple process of setting up controls by displaying pictures and instructions using menus or simple phrases such as "What do you want to turn on?" and "Where is it?" System can be programmed for things to happen at a preset time, daily, weekdays only, weekends, or just on specific days. A "Help" button is provided, if the user becomes confused. If pressed, the needed information will appear on the TV screen. Figure A-6 shows some of the screens used by the program to simplify scheduling.

The HomeMinder features a memo pad function which allows user to input appointments and dates. With the press of a button the screen will read: "What do you want to remember?" and display a list of options such as birthday, anniversary or doctor's appointment. After one is selected, the screen will instruct the user to provide the correct date and time. HomeMinder will then recall the memo and alert the user to review the memo pad display on the day of the event.

HomeMinder can be reached from virtually anywhere across the country by using a touch-tone phone. The system will "answer" after seven to ten rings and respond to "commands," or numbers pressed on the phone. Two separate messages can also be left at the touch of a button: "I can be reached at (telephone number)" or "I will be home at (time)." A pre-determined "password number" prevents unauthorized entry into the system.

HomeMinder can be reached from a rotary dial phone using a tone generator, available at phone supply stores, to duplicate the touch-tone signals.

As with other GE consumer products, HomeMinder is supported by General Electric's national toll-free information service. Consumers can call 800-626-2000, to locate their nearest dealer or receive assistance with product use and service.

GE experimenting with *HomeNet* which is reported to allow microcomputer-based General Electric appliances to communicate with each other through normal house wiring. A "smart" television set, again, may act as the controller.

Fig. A-5. HomeMinder Modules (courtesy General Electric, Video Products Div.).

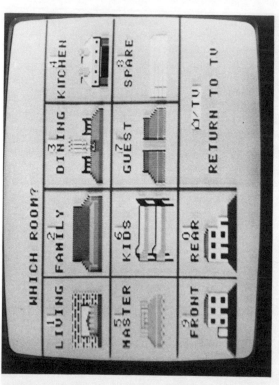

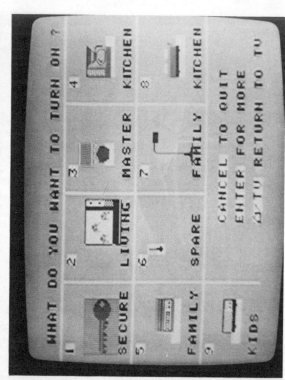

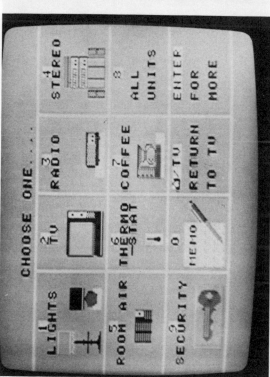

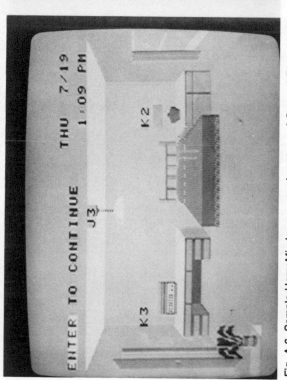

Fig. A-6. Sample HomeMinder screens (courtesy of General Electric, Video Products Div.).

WV-80/KTV
Panasonic

Base Price = 995.00

IT-25U CCTV
Sharp Electronics

Base Price = 525.00

Energy Control System (ECS)
Technicon International
23 Old Kings Highway So.
Darien, CT 06820
202-655-1299

Base Price = 190.00

Panasonics WV-80/KTV includes two cameras, two sets of mounting brackets, and a video monitor. System has built in sequential camera switching. Ports are available for intercom, VCR, or an alarm sensor.

The Sharp Electronics outfit comes with mini-camera, lens and mounting brackets, a nine inch monitor, 33 feet of cable and includes a two way intercom system. Add-ons available.

User of ECS can dial from any touch-tone phone (from anywhere) to control up to 8 X-10 Modules.

Appendix B

Other Methods for Controlling Central Heating and Cooling

This appendix is a bit more technical than the chapters in this book and, depending on the equipment you buy, may require some soldering. However, it does provide an alternative method for the control of both central heating and cooling systems, and does so in a slightly more precise way than explained in Chapter 7. It is suggested that before trying this method, you thoroughly read Chapter 7 if you have not already done so. Then after reading this appendix, decide whether there are any real advantages for you to proceed "the hard way"!

HOW IT WORKS

Chapter 7 gave an explanation of how a furnace (or central air conditioner) and thermostat work to control your home heating (and cooling) needs. The thermostat, by sensing temperature, either switches on or off thus allowing the loop of electrical current to start or stop the furnace. This same method is the one used here. However, this method uses two loops and two thermostats instead of one.

The idea is really quite simple. One thermostat is set at a lower temperature (such as 60 degrees) and another is set at a higher temperature (possibly 70 degrees). The computer, by using a simple relay (controlled by one of the X-10 Appliance Modules) controls which thermostat in turn controls the furnace. As shown in Fig. B-1, the X-10 Module and relay control which electrical loop controls the furnace. The benefit of this simple system is that one thermostat or the other is always in control. Therefore, even if the computer fails, no major problem is created in terms of heating the house.

If your furnace is the type that shuts off when the power in your house fails, this method will not keep it running. However, your furnace will function as it always has once your power returns by either manually being reset or resetting itself.

WHAT YOU NEED TO BUY

Take a look at a couple of things about your furnace. What voltage is sent through the present thermostat? This can be found by looking at the

172

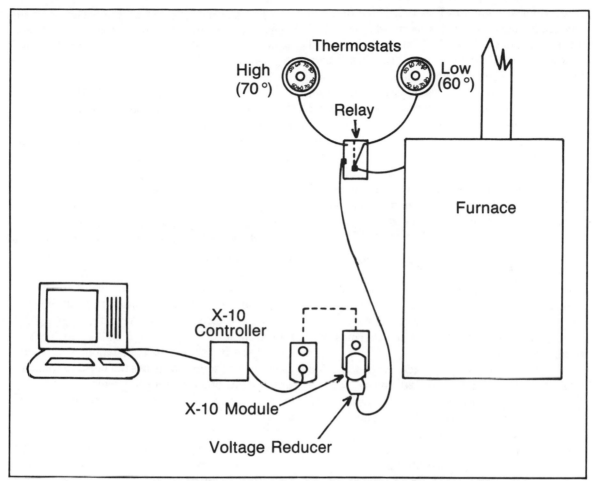

Fig. B-1. Relay control of two thermostats. One or the other thermostat is always in control of the furnace.

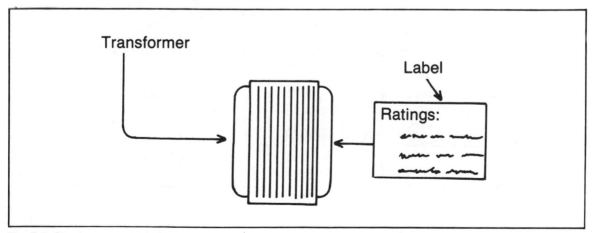

Fig. B-2. Check power supply (voltage reducer) which runs through your present thermostat.

transformer as shown in Fig. B-2. If the rating is between 24 and 30 volts, the thermostat described in this appendix will work. (This equipment will work with most heating systems—even those where the thermostat controls central air conditioning.) If the rating is beyond this maximum or minimum, then check with your local heating supply store and request an alternative thermostat.

A second question is how many heat zones do you have? If you have more than one and you wish to be able to control all of them, then you will need one of the following sets for each heat zone.

Note: It is likely that you can use your current thermostat as one of the two needed.

PARTS LIST

The following parts are needed to complete this project:

☐ Two Honeywell #T87F thermostats. Rating: 24-30 volts.

☐ One relay. Radio Shack carries a wide variety of relays such as a 120 volt ac relay # 275-217 ($5.49); or for low voltage operation, a 12 volt dc relay #275-218 (also $5.49). Low voltage relays will require a voltage reducer (many sold at Radio Shack).

☐ One X-10 Appliance Module

The thermostats can be purchased at many home maintenance or hardware stores, and all other equipment is available at Radio Shack or other electronics stores.

WHAT YOU NEED TO DO

The first thing to do is re-check to make sure that all your equipment matches your system. Be sure to check the voltage rating on the power source to your current thermostat against that of your new thermostats. Read through the manufacturer's directions before proceeding, and follow their instructions. Also check the location of your existing thermostat. The location should be about 5 feet above the floor in an area with good circulation at average temperature. The thermostat should not be located where it may be affected by drafts, hot or cold air from ducts, or radiant heat from the sun or appliances. If your current thermostat appears to be in a bad location, you should consider relocating it.

Figure B-3 shows the installation using an adjacent power source, which is the most convenient. The second diagram shows a remote (basement) location which may prove to be more aesthetically pleasing.

The next step in the installation process is to **disconnect the power supply** before removing the old thermostat and installing the two new ther-

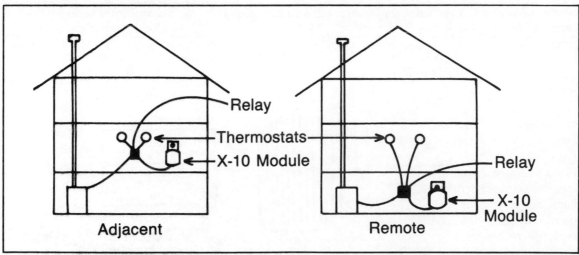

Fig. B-3. Adjacent or remote installation.

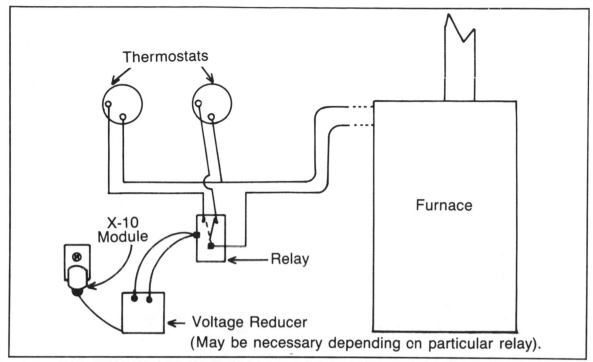

Fig. B-4. Wiring diagram. May differ depending on your particular thermostat system, but the theory is the same.

mostats. This serves two purposes: avoiding shock and preventing the equipment from being damaged. After disconnecting the power supply, remove the old thermostat. Follow the wiring diagram in Fig. B-4 in conjunction with your thermostat manufacturer's instructions. The only difference between the diagram and the manufacturer's instructions are the leads that go to the relay to control one or the other thermostat. (Some thermostats have extra wires which are used to power a clock, to completely shut-down the furnace, or to switch from heating to cooling. If your current thermostat has more than two wires, the relay switch should be linked to open and close the circuit on one of the wires that controls the furnace according to your home's temperature (in line with the thermostat's temperature control switch). Also, if your home has central air controlled through the same thermostat, an extra controlling wire will be present. The relays noted before both have more than one switch included, and this additional air conditioning wire can be linked and switched using the same relay.

Once the thermostats and relay (and voltage reducer, if appropriate) have been wired and mounted, adjust the X-10 Appliance Module's HOUSE and UNIT CODES to an appropriate setting as described in Chapter 6. After checking all wiring, connect the relay (or voltage reducer) to the X-10 Module and, in turn, the X-10 Module into a wall outlet. Set your thermostats, turn on the current, and your heating and/or cooling systems are ready for computer control! If you have more than one heating or air conditioning zone, repeat the instructions above for each zone.

HOW LONG WILL IT TAKE

Once all equipment and tools are ready, the actual time needed to do the furnace and/or central air control assembly should be roughly a half hour for each zone. Of course, if rewiring takes place because of an inappropriate location of the original thermostat, or if wiring needs to be hidden for aesthetic reasons, extra time will be required.

Appendix C
Utility Monitoring Program

Once you install a Home Control system in your home, you may wish to track the volume and costs of your energy consumption from year to year. The following is a menu driven Utility Monitoring Program which was written on the IBM PC in BASIC. With some minor changes, it will work on most any computer. A few MicroSoft BASIC "key" words such as INKEY$, CLS, LOCATE, and LPRINT may not work on your machine. However, by reviewing the BASIC manual that came with your computer, you should be able to make the necessary changes. Also, this program has been written to SAVE or LOAD its data from a diskette. This section of the program will likely need changes if you are using another machine, or especially if you are planning to LOAD and SAVE from tape.

PROGRAM DESCRIPTION

Once the program loads, a menu screen is displayed as shown in Fig. C-1. Press #2. "Edit (Create) Information", will prompt you for the name of the utility, the utility type (water, electric, gas, or oil),

and request a unit of measurement (i.e., kilowatt hours, cubic feet, etc.), and the current year. After you have ENTERed this information you can ENTER the volume and costs (as shown in Fig. C-2) for each month in the prior year, and again (by pressing A and the ENTER key) for the current year. Once you have ENTERed all your information, press F and the ENTER key to return to the main menu.

From the main menu you can SAVE your information to a diskette, and/or PRINT your information to either the monitor or a printer (a printer is optional and is not necessary to RUN the program). The printed output from the program is shown in Fig. C-3. As you can see, the program displays both the prior and the current year's volumes and costs and compares the two. If the prior year's volume or cost for any particular month is zero, then that month will not be included in the calculations.

With this program you can easily keep tabs on how well your Home Control (and/or other) energy conservation program is paying off.

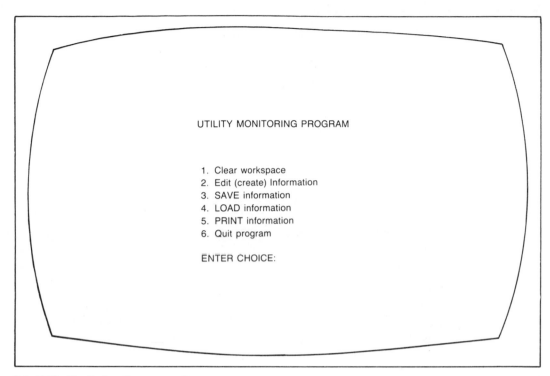

Fig. C-1. Utility Monitoring Program main menu.

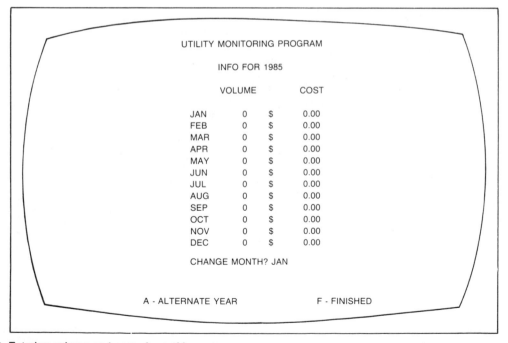

Fig. C-2. Entering volume and cost of monthly energy usage.

UTILITY ANALYSIS

COMPANY: NEW YORK UTILITY CO.
TYPE: ELECTRIC/GAS/OIL/WATER
MEASURE IN: KWH/CUBIC FEET/GALLONS

VOLUME DECREASE/(INCREASE) BY MONTH

	1985	1986	DEC/(INC)	%
	* * * *	* * * *	* * * * * * * *	* * * * *
JAN	1	1	0	0.0
FEB	0	0	0	N/A
MAR	0	0	0	N/A
APR	0	0	0	N/A
MAY	0	0	0	N/A
JUN	0	0	0	N/A
JUL	0	0	0	N/A
AUG	0	0	0	N/A
SEP	0	0	0	N/A
OCT	0	0	0	N/A
NOV	0	0	0	N/A
DEC	0	0	0	N/A
TOT	1	1	0	0.0
AVG	1	1	0	0.0

COST DECREASE/(INCREASE) BY MONTH

	1985	1986	DEC/(INC)	%
	* * * *	* * * *	* * * * * * * *	* * * * *
JAN	1	1	0	0.0
FEB	0	0	0	N/A
MAR	0	0	0	N/A
APR	0	0	0	N/A
MAY	0	0	0	N/A
JUN	0	0	0	N/A
JUL	0	0	0	N/A
AUG	0	0	0	N/A
SEP	0	0	0	N/A
OCT	0	0	0	N/A
NOV	0	0	0	N/A
DEC	0	0	0	N/A
TOT	1	1	0	0.0
AVG	1	1	0	0.0

Fig. C-3. Program output–comparison of energy usage and costs year-to-year.

```
1000 'UTILITY MONITORING PROGRAM
1010 '(c) DAVID B. BONYNGE 1984
1020 KEY OFF:LOCATE ,,0:WIDTH 40:UT$ = "UTILITY MONITORING PROGRAM"
1030 Z$ = STRINGS(40,"*")
1040 Y$ = STRINGS(40," ")
1050 F1$ = "######-":F3$ = "###.#-"
1060 DIM A$(12),A(24,2)
1070 FOR I = 1 TO 12:READ A$(I):NEXT I
1080 CLS:LOCATE 12,8:PRINT UT$:LOCATE 22,8:PRINT "(c) David B. Bonynge 1984"
1090 FOR I = 1 TO 3000:NEXT I
1100 CLS:LOCATE 1,8:PRINT UT$:LOCATE 8,12:PRINT "1.  Clear workspace":LOCATE 10,
12:PRINT "2.  Edit (create) Information":LOCATE 12,12:PRINT "3.  SAVE informatio
n"
1110 LOCATE 14,12:PRINT "4.  LOAD information":LOCATE 16,12:PRINT "5.  PRINT inf
ormation"
1120 LOCATE 18,12:PRINT "6.  Quit program":LOCATE 21,8:PRINT "ENTER CHOICE:"
1130 D$ = INKEY$:IF D$ < "1" OR D$ > "6" THEN 1130
1140 ON VAL(D$) GOTO 2000,3000,4000,5000,6000,7000


2000 'CLEAR WORKSPACE
2010 CLS:LOCATE 12,11:PRINT "ARE YOU SURE (Y,N)?"
2020 D$ = INKEY$:IF D$ <> "Y" AND D$ <> "y" AND D$ <> "N" AND D$ <> "n" THEN 202
0
2030 IF D$ <> "Y" AND D$ <> "y" THEN 1100
2040 LOCATE 12,1:PRINT Y$:LOCATE 12,15:PRINT "PLEASE WAIT":COMPANY$ = "":FOR I1
= 0 TO 24:FOR I2 = 0 TO 2:A(I1,I2) = 0:NEXT I2:NEXT I1:GOTO 1100


3000 'EDIT ROUTINE
3010 YA=YR-1:Z = 0
3020 IF COMPANY$ <> "" GOTO 3120
3030 CLS:LOCATE 1,8:PRINT UT$
3040 LOCATE 8,1:PRINT "COMPANY NAME:":PRINT:INPUT COMPANY$
3050 IF COMPANY$ = "" THEN 3030
3060 PRINT:PRINT "UTILITY TYPE:":PRINT:INPUT KIND$:PRINT:PRINT "USAGE MEASURE IN
:":PRINT:INPUT US$
3070 LOCATE 21,6:PRINT "ARE ALL ANSWERS CORRECT (Y,N)?"
3080 D$ = INKEY$:IF D$ <> "Y" AND D$ <> "N" AND D$ <> "y" AND D$ <> "n" THEN 308
0
3090 IF D$ = "N" OR D$ = "n" THEN COMPANY$ = "":GOTO 3030
3100 CLS:LOCATE 1,8:PRINT UT$
3110 LOCATE 12,10:PRINT "CURRENT YEAR";:INPUT YR:YA = YR-1:IF YR < 1980 THEN 310
0
3120 CLS:LOCATE 1,8:PRINT UT$:LOCATE 3,13:PRINT "INFO FOR ";YA:LOCATE 5,15:PRINT
"VOLUME       COST"
3130 FOR I = 1 TO 12:PRINT "          ";A$(I);"    ";:PRINT USING F1$;A(I+Z,1);:PRI
NT "   ";:PRINT USING "$####.##";A(I+Z,2):NEXT I
3140 LOCATE 22,3:PRINT "A - ALTERNATE YEAR      F - FINISHED":LOCATE 24,9:PRINT"
** CAPS MUST BE ON **";
3150 LOCATE 20,1:PRINT Y$;:LOCATE 20,9:INPUT "CHANGE MONTH";D$:IF (D$ = "A" OR D
$ = "a") AND YA = YR THEN YA = YR - 1 :Z = 0:GOTO 3120ELSE IF D$ = "A" OR D$ = "
a" THEN YA = YR:Z = 12:GOTO 3120
3160 IF D$ = "F" OR D$ = "f" THEN 1100
3170 IF LEN(D$) > 3 THEN D$ = LEFT$(D$,3)
3180 FOR I = 1 TO 12:IF D$ = A$(I) THEN 3190 ELSE NEXT I:GOTO 3140
3190 I1 = I:LOCATE 20,1:PRINT Y$;:LOCATE 20,9:INPUT "VOLUME";A(I1+Z,1):LOCATE 20
,1:PRINT Y$;:LOCATE 20,9:INPUT "CHARGES";A(I1+Z,2):GOTO 3120


4000 'SAVE ROUTINE
4010 CLS:LOCATE 2,15:PRINT "SAVE DATA":LOCATE 12,1:INPUT "FILE NAME";TYPE$
```

Fig. C-4. Program Listing for the IBM Personal Computer. (Continued to page 181.)

```
4020 IF COMPANY$ = "" THEN 1100 ELSE CLS:LOCATE 12,15:PRINT "PLEASE WAIT"
4030 OPEN "O",#1,TYPE$:PRINT#1, COMPANY$:PRINT#1, KIND$:PRINT#1, US$:PRINT#1,YR:
FOR I1 = 0 TO 24:FOR I2 = 0 TO 2:PRINT#1,A(I1,I2):NEXT I2:NEXT I1
4040 CLOSE#1:GOTO 1100


5000 'LOAD ROUTINE
5010 CLS:LOCATE 2,15:PRINT "LOAD DATA":LOCATE 12,1:INPUT "FILE NAME";TYPE$
5020 CLS:LOCATE 12,15:PRINT "PLEASE WAIT"
5030 OPEN "I",#1,TYPE$:INPUT#1, COMPANY$:INPUT#1, KIND$:INPUT#1, US$:INPUT#1,YR:
FOR I1 = 0 TO 24:FOR I2 = 0 TO 2:INPUT#1,A(I1,I2):NEXT I2:NEXT I1
5040 CLOSE#1:GOTO 1100


6000 'PRINT ROUTINE
6010 IF COMPANY$ = "" THEN 1100
6020 CLS:LOCATE 1,8:PRINT UT$:LOCATE 10,12:PRINT"1. MONITOR?":LOCATE 12,12:PRINT
"2. PRINTER?":LOCATE 16,12:PRINT "CHOOSE 1 OR 2:"
6030 D$ = INKEY$:IF D$ <> "1" AND D$ <> "2" THEN 6030
6040 IF D$ = "2" THEN 6210
6050 FOR I2 = 1 TO 2:IF I2 = 1 THEN C$ = "VOLUME" ELSE C$ = "COST"
6060 CLS:LOCATE 1,12:PRINT "UTILITY ANALYSIS":LOCATE 3,2:PRINT C$;" DECREASE/(IN
CREASE) BY MONTH":LOCATE 5,7:PRINT YR-1;"   ";YR;" DEC/(INC)     %":LOCATE 6,8:PR
INT"****    ****  ********  *****"
6070 B1 = 0:B2 = 0:B3 = 12
6080 FOR I = 1 TO 12
6090 B1 = B1 + A(I,I2):B2 = B2 + A(I+12,I2):IF A(I,I2) = 0 THEN B3 = B3 - 1:B2 =
 B2-A(I+12,I2)
6100 PRINT A$(I);:PRINT "  ";:PRINT USING F1$;A(I,I2);:PRINT"  ";:PRINT USING F1
$;A(I+12,I2);:PRINT " ";
6110 DIF = A(I,I2) - A(I+12,I2):PRINT USING F1$;DIF;:PRINT "    ";:IF A(I,I2) =
0 THEN PRINT " N/A" ELSE PRINT USING F3$;DIF/A(I,I2)*100
6120 NEXT I:PRINT
6130 PRINT "TOT  ";:PRINT USING F1$;B1;:PRINT"  ";:PRINT USING F1$;B2;:PRINT " "
;
6140 DIF = B1-B2:PRINT USING F1$;DIF;:PRINT "    ";:IF B1 = 0 THEN PRINT " N/A":
GOTO 6170 ELSE PRINT USING F3$;DIF/B1*100
6150 PRINT "AVG  ";:PRINT USING F1$;B1/B3;:PRINT"  ";:PRINT USING F1$;B2/B3;:PRI
NT " ";
6160 DIF = (B1/B3)-(B2/B3):PRINT USING F1$;DIF;:PRINT "    ";:PRINT USING F3$;DI
F/(B1/B3)*100
6170 B1=0:B2=0:B3=12
6180 LOCATE 23,12:PRINT "Press any key:";
6190 D$ = INKEY$:IF D$ = "" THEN 6190
6200 NEXT I2:GOTO 1100
6210 LPRINT CHR$(27);CHR$(21):LPRINT"                 UTILITY ANALYSIS":LPRINT:LPRINT
:LPRINT "COMPANY:     ";COMPANY$:LPRINT "TYPE:        ";KIND$:LPRINT "MEASURE IN
:   ";US$:LPRINT
6220 FOR I2 = 1 TO 2:IF I2 = 1 THEN C$ = "VOLUME" ELSE C$ = "COST"
6230 CLS:LPRINT"  ";C$;" DECREASE/(INCREASE) BY MONTH":LPRINT:LPRINT"       ";YR
-1;"   ";YR;" DEC/(INC)     %":LPRINT "              ****    ****  ********  *****"
6240 B1 = 0:B2 = 0:B3 = 12
6250 FOR I = 1 TO 12
6260 B1 = B1 + A(I,I2):B2 = B2 + A(I+12,I2):IF A(I,I2) = 0 THEN B3 = B3 - 1:B2 =
 B2-A(I+12,I2)
6270 LPRINT A$(I);:LPRINT "  ";:LPRINT USING F1$;A(I,I2);:LPRINT"  ";:LPRINT USI
NG F1$;A(I+12,I2);:LPRINT " ";
6280 DIF = A(I,I2) - A(I+12,I2):LPRINT USING F1$;DIF;:LPRINT "    ";:IF A(I,I2)
= 0 THEN LPRINT " N/A" ELSE LPRINT USING F3$;DIF/A(I,I2)*100
6290 NEXT I:LPRINT
6300 LPRINT "TOT  ";:LPRINT USING F1$;B1;:LPRINT"  ";:LPRINT USING F1$;B2;:LPRIN
T " ";
6310 DIF = B1-B2:LPRINT USING F1$;DIF;:LPRINT "    ";:IF B1 = 0 THEN LPRINT " N/
```

```
A":GOTO 6170 ELSE LPRINT USING F3$;DIF/B1*100
6320 LPRINT "AVG  ";:LPRINT USING F1$;B1/B3;:LPRINT"   ";:LPRINT USING F1$;B2/B3;
:LPRINT " ";
6330 DIF = (B1/B3)-(B2/B3):LPRINT USING F1$;DIF;:LPRINT "     ";:IF B1/B3 = 0 THE
N LPRINT " N/A" ELSE LPRINT USING F3$;DIF/(B1/B3)*100
6340 B1=0:B2=0:B3=12
6350 IF I2 = 1 THEN LPRINT:LPRINT:LPRINT
6360 NEXT I2:GOTO 1100

7000 'END
7010 CLS:LOCATE 12,11:PRINT "ARE YOU SURE (Y,N)?"
7020 D$ = INKEY$:IF D$ <> "Y" AND D$ <> "y" AND D$ <> "N" AND D$ <> "n" THEN 702
0
7030 IF D$ = "Y" OR D$ = "y" THEN CLS:END ELSE 1100

8000 DATA JAN,FEB,MAR,APR,MAY,JUN,JUL,AUG,SEP,OCT,NOV,DEC
```

Appendix D
Optional Reading

For those of you who wish to build your own Home Control system, the following three part (3 month) article is a step-by-step guide and includes explanations of both hardware and software. Some experience is assumed in terms of your electronic project building capability! This Home Control Computer is programmed through the serial (RS-232) port of a regular computer, and once it has received its instructions, it can operate on its own. It includes sensing capabilities and an X-10 Controller among its features, and all parts (as a kit or assembled) are available through Vesta Technology, Inc., 2849 W. 35th Ave., Denver, CO 80211.

Sarns, Steven E. "Home Control Computer," *Radio Electronics*, Vol. 55, No. 4-6 (April, May, June, 1984).

Most book stores that carry computer books will offer a number of books on *interfacing*. If you wish to understand the electronics between your computer and Home Control or other peripherals, these types of books have a wealth of technical information. TAB recommends the books listed here.

Carr, Joseph J. *Interfacing Your Microcomputer to Virtually Anything*. Blue Ridge Summit, PA: TAB BOOKS, Inc., 1984.

Cunningham, John E., and Horn, Delton T. *Handbook of Remote Control and Automation Techniques 2nd Edition*. Blue Ridge Summit, PA: TAB BOOKS, Inc., 1984.

Leibson, Steve. *The Handbook of Microcomputer Interfacing*. Blue Ridge Summit, PA: TAB BOOKS Inc., 1983.

Wolfe, Gordon W. *Computer Peripherals that You Can Build*. Blue Ridge Summit, PA: TAB BOOKS, Inc., 1982.

Index

Edited by Brint Rutherford